The Age of Discontent

The years following the 2008 financial crisis produced a surge of political discontent with populism, conspiracism, and Far Right extremism
rising across the world. Despite this timing, many of these movements
coalesced around cultural issues rather than economic grievances. But
if culture, and not economics, is the primary driver of political discontent, why did these developments emerge after a financial collapse, a
pattern that repeats throughout the history of the democratic world?
Using the framework of 'Affective Political Economy', The Age of
Discontent demonstrates that emotions borne of economic crises produce cultural discontent, thus enflaming conflicts over values and identities. The book uses this framework to explain the rise of populism
and the radical right in the US, UK, Spain, and Brazil, and the social
uprising in Chile. It argues that states must fulfill their roles as provid-
ers of social insurance and channels for citizen voices if they wish to
turn back the tide of political discontent.

Matthew Rhodes-Purdy is an Assistant Professor of Political Science at
Clemson University. He is the author of Regime Support Beyond the
Balance Sheet (2017).

Rachel Navarre is an Assistant Professor in the Department of Political
Science and Master of Public Administration Program at Bridgewater
State University. She is co-author of Immigration in the 21st Century
(2020) with Drs. Terri Givens and Pete Mohanty.

Stephen Utych is a market researcher with area focus on political psychology, political behavior, and experimental methods. Dr. Utych has
published over thirty peer-reviewed articles.

The Age of Discontent

Populism, Extremism, and Conspiracy Theories in Contemporary Democracies

MATTHEW RHODES-PURDY

Clemson University

RACHEL NAVARRE

Bridgewater State University

STEPHEN UTYCH

Independent Researcher

CAMBRIDGE
UNIVERSITY PRESS

Shaftesbury Road, Cambridge CB2 8EA, United Kingdom

One Liberty Plaza, 20th Floor, New York, NY 10006, USA

477 Williamstown Road, Port Melbourne, VIC 3207, Australia

314–321, 3rd Floor, Plot 3, Splendor Forum, Jasola District Centre, New Delhi – 110025, India

103 Penang Road, #05–06/07, Visioncrest Commercial, Singapore 238467

Cambridge University Press is part of Cambridge University Press & Assessment, a department of the University of Cambridge.

We share the University's mission to contribute to society through the pursuit of education, learning and research at the highest international levels of excellence.

www.cambridge.org
Information on this title: www.cambridge.org/9781009279437

DOI: 10.1017/9781009279383

First published 2023
First paperback edition 2024

A catalogue record for this publication is available from the British Library

Library of Congress Cataloging-in-Publication data
NAMES: Rhodes-Purdy, Matthew, author. | Navarre, Rachel, author. |
Utych, Stephen, author.
TITLE: The age of discontent : populism, extremism, and conspiracy theories
in contemporary democracies / Matthew Rhodes-Purdy, Clemson University,
South Carolina, Rachel Navarre, Bridgewater State College, Massachusetts,
Stephen Utych, Boise State University, Idaho.
DESCRIPTION: New York : Cambridge University Press, 2023. |
Includes bibliographical references and index.
IDENTIFIERS: LCCN 2022030551 | ISBN 9781009279390 (Hardback) |
ISBN 9781009279383 (eBook)
SUBJECTS: LCSH: Financial crises – Psychological aspects. |
Financial crises – Political aspects. | Social conflict. | Radicalism. |
Political psychology. | Emotions. | Conspiracy theories.
CLASSIFICATION: LCC HB3718 .R46 2023 | DDC 338.5/42–dc23/eng/20221116
LC record available at https://lccn.loc.gov/2022030551

ISBN   978-1-009-27939-0   Hardback
ISBN   978-1-009-27943-7   Paperback

Matthew Rhodes-Purdy: To Helen. To solve the problems we lay out in this book, we will need to be brave and bold, and when I think of brave and bold, I think of you.

Rachel Navarre: To Caleb, his imagination, and his stories.

Stephen Utych: To Margot. I hope your generation's future is brighter than the one we paint in this book. If not, I know you will make it so.

Contents

Figures

Tables

Acknowledgements

The ideas and arguments that eventually coalesced into this book have been knocking around in at least one of our heads for more than ten years. During that time, discontent has gone from a relatively niche topic to one of the most pressing threats facing contemporary democracies. As the period we call the "age of discontent" unfolded, discontent rapidly evolved, taking on forms not previously seen (e.g. left-wing populism in Europe and radical right populism in Latin America) and gaining a degree of prominence and power long thought impossible in advanced democracies.

No successful academic book is written without substantial help, and this book required perhaps even more outside assistance than is typical, given its scope and its lengthy germination. We include both group and individual acknowledgements here. As a group, we owe an enormous debt to several people who gave critical feedback on the manuscript as it evolved. Funding for survey and experimental data collection was provided principally by the School of Public Service at Boise State University, with some funding also provided by Clemson University. The empirical, statistical, and experimental findings presented here benefitted greatly from comments made by anonymous reviewers at several journals, including the *Journal of Politics*, *The Journal of Race, Ethnicity, and Politics*, and the *Journal of Experimental Political Science*. George Marcus was kind enough to offer his time at a conference to discuss with us our application of emotions (which relies heavily on this work on affective intelligence theory) to the study of political discontent.

The theory, conceptualization, and presentation of our argument owes a great deal to feedback given during a virtual book workshop attended by Ryan Carlin, Ashley Jardina, Shana Gadarian, Jen Merolla, Kenneth Roberts, Fernando Rosenblatt, and Lisa Zanotti. In particular, the argument as it relates to Latin America, several of the terms and arguments used throughout, and the presentation of experimental results in Chapter 4 have been vastly improved by their thorough and insightful comments. We cannot thank them enough, and we go on the record here as owing each of them a very substantial favor.

Matthew Rhodes-Purdy: I wish first and foremost to thank Kurt Weyland, who has been kind enough to continue reviewing virtually everything I write as though I were still a graduate student. Any tendency I may have to get lazy in the logical construction of arguments or the precision of my prose has been held firmly in check by the knowledge that, no matter how significant, Kurt will find it. I also owe him considerable thanks for giving me something that many advisors withhold: the freedom to disagree. Kurt and I have butted heads about any number of conceptual and theoretical issues (the definition of populism we use, for example, will no doubt provoke an exasperated sigh), and yet Kurt has always challenged me with respect and a willingness to agree to disagree.

I also wish to thank Fernando Rosenblatt, for sharing not only his time but also his friendship and even briefly his office space. Our discussions of democracy and how it might be deepened and made more participatory and inclusive have such a profound impact on how I think about democratic discontent that they influence virtually every aspect of this book. Thanks are also due to Fernando for his expertise in Uruguay politics. In a similar vein, I would like to thank Wendy Hunter for her careful critique of the Brazilian case study included in Chapter 7. Prior to this book I had not conducted research on Brazil, and her comments on this chapter were essential. I would also like to thank Ryan Lloyd for periodically answering questions I had about Jair Bolsonaro.

Finally, I would like to thank my wife Lindsey, and my children Hank and Helen, who have spent over a decade (or in the case of the kids, their entire lives) being subjected to ramblings, lectures, tirades, status reports, and various other less-than-fascinating interactions regarding this project. Without your patience, support, and (occasionally) tolerance, this book would not exist.

Rachel Navarre: I too must thank my academic advisors, Terri Givens and David Leal. They gave me a place to belong in graduate school, as well as the support needed to make it through. They have helped with research and opportunities, as well as the big ideas. They have been a key aid in learning both how to do research and navigate the academy.

I would also like to thank my circle at the University of Texas at Austin and my current colleagues at Bridgewater for their support and camaraderie throughout graduate school and beyond. I owe Matt a debt of gratitude for inviting me to this project, even though we still disagree on how much direct democracy is too much. Clare Brock has been essential in helping me think things through and being a sounding board for research and life.

The person that provided the greatest support for this project is of course my spouse, Jeremy. Jeremy not only moved with me to a place where seafood is unseasoned but supported and tolerated my discussions of this project. His knowledge of the Far Right in America proved invaluable, as well as his ability to provide feedback as a non-academic. Even though the past few years have been difficult for everyone, there is no one else I'd rather spend a pandemic lockdown with than him and our son, Caleb.

Stephen Utych: I would first like to thank Cindy Kam. Without her mentorship, I can't imagine that I would have accomplished anything as a scholar. From day one as a twenty-four-year-old graduate student, Cindy has had my back and given me the knowledge and support I need to be the best scholar I could be. She is present in all of the work I do, and has been instrumental in shaping this book, providing detailed feedback multiple times on numerous chapters. Her insights, kindness, and support throughout my career have given me the confidence to take risks as a researcher, and the knowledge to know which risks are worth taking.

Damon Roberts and James Fahey have also been instrumental in helping me think through this book, and how to present findings that resonate with a large audience. Their insight is unparalleled, and every time I talk about research with Damon and James, I learn something new. Having colleagues and friends like Damon and James makes this career less lonely, and being able to informally discuss our work, especially when we hit roadblocks, has been a great benefit to me.

Speaking of friendships, I'd be remiss to not thank my closest friends from graduate school – Drew Engelhardt, Scott Limbocker, Bryan Rooney, Marc Trussler, and Bryce Williams-Tuggle. We work in a variety of different fields in political science, but they are always a quick text away from answering the questions, from silly to serious, I have as I'm working through a project. They may not even realize the ways in which they have helped this work come together.

My spouse, Alexandra, has been the constant in my life throughout the time I've spent writing this book. We have been through so many changes together, but she has served as a constant source of happiness and support. Marrying her was the greatest decision I have ever made, and her willingness to listen to me ramble about my work has been invaluable in writing this book. I could not ask for a kinder, smarter, funnier, and more incredible partner.

Lastly, I thank my daughter, Margot. While she has been, admittedly, useless as a source for in-depth analyses of geopolitical events (her preferences are stuffed animals and coloring books), she has nonetheless been instrumental to me as I've written this book. My life changed the day Margot entered it, and she has truly taught me the value of balance and family. Without her, my life would have a lot less joy. For that, I am thankful.

Abbreviations

CONCEPTS, THEORIES, AND APPROACHES

AIT	affective intelligence theory
APE	affective political economy
AUI	attitudes towards unauthorized immigrants
DSV	double simultaneous vote
FR	far right
ISI	import substitution industrialization
PR	proportional representation
PRR	populist radical right
PSV	perceived strong voice

PARTIES, MOVEMENTS, AND LEADERS (WITH COUNTRIES AND ORIENTATIONS)

Acronym	Full Name	Orientation
BE	Left Bloc (Portugal)	Left
BLM	Black Lives Matter (USA)	Left
CA	Open Meeting (Uruguay)	Conservative Right
CiU	Convergence and Unity (Spain)	Center-Right/Catalan Nationalist
Cs	Citizens (Spain)	Center/Liberal Right
FA	Broad Front (Uruguay)	Left
NDP	New Democratic Party (Canada)	Left/Center-Left
OWS	Occupy Wall Street (USA)	Left/Populist Left
PP	People's Party (Spain)	Center-Right

PS	Socialist Party (Portugal)	Center-Left
PSOE	Socialist Workers' Party of Spain	Center-Left
PT	Workers' Party (Brazil)	Left/Center-Left
STS	Stop the Steal (USA)	Populist Right
UKIP	United Kingdom Independence Party	Populist Right

DATA AND METHODS

CFA	confirmatory factor analysis
PANAS	positive and negative affect schedule
PSAS	Political System Attitudes Survey
SE	standard error
SEM	structural equation model

I

Introduction

The administration of Donald J. Trump began and ended the same way: with "American carnage." On his inauguration day, Trump stood at the steps of the Capitol Building and used this phrase to describe the situation of the country, a state of affairs he alone could redeem. Four years later, Trump supporters stormed the same building in an attempted insurrection, inflicting hundreds of injuries upon police officers and thousands of dollars in damage, and producing some of the most harrowing newsreel footage in the history of the United States. The attack on the Capitol was a culmination of Trump's entire political career. Throughout his presidency, Trump attacked the media, slandered the electoral process, thumbed his nose at institutional safeguards, forced aside members of his own party who refused to show him enough deference, and even encouraged violence against opponents. The violence at the Capitol was not an anomaly, but merely an extreme example of a kind of politics that had become depressingly common around the world as the 2010s closed. During this decade, a steady stream of populists, extremists, conspiracy theorists, and authoritarians challenged mainstream leaders and parties around the world, with varying degrees of success. Political tendencies long thought decently buried (e.g. nativism, ethnonationalism, and populist authoritarianism) rose like vampires, intent on battening onto the neck of the democratic world.

Current scholarship has largely separated the study of these political trends into distinct topics (e.g. populism, the far right (FR), conspiracism, regime support, contentious politics). Yet despite differences in ideology, social base, country of origin, strength of tether to reality, propensity for violence, etc., all the members of the political rogue's gallery that we have assembled so far share a conceptual core. Each evinces a profound rejection of the sociopolitical status quo.

We call this rejection democratic discontent. No one who lives under democratic rule for long can avoid shaking their head in frustration at some foolish policy or political leader. But these are relatively minor and transient irritants that will always occur when large groups of humans gather to make collective decisions. Discontent has four aspects that distinguish it from the ordinary annoyances that all citizens of democracies suffer from time to time. First, discontent is broader. To the discontented, *all* policies are bad, all leaders are crooked, and democratic institutions (which in free societies are supposed to evict crooked leaders who make bad policies) are woefully insufficient to right the ship of state. Second, discontent runs deeper; it casts policies not as ill advised or flawed but intentionally harmful, and political leaders not as incompetent but as actively malign. And it suggests that the mechanisms and procedures of democracy are not merely imperfect but irreparably and fundamentally broken. The discontented individual sees little hope of correcting course through politics as usual. They see bad leaders triumph election after election, with no end in sight.

Third, discontent is cumulative. Dissatisfaction waxes and wanes as the winds change and parties cycle in and out of power. Discontent, on the other hand, builds over time as repeated disappointments become disaffection. Each failure of the political system to rectify wrongs erodes systemic trust and confidence in the political class. This forms something of a paradox, because as we argue throughout this chapter and the remainder of the book, discontented politics also tends to erupt rapidly. As such, any explanation of discontent needs to consider both long-term processes by which democracies lose legitimacy as well as the immediate triggering events.

Lastly, and perhaps a bit confoundingly given all the *sturm und drang* depicted so far, discontent is latent, or unobservable. Discontent is a vague and inchoate evaluation of the political environment: it is a free-floating, ill-defined sense that a democratic regime has gone badly off course. Unusually for a book's eponymous concept, we make no attempt anywhere here to measure discontent itself. We do not expect ordinary citizens to articulate such an amorphous notion. Instead, discontent must be imbued with meaning through social and political narratives (Shiller 2020).

Discontented citizens will seek out ideas, identities, and narratives that reflect their own disgust with the status quo, while simultaneously providing them with the detailed explanations of why things have gone so awry and what can be done about them. Discontented citizens do not produce these narratives themselves; rather, they pick and choose from the menu of narratives made available to them by elites, media, and, increasingly, social media networks. Any real-world manifestation of discontent will reflect the idiosyncratic character of the narrative menu in a given context, shaped by party system dynamics, mass media, political history, specific cultural cleavages, etc. This heterogeneity of expression obscures shared traits and causal origins.

While discontented manifestations reflect their environments, we can still categorize them using a few basic points of divergence. First, discontent requires a target, someone (or something) to blame for the poor state of society. Taking a cue from the literature on political support (Klingemann 1999, Easton 1975), we can array targets on a continuum from specific (i.e. existing persons or organizations) to diffuse (abstract ideas and concepts). On the specific side, if the political class is blamed, discontent manifests as anti-elitism. When this combines with a belief in the moral and political superiority of "the people," an imagined unity of ordinary citizens, it becomes populism (Hawkins 2018, Mudde 2007). If a person blames minorities or immigrants, discontent manifests as "prejudice," an umbrella term we use to describe negative intergroup attitudes held by privileged groups against marginalized groups. Populism and prejudice can combine, as discontented individuals can blame more than one entity (thus leading to the populist radical right, or PRR).

Going toward the more diffuse end of the spectrum, discontented persons can blame "the system," that is, the institutions and practices of an existing democratic regime. This produces "regime antipathy," an extreme negation of regime support. Note that regime antipathy is not the same as a lack of "support for democracy," an unfortunately misleading but oft-used term for a person's commitment to democracy as an ideal. A loss of faith in democracy as an ideal is not in and of itself a form of discontent, but rather a possible *consequence* of discontent.[1]

At its most diffuse, discontent can touch the very bedrock of a person's perceptions of their social environment, leading them to question the trustworthiness of empirical reality. As we discuss later in this book, this is particularly likely when a person is disappointed by a movement or

---

[1] For a more detailed discussion of the interrelationships between regime support and commitment to democracy, see Rhodes-Purdy (2017c, ch. 2). We also further discuss all these definitional issues in more detail in Chapter 2.

leader who promises to vanquish the believed source of discontent. Faced with a hopeless situation, individuals will give credence to any narrative that promises an explanation; even the most byzantine and bizarre conspiracy theories can gain traction if they can provide an escape from the intolerable anxiety that accompanies despondency.

Discontented movements vary in how elaborate or specifically ideological they become, but the most successful tend to focus heavily on their villains and the goodness of their supporters, with policy details left deliberately vague. This helps avoid triggering latent disputes among often diverse groups of supporters who may have little in common beyond shared targets of rage. As such, discontented movements act as *emotional* coalitions, based on resentment toward specific actors, rather than positive solidarity or ideology.

1.1 WHY WE WRITE: DISCONTENT AND DEMOCRACY

Spans of time are often named after the social trends that define them: the gilded age, the roaring twenties, the lost decade, and so on. For the period from 2008 to the present, it would be difficult to find a better title than "the age of discontent." The problems addressed in this book are complex, but they can be boiled down to three short questions: how did the age of discontent rise, how do we put an end to it, and how can similar ages be avoided in the future? We seek to answer these questions not as an abstract academic exercise, but to provide insight for policymakers, activists, and ordinary people about how we, as citizens of democratic polities, might turn away from the acrimony and chaos of the current moment.

In this effort, we are hardly alone. Considerable research has been done in recent years about the impact that discontented political movements have on democratic politics. There are undeniable ways in which discontent can help deepen democratic practices. The current wave of protests in Chile, though often chaotic and occasionally violent, did succeed in breaking the elite consensus over systemic preservation, giving the country the chance to (at long last) discard an illegitimate constitution forged under the aegis of a brutal military dictatorship. Movements and leaders who mobilize citizens on the basis of discontent may activate marginalized social sectors, helping them overcome organizational deficits and collective action dilemmas, thus leading them to become more engaged in politics (Piñeiro, Rhodes-Purdy, and Rosenblatt 2016, De la Torre 2019, 153–154). A small but vocal group of scholars of populism, one of the most important discontented variants we study here, have gone so far as to argue that it alone can unify those without voice, and thus may be a purer form of democratic politics than liberal democracy (Mouffe 2000, Laclau 1977, 2005, Laclau and Mouffe 1985, Panizza 2005). And of course, marginalized ethnic, racial, and gender groups can hardly be faulted for disdaining political systems that treat them as inferiors and deny them full participation in public life.

While these potential benefits cannot be ignored, the academic consensus on the effects of discontent on democratic quality and stability is overwhelmingly negative. Discontent is by its very nature an aggressive and overriding political tendency: the need to remedy profound grievances and salvage "true democracy" must necessarily take precedence over liberal niceties like tolerance of opposition, deference to institutional rules, and even the peaceful transition of power. As such, a barrage of scholarship has lately highlighted the damage that discontented politics can wreak on democratic regimes and practices (e.g. Levitsky and Ziblatt 2018, Mounk 2018, Müller 2016, 2021). Even scholars who argue that institutions in some countries are strong enough to withstand an assault by politically discontented movements recognize the potential for disaster in institutionally weaker contexts (Weyland and Madrid 2019). The verdict on other forms of discontent is even harsher: few are willing to argue that the rise of the FR or of paranoiac movements like QAnon are anything but destructive to genuine democracy. Taken to the extreme, discontent can even justify politically motivated violence, including hate crimes against minorities or immigrants, destructive and riotous contentious politics, and even attempts to forcefully undermine democracy. While recognizing the complex interplay between discontent and democracy, we accept as settled that the two do not mix well. At best, discontent is a red flag, a sign that democracy has failed to win the support of significant sectors of the population. At worst, discontent can pose a major threat to the stability and even survival of democratic politics.

Before we move on, we need to address one final issue regarding our motivation for writing this book. Social scientists typically maintain as best they can an air of objectivity, and thus avoid taking sides in any controversies they study. We have no wish to go against this convention, but we are compelled to do so in one specific instance. We concur with an analogy drawn at a recent civil trial of the Alt-right and white supremacists who organized the "Unite the Right" rally in Charlottesville, by an expert on extremism who compared his work to that of a cancer researcher: one can study a topic with scholarly rigor and still be highly motivated to combat it. As such, we reject the prejudicial and authoritarian leanings of many of the movements we analyze here.

We find it necessary to state this bluntly (and hope the reader will forgive our candor) because we dwell at some length on the economic distress many of the discontented face. Such discussions have become controversial, as many believe that such discussions are intended to excuse or minimize the biases or bigotries of the discontented. No matter how much we may sympathize with the economic travails of those experiencing discontent, that sympathy should not be misconstrued as excusing antidemocratic or authoritarian ideas or actions.

We also refuse to fall victim to reflexive "both sides-ism" when we discuss discontent on the left and right. As much as we can, we do not ignore commonalities between the two: both left- and right-wing discontent can pose a threat to democracy, especially when such movements are headed by charismatic leaders with little regard for the rights and liberties of anyone who opposes them. Yet in most contexts, the threat posed by the right is far greater than that posed by the left. The policies of the right pose a significantly greater threat to the health, safety, and even survival of large swaths of the population than those of their leftist counterparts. And at least in the current age of discontent, the discontented right has shown a much greater propensity for political violence against both opponents and the agents and institutions of the democratic state.

1.2 BACKLASH OR LEFT BEHIND? CULTURE VS. ECONOMICS IN THE STUDY OF DISCONTENT

The causes of discontent are relatively understudied compared to its consequences. This is especially true of our unified conception of the subject; scant research exists analyzing various subcategories of discontent, although this field of study has begun to advance significantly recent years.[2] Work that does exist tends to address specific attitudes or behaviors that evince discontent, rather than discontent itself, such as support for Donald Trump (Abramowitz 2018, Sides, Tesler, and Vavreck 2019), Brexit and the United Kingdom Independence Party (Goodwin and Milazzo 2015, Ford and Goodwin 2014), right-wing cultural backlash (Inglehart and Norris 2019,

---

[2] Cas Mudde's work on nativist populism is an exception to this, as it takes both the nativist and populist elements of this political trend seriously (Mudde and Rovira Kaltwasser 2013a, 2013b, 2018, Mudde 2007).

Gest 2016, Cramer 2016, Jardina 2019), and conspiracism (van Prooijen 2018, Uscinski and Parent 2014, Douglas et al. 2019, Douglas, Sutton, and Cichocka 2017). These works tend to focus on the details of the topic they study while paying less attention to their common core. This is the gap we hope to fill with this book. While the specifics of each discontented subtype are important, we take a step back, look for common connections, and derive from those a general theory of how discontent emerges.

1.2.1 The Left behind Hypothesis

By reviewing extensive literatures on the plethora of discontented politics (see Chapter 3), we identify an overarching debate about what led to the proliferation of anti-system politics in the 2010s: culture (the Backlash hypothesis) or economics (the Left Behind hypothesis). The latter hypothesis is simple enough: scholars in this camp argue that discontent is the product of long-term economic change (mostly due to globalization but in many cases aided and abetted by policy choices of national governments) that create patterns of winners and losers. Discontent is for "losers," that is, those individuals who belong to economically marginalized social groups (Roberts 2019) or were harmed or put at risk by the global shift toward neoliberal, laissez-faire capitalism (Eichengreen 2018, Hacker 2008, Crouch 2009, 2011). The left behind are typically not the most deprived members of society but are instead middle-class members of the ethnoracial majority. Consistent with relative deprivation theory (Macdougall, Feddes, and Doosje 2020, Elchardus and Spruyt 2012, 2016, Spruyt, Keppens, and Van Droogenbroeck 2016, Gurr 1971), being left behind is shaped more by comparison with elite social classes and frustrated expectations than by absolute deprivation. Fearing for their livelihoods and with ever-decreasing assistance from increasingly stingy welfare states, the left behind became resentful and distrustful of political systems they felt had abandoned them (Hacker and Pierson 2020, Crouch 2018), but these sentiments for the most part remained below the surface of mainstream politics until 2008. This is consistent with earlier works on democratic discontent (especially populism) that highlight the importance of economically transformative periods in forging populist alliances (Collier and Collier 2002, Kazin 1998, Hicks 1931b, Spalding 1977). In other words, the Left Behind hypothesis can be seen as an extreme form of economic voting (Anderson 2007), where citizens come to view the elite as an undifferentiated class and seek to punish them all for their economic failures.

Throughout this book we speak of the era of the "Great Recession," but the last word should probably be plural. During the period we cover (roughly 2008–2020), there have been no fewer than three major economic crises with global reach: the eponymous financial crisis, the collapse of the commodities boom in 2014, and the Covid-19 crisis which produced the most sudden and severe recession in modern history as the pandemic expanded in the early part of 2020. The Left Behind hypothesis argues that economic crises caused the long-term economic strains mentioned earlier to boil over into open rebellion against neoliberal democracy, although this rebellion was often directed less at corporate masters and economic elites than at perceived competitors, namely immigrants and racial minorities.[3] The fact that discontent emerged just as the economy sank is, therefore, hardly a coincidence.

Evidence for the Left Behind hypothesis comes primarily in two forms. The first includes analyses of the demography of supporters of discontented political movements (e.g. Brexit, the Tea Party, Donald Trump). Such research shows that discontented individuals are disproportionately likely to have demographic profiles (e.g. low education, modest skills, employment in declining trades, etc.) that leave them particularly exposed to the tumults of both long-term economic change and the acute impacts of the 2008 crisis (Ford and Goodwin 2014, Sides, Tesler, and Vavreck 2019, Williams 2019). Ethnographic approaches to these groups, while also highlighting cultural factors (as we discuss shortly), point to the sense of economic abandonment many of these individuals feel (Skocpol and Williamson 2012, Cramer 2016).

The second major set of evidence comes from sophisticated quantitative studies at the meso level, that is, where the units of analysis are geographical areas, typically counties, regions, or metropolitan areas. These analyses often include measures of potential cultural threats such as ethnic diversity, allowing a direct comparison between economic and cultural causes. The results are consistent, at least on economics: culture sometimes matters and sometimes does not, but economic factors are almost always crucial (Colantone and Stanig 2018a, 2018b, Becker, Fetzer, and Novy 2017, Georgiadou, Rori, and Roumanias 2018, c.f. Miller 2020).

[3] Taken as such, the Left Behind hypothesis, while useful shorthand, is not totally accurate: it deemphasizes the importance of economic crisis in triggering longstanding economic grievances. Left Behind Then Rudely Shoved Down might be a better label, but in the interest of avoiding long acronyms we use the shorter term to refer to this combination of long-term, slow-burn economic marginalization and sudden economic calamity throughout this book.

TABLE 1.1 *List of discontented political movements and leaders by economic crises*

Crisis	Movements and leaders
Panics of 1873 and 1893	The People's Party, Greenback/Free Silver, Temperance Movement (USA)
Post-World War I inflationary crises	Italian fascism, Nazism
Great Depression	Nationalism: Father Coughlin, Charles Lindberg/America First Left-wing populism: Huey Long
World War II commodities slump	Classical Latin American populism: Perón (Argentina), Vargas (Brazil)
The lost decade (Latin America)	Neopopulism: Menem (Argentina), Fujimori (Peru)
Neoliberal reform era (Latin America)	Chávez (Venezuela), Morales (Bolivia), Correa (Ecuador)
The Great Recession	Anti-austerity populism: Sanders (USA), SYRIZA (Greece), Podemos (Spain) Ethnonationalist populism: Trump (USA), VOX, Alternative for Germany (Europe), UK Independence Party Postcommunist national populism: Orbán (Hungary), Law and Justice (Poland)
Collapse of the 2000s/2010s commodities boom	Bolsonaro (Brazil); Obrador (Mexico), Kast/Boric (Chile), Castillo (Peru), Nayib (El Salvador)

Perhaps the best evidence for the notion that economic trauma is the primary driver of discontent is historical patterning. To demonstrate this, we provide a list of discontented political movements throughout history, from the regions we study in this book (namely Europe and the Americas), and the economic crises with which they coincide (Table 1.1).

The co-occurrence of economic and democratic discontent shown in this table is suggestive, but not conclusive. The rise of European fascism was clearly influenced by humiliating defeats in World War I, for example, while PRR in Europe spiked after a recession but also during an influx of refugees from the Middle East. Nevertheless, the volume of discontent in the wake of economic turbulence is enough to justify taking the economic argument seriously. This is especially true of the most severe recessions: in those cases, the political and economic status quo often suffers a two-pronged assault, with both left- and right-wing discontented movements battling each other to try to define the new reality that seemingly must replace business as usual.

1.2.2 Mapping the Rise of Discontent since the Great Recession

Even a cursory analysis of voting data from before and after the economic crises of the 2010s shows that history has repeated itself. To demonstrate this, and to give the reader a clearer overview of populism in Europe and the Americas since the Great Recession, we collected voting data for both regions, beginning in 2008 and ending in 2018. We collected data from parliamentary elections (Europe and Canada) and first-round presidential vote share (the USA and Latin America). We also identified discontented and mainstream candidates and parties. For Europe, we used PopuList 2.0 (Rooduijn et al. 2019) to identify populist parties and ParlGov development version 15. Sep. 2021 (Döring and Manow 2021) for party vote shares. For Latin America, we constructed a list of discontented leaders ourselves based on our own knowledge of the region.[4] Using Tableau mapping software, we produced two sets of maps for each region: one from the beginning of the crisis era in 2008, and another at the latest point in the crisis era for which data were available, in 2018. Lighter shades indicate a smaller vote share for discontented parties and leaders, while darker shades indicate greater support. These maps are presented in Figure 1.1.

We can draw two important conclusions from these maps. First, the emergence of discontent during the 2010s was both substantial and, if not uniform, at least very widely distributed. And these increases were not driven by extreme swings in a small number of cases (although some countries did swing more than others), but rather by a general increase in the fortunes of discontented movements and leaders in both regions. In 2000, populist parties received, on average, 10.4 percent of the national vote in Europe. That figure increased gradually to 15.3 percent in 2007, just before the crisis struck. By 2019, that percentage had increased to 25.3 percent; populist parties, on average, obtained more than a quarter of the national vote. Although not apparent on the static maps, the animated maps reveal three broad groups of populist advances during the 2000s. First, we see a surge of nationalist populists in the postcommunist world (e.g. Orbán in

[4] For a list of discontented leaders, see the online appendix (https://dataverse.harvard.edu/dataverse/ageofdiscontent/). Animated versions of the maps provided here, with data for each year between 2000 and 2020, can be found at: https://public.tableau.com/app/profile/rachel.navarre.

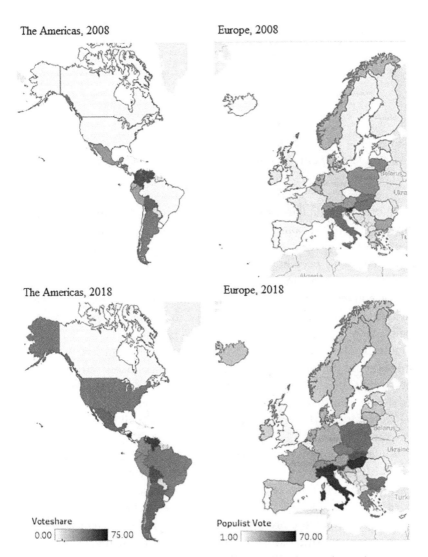

FIGURE 1.1 Maps of support for discontented leaders and populists.

Hungary, Peace and Justice in Poland) that predates the eurozone crisis but which accelerated after the crisis. Second is a wave of left-leaning anti-austerity parties like SYRIZA in Greece and Podemos in Spain that rose in the immediate aftermath of the eurozone crisis and are concentrated in the countries that were worst hit by it. Finally, we can see the advance of the nativist PRR in northern, central, and later southern Europe.

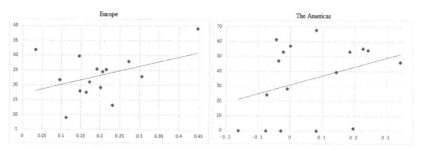

FIGURE I.2 Scatterplot of crisis severity and discontented vote share.

Figures were similar for populist candidates in the Americas: in 2014, the last year of the commodities boom, populist candidates received an average of 21 percent of the first-round vote; in 2019, that figure had increased by 50 percent, to 30.9 percent. In 2000, only two populists held power in the Americas; by 2019, this figure has risen to eleven, out of eighteen countries included in the sample. Here again, we see distinct clusters. Prior to 2014, most of the successful populists in the region were left-wing nationalist holdovers from the *chavista* wave of populism. This wave, led by Chávez in Venezuela and Evo Morales in Bolivia, rose during the latter stages of the neoliberal reform crisis of the 1990s. The second major cluster emerges only after the commodities crisis began in 2014, and is characterized by unusual diversity, ranging from far left (López Obrador in Mexico, Castillo in Peru) to PRR (Bolsonaro in Brazil).

While these maps show a general trend toward greater discontented voting after the economic crises after 2008, they do not provide much information about the relationship between discontent and the severity of the crisis. As such, we combined these election data with a measure of gross domestic product (GDP) per capita, in current US dollars, taken from the World Bank's database. We then calculated the difference between the highest level of GDP from before the relevant crisis (from 2000 to 2008 for western Europe, the USA, and Canada, 2013 for Latin America) and the lowest level after the crisis. This produced a measure of the severity of the crisis in each country. We then produced a scatter plot with discontented vote share; the charts are presented in Figure I.2.

These charts show a clear correlation between crisis severity and discontented vote share. Correlations were modest for both Europe (r=0.199) and Latin America (0.187). However, in each case several outliers obscure the association. Costa Rica, Iceland, and Portugal (all relatively strong and responsive democracies, a mitigating factor we discuss in Chapter 9) have much less discontent than their economic fortunes would predict. On the other hand, the discontented vote share in Nicaragua and Italy are inflated far above the correlation line, most likely due to the lingering effects of pre-crisis populism on party systems and the integrity of elections. Removing these atypical cases produces a correlation between crisis severity and discontented vote share of 0.397 in western Europe and 0.488 in Latin America.

While these correlations are by no means incontrovertible evidence for the Left Behind hypothesis, they do (along with the historical patterning and meso-level analyses described earlier) make a strong a priori case that one must take economic crises seriously.

1.2.3 The Backlash Hypothesis and Cultural Discontent

Yet when we descend from the macro-historical to the micro level, where individuals are the unit of analysis, these effects tend to disappear. In studies comparing economic and cultural attitudes' effects on discontent in surveys (e.g. Inglehart and Norris 2019, 2016, Miller 2020, Georgiadou, Rori, and Roumanias 2018), cultural factors like hostility toward immigrants or racial resentment nearly always have a much more significant influence than economic attitudes. This leads to the second major hypothesized explanation for the rise of discontent: the Backlash hypothesis. The most thorough explication of this approach has been provided by Inglehart and Norris (2019). Inglehart and Norris argue that social modernization has produced uneven distribution of postmaterialist values. According to the Backlash hypothesis, the left behind are not defined by their economic precarity but by their traditionalism and authoritarianism, becoming alienated as their values have been increasingly marginalized (Hochschild 2018, Williams 2019, Goodhart 2017).

This cultural discontent, which we define as a sense that one's beliefs, values, and identities are not respected by society, leads to viewing cultural conflicts in stark zero-sum terms. The discontented among the ethnoracial majority, particularly those who identify as conservative or tend to lean to the right, give little credence to the claims of tolerance and celebration of diversity emanating from elite multiculturalists; to them, multiculturalism tolerates anything except traditionalism. Demographic and value changes in society are thus interpreted as part of a large-scale conflict between "ordinary folks" and a shadow group of "others," often called globalists,[5] along with their allies among minority groups and the urban professional classes. In this fight no one can win without someone else losing: advances by marginalized minorities, upward mobility of immigrants, and increasing acceptance of LGBTQ individuals are viewed not as the resolution of old injustices but as deliberate attempts to undermine the unity of the nation and thus weaken its opposition to globalism (Gest 2016, Golder 2016). Politics cease to be a competition between distinct visions of the public good, instead taking on a factional[6] character, becoming a competition between unified and antagonistic groups with no shared identity to speak of (Forgas, Crano, and Fiedler 2021, Abramowitz 2018). Progressives are not immune; those on the left can also experience their own brand of cultural discontent, manifesting as hostility toward conservative-leaning groups (e.g. the religiously devout, rural dwellers, blue-collar workers) or even left-wing authoritarianism (Costello et al. 2021).

Although these cultural issues have typically been more common in developed states in Europe and the North Atlantic, recently Latin American outsiders like Jair Bolsonaro of Brazil have also taken to criticizing anti-racism efforts and "gender ideology," rather than more historically typical conflicts over wealth distribution. The consequences of this are many: increasing authoritarianism (Adorno et al. 2019, Altemeyer 1981, 1996, Inglehart and Norris 2017), adoption of explicitly white racial or ethnonationalist identities (Jardina 2019, Golder 2016, Kinder and Kam 2009, Tesler 2016), and rising support for both politically discontented leaders/movements and even political extremism.

Like the Left Behind hypothesis, the Backlash hypothesis has some significant problems and shortcomings. We explain these in some detail in Chapter 2, but briefly put there are lingering concerns about the causal mechanisms involved. Inglehart and Norris' work has recently been challenged on empirical grounds (Schäfer 2021), and more broadly speaking the generational conflict that lies at the heart of the theory does not fit

---

[5] As we note throughout this book, the "globalists" of PRR conspiracy theories are often indistinguishable from Jews in established FR anti-Semitic conspiracy theories. The use of the new term allows the PRR to activate the same latent paranoias and prejudices as earlier FR movements while providing plausible deniability of anti-Semitism.

[6] The authors of the cited work use the term "tribal," which we avoid due to its anti-Indigenous connotations.

with the strong support for the FR seen among younger voters in many European countries. Most crucially for our purposes, all variants of the Backlash hypotheses involve mechanisms that unfold gradually over time, and thus cannot explain why discontent, culturally focused or otherwise, should so reliably erupt in the aftermath of economic crises.

1.3 OUR APPROACH: THE AFFECTIVE POLITICAL ECONOMY OF DISCONTENT

Both the Left Behind and Backlash hypotheses make important contributions to our understanding of discontent, but the analytical impasse we described earlier means these approaches raise more questions than they answer. If one or the other were clearly more important for solving the puzzle of democratic discontent, we would expect stronger or more consistent evidence in its favor. Instead, we find strong evidence for both in different sorts of studies: meso-level studies favor economics, micro-level analyses give the prize to culture, while ethnographic studies tend to be a mixed bag. How can two competing and contradictory theories both be supported by such strong evidence at different levels of analyses?

To begin resolving this paradox, we resort to an old parable. What we find in the study of discontent is two blind people touching an elephant: one touches the trunk, and believes the animal to be a snake, while the other touches the leg, and describes a tree. Both the Left Behind and Backlash hypotheses capture something important about discontent but fail to see the connections between economics and culture: in each case, meso- and micro-level studies find only the part of the puzzle that is easy to see with the particular methods used. Our primary goal in this book is to illuminate those connections. At no point in this book do we castigate one or the other hypothesis as fundamentally flawed. Our goal here is not to vanquish, but to reconcile.

This is easier said than done: economic and cultural approaches to politics typically rely on fundamentally opposing assumptions about what motivates human behavior. Economic approaches need not be strictly rationalist, but they do tend to assume that material self-interest is the primary motivation for most people. Cultural explanations usually assume that values, ideas, and beliefs drive human behavior, rather than the calculating selfishness one finds in *Homo economicus*. Trying to force these approaches together thus risks inelegant and self-contradictory theories, rather than clear resolutions.

1.3.1 Why Political Psychology?

To craft a more unified theory of discontent, we adopt political psychology as our foundational approach, a decision which requires a brief defense. Studies of discontented political tendencies like populism have often focused more on leaders and institutions (e.g. Weyland 2017, Weyland and Madrid 2019, Rhodes-Purdy and Madrid 2020, Mudde and Rovira Kaltwasser 2013c) or on political parties (Mudde 2007) rather than on the behavior of ordinary citizens. When such scholarship does address public opinion, it often sees it as a relatively constant feature in society, changing little and relevant only when activated by elites (Hawkins, Rovira Kaltwasser, and Andreadis 2018, Mudde 2010). Our findings suggest otherwise. We show that discontent can and does respond to elements of the social environment in experimental settings, and these effects are reflected in observational studies as well. The role of elites and parties is not neglected in this book; we understand that powerful actors play an important role in shaping narratives and providing (or failing to provide) channels for public discontent.

Yet ultimately, ours is a story about ordinary citizens believing things and doing things they previously did not. It seems appropriate when trying to explain these changes to rely on a field of study that makes human motivation a core area of study. Political psychology has the further advantage of studying, rather than assuming, the source of motivation, unlike economism or culturalism. Due to this, political psychology relies on empirical studies to investigate why humans act the way they do in all its messy complexity.

1.3.2 Affective Intelligence Theory: The Emotional Link between Economics and Culture

Our resort to political psychology does not provide an instant escape hatch from the paradox formed by the Left Behind and Backlash hypotheses; we still need to explicate a clear and convincing link between economics and culture. To do so, we rely on emotions as the connective tissue between these disparate arenas of human experience. Specifically, we invoke emotions as described in affective intelligence theory (AIT), as primarily developed by George Marcus, Michael MacKuen, and Ted Brader (Brader and Marcus 2013, Marcus 2010, Marcus and Brader 2014, Marcus, MacKuen, and Neuman 2011, Marcus and MacKuen 1993).[7]

---

[7] We discuss our choice to invoke emotions generally and AIT specifically in Chapter 3.

Although we explicate AIT fully in Chapter 3, a brief introduction is necessary here because AIT differs radically from how most of us think about emotions. Most people (and most alternative approaches to the study of emotion) understand emotions roughly as follows: a person has an experience which they consciously consider and interpret, which then provokes an emotional response, which then motivates behavior. AIT counters this understanding by reversing the order of these elements, arguing based on neuroscientific research that emotions precede conscious thought. In fact, emotions are not discrete events that happen and then end but continuously operating monitoring processes, constantly scanning the environment for specific cues while shaping motivation *and* cognition. All of this happens before consciousness has a chance to intervene. This at least partly explains why most people so misunderstand how their own emotions work: the part of the brain responsible for "understanding" things, including elements of one's own mind, are pathetically slow. Emotions, on the other hand, do their work so quickly and in most cases so subtly that their work begins and ends before the conscious mind even recognizes that anything has happened.

AIT posits three such monitoring systems: anxiety, enthusiasm, and anger, which we refer to as resentment.[8] These systems monitor for unfamiliarity, reward, and norm violations, respectively. Each has a unique effect on motivation and cognition. Enthusiasm and resentment both encourage a reliance on preexisting habits of mind and cognitive shortcuts. Both enhance general motivation (i.e. lead to a desire to act) but in opposite directions: enthusiasm encourages further reward seeking to sustain its arousal, while resentment encourages punitive aggression against those who transgress against norms to extinguish itself. Anxiety, on the other hand, reduces the desire to act, leading the individual to focus more on cognition instead. It leads to a rapid information search, a scan of the environment to attempt to collect more data in order make the unknown known. More crucially, an anxious mind avoids motivated reasoning and is thus less reliant on previously held biases (Marcus 2021). The insight from AIT of most relevance here is that emotions triggered

---

[8] We discuss our renaming of anger in more detail in Chapter 3. Briefly put, we are hesitant to depart from accepted terminology, but this book is directed at a broad audience who likely hue to a more conventional understanding of emotions. Anger has connotations of intensity and sudden upsurging and subsiding, while resentment (like anxiety) better reflects the enduring, "slow-burn" character of emotions as monitoring systems as depicted in AIT. Readers should be aware from the outset that our use of the word "resentment" does not match how the term is used by other authors.

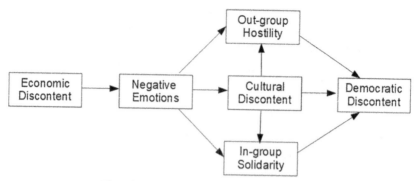

FIGURE 1.3 Flowchart of the APE theory of democratic discontent.

by phenomena in one domain of experience can influence a disparate domain of experience through motivation and cognition, *even if an individual does not cognitively link the two domains.* In other words, emotional reactions to economic trauma could conceivably influence how a person thinks and acts regarding cultural issues even if that individual is totally unaware of the link.

This linkage is exactly what we propose in this book, and what we argue resolves the dispute between the two hypotheses discussed earlier. Our approach uses emotional spillover, or the fact that emotions shape cognition and behavior outside the context that aroused the emotional response, as a bridge between economics, culture, and politics, which leads us to call our general approach "affective political economy" (APE). We see these factors working in sequential fashion, with economics at the beginning of the chain, producing emotional responses that influence cultural attitudes, which in turn produce populist attitudes. We provide a flowchart (Figure 1.3) summarizing our theory, which will help guide readers through the complex discussions later in this chapter and in our theoretical chapters (Chapters 2 and 3).

We argue that economic discontent, driven by long-term economic change and triggered and exacerbated by economic crises, is often the root cause of democratic discontent. However, its influence is mostly indirect, hence the lack of apparent economic effects in public opinion studies. Instead, the role of economic discontent is based in persistent emotional responses. Crises tend to result in a proliferation of social narratives about the actors responsible for precipitating the crisis, political elites who fail to respond with needed help or favor undeserving groups or actors, and a plethora of other narratives seeking to place blame for the crises, thus triggering resentment. Simultaneously, uncertainties regarding the causes of crises, possible solutions, and the likelihood of future economic calamity generate intense and widespread anxiety.

AIT tells us that the cognitive and behavioral changes induced by these emotions are not restricted to the economic events that produced them. Both anxiety and resentment have strong potential links with "hot button" cultural issues. The aggression, hostility, need to take punitive action, and reliance on preexisting biases engendered by resentment readily lend themselves to stories about immigrants stealing jobs, minorities getting an "easy ride," or (on the other side of the ideological spectrum) racists spewing hate unchecked and religious fanatics discriminating against women or LGBTQ individuals. Resentment also increases risk acceptance (Seawright 2012), which could lead to willingness to support political outsiders or risky forms of political behavior like aggressive protest. Furthermore, resentment (and possibly anxiety) trigger not only cultural discontent but greater hostility to out-groups and solidarity with one's own ethnic group (Marcus, Valentino, and Vasilopoulos 2019, Vasilopoulos et al. 2018, Albertson and Gadarian 2015).

Anxiety engenders a willingness to entertain new ideas and narratives, especially if those narratives concern threats, as there is evidence that the information search triggered by anxiety also increases attention to threatening information (Albertson and Gadarian 2015, Gadarian and Albertson 2014). By focusing on information that one finds threatening, anxiety could paradoxically *reinforce* existing beliefs through selective attention to threatening information. In other words, economic discontent does its work not by directly triggering democratic discontent but by turning up the heat on whatever cultural conflicts are relevant in a given context.

From here, the connection between cultural and democratic discontent is straightforward: disenchantment with politics as usual is a predictable response to feeling as though elites and the political system prioritize the values of "the other" while neglecting and even spurning one's own values. At this point, the only question left is what specific variety (or varieties) of discontent will emerge, as political antipathy melds with preexisting social attitudes and beliefs. Panizza (2005) calls populism the "mirror of democracy," but a more apt metaphor might be that discontent casts existing political norms, practices, and elites in the role of Dorian Gray, with discontented movements their portrait: an amalgamation of the nasty, dysfunctional, and hostile elements of politics that typically lie dormant during better times.

None of this is to argue that cultural conflicts are absent or unimportant when the economy roars: one can find conflicts over race, immigration, acceptance of LGBTQ individuals, secularism, and any number of issues in good times as in bad. Nor do nice tolerant democrats suddenly strap on jackboots and become ravening fascists when the unemployment rate begins to rise. Even in the social democracies of Scandinavia, where strong and comprehensive welfare states provide considerable protection for most citizens, culturally discontented political movements have become political fixtures.[9] Yet economic turmoil is like gasoline poured on a fire: it hardens the battle lines between social groups, raises the stakes of those conflicts, and increases the demands for political leaders and systems to pick sides.

1.4 LOWERING THE TEMPERATURE: MANAGING DEMOCRATIC DISCONTENT

Explaining democratic discontent is a worthy academic goal, but from a more practical standpoint it is only a means to an end: namely, avoiding the havoc that discontented movements can wreak on democratic societies. While we address this issue more thoroughly in the conclusion to this book (Chapter 10), there are two practical conclusions we draw from our theory that bear noting here. First, the Left Behind and Backlash hypotheses are wildly different in terms of manageability. If discontent is driven entirely by culture, then the options for ameliorating the problem are limited and unpalatable. Should societies accommodate cultural backlash even if that means violating the rights or trammeling the march toward social equality of marginalized groups? Or should societies throw up roadblocks, double-down on the use of courts, party elites (Levitsky and Ziblatt 2018), or unelected bodies like the Department of Antiracism proposed by Kendi (2019) to keep conservative traditionalists from violating the rights of others?

Given the threats faced by contemporary democracy, we certainty understand the impulse to keep extremists and political arsonists at bay by any means necessary. Yet our approach suggests that such reforms would be counterproductive. Cultural conflicts are always difficult, but as we show throughout this book, the intense animosity surrounding them gets considerably worse when people are under economic pressure. Furthermore, economic problems tend to weigh heavier on citizens when the quality of democracy is poor. An extensive emerging literature on procedural justice in democracies has shown that economic problems are perceived as far graver when citizens feel that democratic regimes

---

[9] For an insightful discussion of the economic causes of PRR success in Scandinavia, see Roberts (2019).

provide them with little meaningful influence on politics (Magalhães 2016, Magalhães and Aguiar-Conraria 2018, Rhodes-Purdy 2021c). Democratic deficiencies can also generate democratic discontent directly in their own right (Roberts 2015, 2019, Busby, Gubler, and Hawkins 2019). This book reinforces these findings: we demonstrate throughout our empirical chapters that a lack of an institutionally guaranteed voice for citizens exacerbates democratic discontent in several ways.

The upside is that our suggested solutions to the problem of discontent are far less distasteful than those implied by a cultural origin, if not necessarily uncontroversial. Simply put, we argue that state action to improve economic security and to enhance the role of citizens in a democracy is the most promising ways to avoid future episodes of extreme discontent. Such actions would mutually benefit both sides of the cultural divide while centering costs mostly on the elite. In so suggesting, we are standing against some powerful orthodoxies. Economically, the trend until very recently has been *away* from providing greater citizen protection through social welfare: as noted earlier, the age of discontent came after nearly thirty years of neoliberalism, where states were marginalized in their roles as economic managers and social safety nets weakened in the interest of budget discipline (Eichengreen 2018, Crouch 2011, Hacker 2008). Politically, many scholars of democracy have advocated the opposite approach to what we suggest here, arguing that citizen voice must be *reduced* to protect democracy from charismatic demagogues (Levitsky and Ziblatt 2018, Mounk 2018, Rosenbluth and Shapiro 2018, Riker 1988, Schumpeter 2008).

We are not naive and do not overestimate the power such reforms have. Removing oxygen from a fire will extinguish it, but anything that burned in the conflagration will always be ashes. Our current moment of discontent may have already become self-sustaining: something to simply be endured and worked through. Yet, even if this moment passes we are likely to find ourselves here again at some point in the future; the good times never roll forever, and economic crises are, in the long run, inevitable. We hope this book motivates activists and policymakers to focus on reforms that could mitigate the damage of future crises.

1.5 PLAN OF THE BOOK: STRUCTURE, METHODS, AND CASE SELECTION

Section 1.4 provided a preview of the solutions our theory suggests, but its inclusion puts the cart before the horse. Solutions suggested by a theory should never be considered until that theory is well and thoroughly tested, which is the primary purpose of the later chapters of this book. These tests involve both qualitative and quantitative analyses, which presents us with a dilemma. We cannot expect our theory to be taken seriously without providing the best possible evidence to support it, which requires some complex statistical methods. Yet we also want this book to be accessible to a broad scholarly audience, including those who have little experience or interest in methodology. As such, in this section we lay out the structure of the remainder of the book, briefly illustrating how we use evidence and providing guidance for which sections different sorts of readers might wish to pay the most attention.

Chapters 2 and 3, along with this introduction, set out our primary theoretical argument. Chapter 2 establishes our conceptual schema, discussing our definitions of economic, cultural, and democratic discontent, how discontent manifests in different specific ideas (e.g. as populism, support for the FR, conspiracism, etc.) and behaviors, including support for political outsiders, involvement with extremist movements, contentious political behavior, and even political violence. It also introduces the conflict between the Left Behind and Backlash hypotheses in detail, arguing that both fail to capture a complete picture of discontent.

Chapter 3 lays out our theoretical framework. This includes an indepth explication of the multistep structure of the theory, where economic discontent engenders emotions, which in turn cause cultural discontent to flare up, with culture the proximate cause of democratic discontent. This chapter also explicates how democratic quality and voice can either ameliorate or intensify these relationships. These two chapters are likely to be of greatest interest to those studying discontent from a theoretical perspective; other readers with less interest in theoretical details might wish to skim Chapter 2 but pay greater attention to Chapter 3.

We spend the remaining chapters of the book testing and applying the theory developed in Chapters 1–3. We adopt a mixed methods approach, using both quantitative and qualitative techniques, although we rely more heavily on the former. Chapter 4 is the most statistically dense chapter of the book. In this chapter, we use survey experiments to test each stage of the theory as outlined in Figure 1.1. All experiments were conducted in the United States (a limitation we at least partially overcome with observational data taken from other countries), using a variety of platforms, including convenience samples (Mechanical Turk) and nationally representative samples. As we do in other chapters when presenting our analyses, we try to present results as simply and straightforwardly as possible. Nevertheless, readers who do not have a great deal of experience with experimental techniques may wish to focus on our discussion of results while skimming the remainder of this chapter.

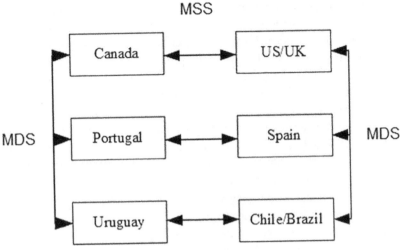

FIGURE 1.4 Chart of case comparisons.

Chapters 5–8 present our case studies. These chapters serve two purposes. Our primary goal is to demonstrate in these chapters the practical utility of APE for explaining political outcomes in real-world cases. We apply our theory to elucidate the often subtle and disguised ways in which economic problems worm their way into a host of other social problems, especially cultural conflicts. To that end, we rely primarily on analysis of within-country (or region) survey data, including original data collected as part of our Political Systems Attitudes Study (PSAS) project (Rhodes-Purdy, Navarre, and Utych 2020).

Our secondary objective with these chapters is to provide further insight into the causes of democratic discontent at the national level through comparative analysis. This goal drove our selection of cases, which we chose to develop a series of most different systems (MDS) and most similar systems (MSS) designs. A chart of these comparisons is presented in Figure 1.4.

Our core cases come from different regions, and have different levels of economic development, political histories, cultural heritages, and so on. Few characteristics are shared by these countries, save two: major surges of democratic discontent and severe economic crises. Observational data from each country, including original data collected as part of the PSAS and national election studies, support our theory.

To avoid problems related to selection on the independent variable, in Chapter 8 we include a trio of cases that form three paired MSS comparisons with our core cases, as well as a second MDS comparison among themselves:

Canada, Portugal, and Uruguay. These cases illustrate two factors that can reduce the translation of economic crises into cultural and democratic discontent. First, political responses are crucial. Political systems that rise to the challenge presented by crises, accepting and adapting to new realities (especially the discrediting of neoliberalism and austerity), can retain the support of their publics even if the economic damage is severe. The three countries we include in this chapter differ from our core set of cases in that they all resisted (eventually) the demands of international organizations and right-wing political actors to slash budgets and raise taxes in the midst of major recessions. Our second factor facilitated this political flexibility: democratic responsiveness through effective left or center-left parties. In all three "negative" cases, left-wing parties were able to either continue their resistance to neoliberal orthodoxy or depart from an earlier acceptance.

In Chapter 9, we circle back to the United States to examine the dynamics when politically discontented movements take power. Although we spend much of the book emphasizing the importance of economic turmoil in generating discontent, in this chapter we find that once in power, discontent can enter a self-perpetuating vicious cycle due to deliberate polarization of society by discontented leaders. The cycle intensifies not just by radicalizing the followers of the dominant discontented movement, but by pushing the opposition further from the ideological center as well. We also investigate the role conspiracy theories play in perpetuating this vicious feedback loop.

In the final chapter, we summarize our findings (briefly), but focus mostly on their implication for the future of democracy. Among other things, we argue against the short-sighted desire to rely on antidemocratic barriers from both left and right to manage social problems and prevent the rise of charismatic demagogues. We also raise questions about whether neoliberalism is, in the absence of common enemies like communism or fascism, compatible with democratic survival in the long term. Markets and democracy form a dilemma: each appears to be a necessary precondition of the successful operation of the other (Iversen and Soskice 2019), yet each also faces constant pressure to erode and negate its opposite. The intrinsic economic insecurity that results from the erosion of the welfare state, along with the hollowing out of democratic systems and the rejection of citizen voice necessary to sustain extreme economic liberalism, threaten to produce a sort of Sisyphean feedback loop, where democracy continually pushes against the corrosive effects of discontent even as the dictates of laissez-faire economics subvert those efforts. We conclude the book speculatively (but a bit more hopefully), noting specific reforms that we hope will allow us to close the book on the age of discontent.

2

Left Behind vs. Backlash

Economic and Cultural Theories of Democratic Discontent

Over the next two chapters, we outline our theory of democratic discontent.[1] Our first task here is to get ourselves, and more than half a dozen bodies of scholarship, organized. Existing scholarship on discontented political tendencies is highly compartmentalized: studies of specific variants of discontent (e.g. populism, conspiracism, support for the FR) tend to be siloed off from one another, with relatively little cross-topic attention despite the obvious synergies between them. The result is that consistent findings appear sporadic, inconsistent findings go unnoticed, and conceptual blurriness is pervasive. We begin by establishing a conceptual schema of democratic discontent (or simply discontent, which we use hereafter without the modifier interchangeably with democratic discontent).

We then turn to existing arguments about the origin of discontent. Our goal here is not to review every theoretical debate in agonizing detail; this is a book about discontent, not any specific manifestation of it. We review these literatures with an eye toward overlap: we try to identify which debates recur in multiple studies, over multiple fields. By putting unique aspects of each literature to the side, it becomes clear that battle lines are repeatedly drawn between economics and culture. Are people turning against the political mainstream, defined by neoliberal capitalism, liberal democracy, and (increasingly) multiculturalism because they believe their economic interests have suffered under the strain of competition from

---

[1] Portions of this chapter have appeared in previously published articles (Utych, Navarre, and Rhodes-Purdy 2021, Rhodes-Purdy, Navarre, and Utych 2020, Navarre, Rhodes-Purdy, and Utych 2020). Sections are reprinted with the permission of the relevant journals.

immigrants or developing countries? Or is it because they feel their values and identities are under attack by an elite cabal of globalists and their urbane, cosmopolitan allies? We find no satisfactory resolution to these questions in existing research; we propose and defend such an answer in the remainder of this book.

2.1 THE STRUCTURE OF DISCONTENT

Discontent is a risky concept; we are attempting to incorporate a bewilderingly diverse array of attitudes and behaviors under a single term. The potential for impermissible conceptual stretching (Sartori 1970), making different types of things appear more similar than they really are when attempting to move across contexts, is significant. With that in mind, we take a relatively conservative approach to conceptualization: we avoid using less strict forms of taxonomy like radial or family resemblance categories (Collier and Mahon 1993), in favor of a (mostly) strictly hierarchical schema, with higher-order concepts made more broadly encompassing by reducing their specificity, or in Sartori's terms, by moving up the "ladder of abstraction."

The behaviors and attitudes we analyze in this book cross the ideological spectrum, appeal to a diverse array of cultural and social groups, and encourage distinct types of electoral and contentious political behavior. Adherents of many of these movements despise their opposite numbers and would vehemently reject any proposed similarities; culturally focused left populists, for example, would balk at being lumped in with the PRR. There are certainly important conceptual and moral differences between variants of discontent. Yet, discontented movements all share a deep-seated lack of support for or antipathy toward major components of the dominant political order. In psychological terms, discontent is an attitude, with strong negative valence (i.e. characterized by unpleasant emotions like anger and anxiety), that is directed at some element of the political mainstream in a given person's society. As we discussed in Chapter 1, discontent itself is a malformed reflection of the political status quo. The specific type of discontent, and the ideologies and narrative that imbue it with meaning, tend to be a negative image of the political status quo. This becomes especially important in our case-focused chapters, where we find that the details of how and in what form discontent manifests is heavily influenced by the local political context.

As we discuss specific manifestations of discontent throughout this chapter, we often find multiple competing definitions. Some of these debates are of relatively minor importance to our theory but have considerable relevance for measurement issues; we leave these issues to the empirical chapters where we discuss measurement issues. However, definitional issues related to some specific manifestations (such as populism and conspiracism) have major relevance to theory; what factors explain the manifestation of these attitudes may well depend upon how they are conceptualized. In those cases, we discuss definitional debates in some detail in this chapter. Before going further, we need to briefly discuss our overarching criteria for evaluating existing conceptualizations of specific forms of discontent. In crafting our own definitions or selecting among existing definitions of our various manifestations of discontent, several criteria are relevant:

- *Dynamism.* As discontented movements can emerge quite rapidly, we prioritize conceptualizations that allow for relatively rapid change in magnitude or salience.
- *Comparability.* We favor conceptualizations of discontent manifestations that avoid case-specific details (e.g. definitions of conspiracism that reference specific conspiracy theories which may be totally irrelevant in most countries). We also avoid definitions with clear ideological content, which would prevent comparison of ideologically disparate but otherwise similar attitudes and behavior (e.g. populism as practiced by the left and the right).
- *Discriminant validity.* We discuss an array of manifestations, some of which frequently co-occur (e.g., ethnocentrism/nativism and populism are very closely correlated, at least in Europe). As such, we require concepts that can clearly demarcate one form of discontent manifestation from others.
- *Psychological basis.* Our framework relies heavily on social psychology and the psychology of emotions. As such, we prefer conceptualizations that are rooted in psychological theories and concepts, or are at least easily reconcilable with them.

2.2 ATTITUDINAL MANIFESTATIONS OF DISCONTENT: REGIME ANTIPATHY, POPULISM, AND CONSPIRACISM

Democratic elites and regimes have not always navigated turbulent waters successfully, especially in the era of the Great Recession. Elucidating the causes of these failures (or why people perceive certain outcomes as failures) is among our most important contributions. However, before we begin any analyses, we must carefully delineate different concepts that each capture disenchantment with democratic politics to some degree, and there are crucial differences that we need to address. We define three such concepts here: regime antipathy/regime support, populism, and conspiracism.

2.2.1 Fighting the System: Democratic Regime Antipathy

First, citizens may become disenchanted with democratic regimes themselves. We call this democratic regime antipathy. The concept of regime support, or a generalized positive attitude toward the actual rules and practices of a given democratic regime, has a long history in the study of politics, going back to early political behavior researchers such as Easton (1975), and the literature on the topic is considerable. We do not address this topic in great detail here (see Norris (1999), Booth and Seligson (2009), Pharr and Putnam (2000), and Rhodes-Purdy (2017c) for detailed treatments) because the movements that have arisen since Great Recession have not, for the most part, targeted their ire directly (or at least not exclusively) at political regimes. That said, regime antipathy contributes to the rise of discontented politics, and we discuss elements of it in various sections of this book. For now, however, we turn to a much more relevant form of explicitly democratic discontent: populism.

2.2.2 Against Elites: Defining Populism

We would happily forgive the reader if their first response to the subtitle of this section was wailings and lamentations. Why, one might reasonably ask, do we need yet *another* discussion of the definitions of populism? As much as we would like to simply embrace one of the existing definitions of populism and move on, we cannot: problems and limitations are prevalent in all conceptualizations, and these need to be discussed and resolved before we move on. Of all the definitions of populism that have been used at one time or another, we can boil down those that are still in widespread use to two. The first is the political strategic definition, articulated most clearly by Weyland (2017, 2001). The strategic approach defines populism as a relationship between a leader and their followers that is unmediated by organizations, especially political parties.

We do not use this definition for several reasons, the most important of which is a lack of cross-regional comparative utility. While well suited for Latin America, it is not as broadly applicable in the North American or European contexts. In these regions, both left- and right-wing populism can be either personalist or based in parties or social movements (e.g. the Tea Party and Occupy Wall Street in the United States). We have no doubt that charisma and personalism matter, hence the lengthy discussion of this definition. We will, in fact, dwell on the issue of charismatic bonding at some length in various parts of this book. We simply do not feel that populism is the best term for either personalism or charismatic attachment, which are better described by the terms just used. Even discounting its use as a definition, the strategic approach has some important lessons for understanding populism. First, we heed Weyland's proposition that populism is best understood as a fundamentally political phenomenon; we will come back to this idea when discussing the ideational approach. Perhaps more crucially, we find personalism and charismatic attachment to be closely associated with populism, although we argue (in later sections) that this association is causal rather than conceptual.

The second definition, and the one which is closest to our own, is the ideational approach, pioneered by Mudde (Akkerman, Mudde, and Zaslove 2014, Mudde 2007) and Hawkins (Hawkins et al. 2019, Hawkins 2009, 2010, Hawkins and Rovira Kaltwasser 2017). The ideational approach holds that populism is a political logic characterized by a moral conflict between an evil and corrupt elite and a totally good and morally upright people. The ideational approach is ideal[2] for our purposes: it can be used to characterize the thoughts and opinions of ordinary citizens (which is crucial for political behavior research such as ours), as well as the manifestos and public appeals of social movements, political parties, and leaders. And the specific ideas that undergird the ideational approach (solidarity with the people, hostility toward and suspicion of the elite) are clearly reflected in core psychological concepts (e.g. in-group solidarity and out-group hostility, anger, resentment, punitive aggression, etc.).

This is not to imply there are no problems with the ideational approach. It fits three of our criteria well, but it has real problems with discriminant validity. Weyland (2017) provides an effective critique of many of the ideational approach's major issues, but none are so troubling as its tendency to produce false positives; for example, some measures would define George W. Bush as a populist. These problems are exacerbated by the fact that many operationalizations of the approach (Hawkins 2009, Akkerman, Mudde, and Zaslove 2014) weight the people-centric aspect of the concept a bit too heavily. The result is that the ideational definition

---

[2] Pun intended.

can conceivably fit many radical political movements, including Marxist socialism/communism and Nazism/fascism. Finally, the definition has some issues when applied to the PRR in Europe (and the USA, if one includes Donald Trump under this rubric). At the same time, the bipartite division of society in the ideational approach does not neatly fit the PRR's emphasis on nonelites like immigrants and racial minorities who are neither elites nor part of the people. The lack of clarity can be partly attributed to the ad hoc development of the approach, which emerged inductively from analyzing the rhetoric and practices of populist parties and from the critical and discursive political theory of Ernesto Laclau and the Essex school (Laclau and Mouffe 1985, Laclau 2005). The absence of a complete psychological model of discontent hampers the ideational approach's ability to distinguish between forms of discontent, while also making theory development more difficult, as we discuss later.

Given this, we specify a slightly modified version of the ideational approach as our working definition. First, we argue that populism is neither a form of discourse nor ideology: instead, it is a psychological attitude, or more accurately a combination of two attitudes, one directed toward the elite, and one directed toward an imaginary unified "people." We concur with the basic ideational definition that populism involves an intense conflict between these two groups, but we minimize the problem of false positives by heeding Weyland's argument that populism is an inherently political phenomenon. We therefore define populism as a belief that members of the *political* elite have betrayed "the people," whom they are supposed to represent, in favor of some other set of interests. The betrayal can be selfish (political elites simply care about their own interests, rather than those of the people), but is more commonly done in favor of some group of "unpeople." The unpeople are those who, though not part of the political elite, are seen as undeserving of participating in democracy for some reason. They may be seen as corrupt or greedy (e.g. bankers, financial elites, multilateral corporations), or as insufficiently supportive of national culture, due to their loyalty to vague globalism or to specific groups that are seen as outside the people (e.g. immigrants, minorities, members of the LGBTQ community). All three categories are culturally constructed; the people have an imagined unity that never exists in reality (Müller 2016).

Our definition has several important advantages over the dominant version of the ideational approach. First, by centering our definition on the political realm (as Weyland suggests), it gains greater discriminant validity. Populism is centered on an evaluation of political elites and a perceived betrayal of the principal–agent relationship that lies at the heart of representative democracy (Plotke 1997). This would exclude Marxists (for whom democracy is a bourgeois conceit) and fascists (who detest democracy as a perversion of the natural hierarchy). Nevertheless, our definition is broadly applicable: populists of all ideological stripes and regional backgrounds comfortably fit this attitude. Second, the centrality of betrayal provides significant analytical leverage, as the psychological effects of betrayal are well known (we discuss this in Chapter 3). Third, this definition satisfies our dynamic criterion. As an attitude, we expect populism to be influenced by fixed characteristics, but also to change over time (perhaps quite quickly) as circumstances change. Finally, we lose nothing in terms of operationalization: our definition actually more closely matches the best scale of populist attitudes, the Castanho Silva et al. (2018) scale, which references political elites and politics in many of its questions.

Populism so defined has some clear overlap with the concept of regime support we (briefly) discussed earlier. Certainly, a lack of faith in "the system" could easily be found in the rhetoric of a populist or a disenchanted democrat. There are subtle differences between the two. First, regime antipathy is directed primarily at institutions and practices, while populism is far more personal, its antagonism being directed toward the political elite. And second, populism is more specific: it tells a particular story about society's problems, based on the betrayal of elites, whereas regime support is deliberately vague, and reflects merely a negative evaluation of regime institutions that may arise from a variety of causes in different contexts and individuals.

2.2.3 What They Don't Want You to Know: Conspiracism

Sometimes discontent targets reality itself. Along with populist ideas and fury at democratic regimes, the era of the Great Recession has seen the rise of unsupported (and often bizarre) conspiracy theories (Castanho Silva, Vegetti, and Littvay 2017; Filer 2018). While belief in these theories may not have become more prevalent across society (Uscinski and Parent 2014), they have recently moved from the dark fringes of society to the center of democratic politics, to the point where even the most febrile conspiracies have been embraced by mainstream politicians (Rosenblum and Muirhead 2019). Conspiracy theories have arisen on the left (e.g. some elements of the anti-vaccination and anti-genetically modified organisms (GMOs) movements) and the right (e.g. QAnon, Stop the Steal, the Great Replacement).

We refer to the tendency of an individual to believe in multiple unfounded conspiracies as conspiracism. Conspiracism is not always a form of democratic discontent; theories such as alien abductions or fears about GMOs are not directly political and are often simply born of paranoia or gullibility. Nevertheless, we treat conspiracism as a manifestation of discontent because belief in these narratives clearly displays a lack of trust in the political system and a willingness to believe that political opponents are almost supernaturally evil. The fact that conspiracism seems to be highly correlated with other manifestations of discontent, especially populism, further compels us to include it in our schema (Castanho Silva, Vegetti, and Littvay 2017).

There is no one accepted way to classify competing explanations for conspiracy theories. To simplify things, we have decided to divide explanations of conspiracy into two groups: cognitive traits, which encompasses the epistemic motivation such as need for cognitive closure and intentionality bias (Douglas, Sutton, and Cichocka 2017), and protective motivation, which sees conspiracies as "a form of threat perception, and fears [that] are fundamentally driven by shifts in relative power" (Uscinski and Parent 2014). In short, protective motivation see conspiracy theories as coping mechanisms, or ways for individuals to understand and interpret negative social outcomes in a way that allows them to escape from intolerable anxiety and demotivation. This protective aspect of conspiracism has a great deal of potential synergy with discontent: it can form part of an explanation for why "the people," who should be sovereign in a democracy, are ignored and disdained instead of exalted. In addition, conspiracy theories can fill the gap and explain the seeming contradiction between the people being the majority but also being the "losers" or taken advantage of, as seen in populism. As we discuss in Chapter 9, this can be particularly important for helping the leaders of discontented movements maintain their followers' loyalty when they fail to achieve significant policy victories.

It is important to note that many conspiracies theories can have seeds of truth in them. The US government *has* helped overthrow regimes and attempted to assassinate world leaders. Scientists *did* use unknowing African Americans and poor Guatemalans to test the effects of untreated sexually transmitted diseases. Levees *were* blown up in 1920s Louisiana to redirect the flooding Mississippi into more rural areas and not the cities. Due to histories like this that have had greater impact on ethnic minorities and the poor, it is no surprise that minorities are more likely to believe in conspiracy theories (Orr and Husting 2018, Crocker et al.

1999). Questioning government and elites is an essential part of accountability and is necessary for the rule of law and transparency; however, in the hands of the discontented, conspiracy theories do not represent reasoned skepticism but rather serve as a way to explain why the "silent majority" is not winning despite its larger numbers.

We freely admit that we are further out on a limb by including conspiracism in our framework than we are with populism. Yet when we examine the dynamics of conspiracism empirically, it acts much as we would expect were it a form of discontent. We are confident that, once we have laid out all the evidence for our approach, most readers will agree with our treatment of conspiracism as a form of discontent.

2.3 BEHAVIORAL CONSEQUENCES OF DISCONTENT

Before we conclude our conceptual discussion, we must discuss one final issue: the connection between attitudes and behavior. Even with relatively specific attitudes, any number of factors can intervene to influence how they manifest as political actions taken by those who hold them. In our case, discontent is a deliberately nonspecific attitude and thus its translation into behavior is even more nebulous. We have two major complications to deal with: the complex interaction of specific manifestations of discontent, and whether discontent is channeled into conventional or unconventional participation.

2.3.1 Electoral Support for Discontented Leaders and Movements

To this point, we have maintained a rigid, classical conceptual schema, with discrete manifestations of discontent nestled within the larger umbrella concept. This strategy is essential for analyses of relationships between these discontented attitudes, such as those we provide in Chapter 4. Yet we seek to do more than simply analyze relationships: a substantial portion of this book is dedicated to applying those analyses to describe actual discontented political movements in real-world cases. And reality can be damnably resistant to such neat categorization. Rambunctious populists, conspiracy theorists, and the rest of their ilk refuse to stay in any neat little box in which we may wish to put them. Instead, they treat our schema like a buffet, taking a bit from each category, with untidy results.

Thus, when categorizing actual discontented movements, we relax one requirement of strict classical categories: mutual exclusivity. Virtually all the movements we discuss in this book are permutations of discontent, mixing and matching to suit their interests and identities. Trumpism, for example, is a mélange of economic discontent, conservative cultural discontent, populism, and conspiracism. As mentioned earlier, the specific permutations of discontent in any given case are likely driven by the details of the case-specific status quo and the discontented narratives that are readily available in a given context; as such, we leave detailed explication of permutations to our case-focused chapters. We will note here that this relaxation of strict classicalism informs our analyses. When trying to explain when and why a movement arose when it did, we must be aware not only of the manifestations of discontent which the movement displays (and the causal antecedents thereof); we must also pay close attention to possible interactions between them.

Regardless of how discontent manifests in different permutations of attitudes, eventually it must lead to some change in actual political behavior among large groups of people to have an impact. The most obvious mechanism for converting thought to action is by voting for leaders, parties, and movements who reflect (and reciprocally shape) discontented ideas and attitudes. We analyze many such leaders and organizations throughout this book.

2.3.2 Into the Streets: Conventional Participation and Contentious Politics

That said, discontent is a uniquely difficult form of politics for democratic institutions to channel. Discontent inherently involves a certain antipathy or distrust toward "the system," and we might therefore expect discontented individuals to be extremely wary of "mainstream" political actors or institutions who they perceive as corrupt or even evil. Situational factors exacerbate this: discontent is not likely to arise or become prominent in healthy democracies where political elites are responsive and there are institutional mechanisms for citizen voice. Leadership in discontented societies is likely to be disconnected from ordinary citizens and unwilling or unable to adapt to new realities. This can easily set in motion a vicious cycle, in which discontented individuals forsake conventional participation, which in turn makes it easier for leaders to ignore the discontented, who pull even further away from mainstream politics as a result. This cycle can be broken in two primary ways. The first is when political entrepreneurs with little loyalty to existing power holders decide to enter the fray, drawing the disillusioned under their banners.

The second method is for the discontented to engage in contentious politics. The notion that contentious behavior strongly implies discontented attitudes is well supported by research, as many scholars have found that democratic discontent, especially regime antipathy, is highly correlated with contentious political behavior (Crow 2010, Muller and Opp 1986, Opp, Burow-Auffarth, and Heinrichs 1981, Rhodes-Purdy 2012, Tarrow 1998, 2000). Social movements throughout history have taken their frustrations onto the streets. In this book, we specifically discuss the Black Lives Matter (BLM) movement and the *estallido social* in Chile that eventually resulted in a plebiscite to draft a new constitution at considerable length; we also discuss conservative protest movements against mask mandates in Chapter 9.

2.4 CHALLENGING THE GLOBAL ORDER: DEMOCRACY, NEOLIBERALISM, AND MULTICULTURALISM

While discontent can take many forms, all of them display a marked antipathy toward "politics as usual." Clearly something is rotten in the states of Europe and the Americas; at least many of the citizens of these countries believe this. Obviously "politics as usual" varies a great deal across the countries we analyze, and the differing impact of the Great Recession, refugee crises, and domestic political turmoil have shaped and molded discontent in different ways as a result. Yet there are global aspects that influence all countries. These are the elements of the liberal democratic capitalist system which has its origins in the allied victory of World War II and developed further as it embraced neoclassical capitalism and globalization during the 1980s and multiculturalism in the twenty-first century.

We have no desire to write a jeremiad. Globalization has lifted millions out of poverty, democracy has become more widespread than at any time in human history and has freed countless people from oppression, and multiculturalism has allowed marginalized groups in societies around the world opportunities to participate fully in public life without discarding their dearly held values and customs. That said, this book is concerned with those who feel threatened or attacked by some element or elements of the global order, and how those feelings intensified under the economic turmoil of the Great Recession era. Therefore, the upsides of the world order, no matter how significant, are not very relevant for our purposes.

Since the turbulence of the 1960s until well into the 1990s, there was little internal dissention among the acolytes of the liberal order, as the overarching conflict between first fascism (during the order's formation after World War II) and then communism (during the Cold War) unified liberals against common enemies. The fall of the Soviet Union in the early 1990s did not immediately fracture the liberal consensus. Many scholars argued that humanity had reached the end of its history as all conceivable alternatives to liberal capitalism and democracy had failed (Fukuyama 2006). Given recent events this argument can seem naive, but at the time the argument was made, the thesis seemed plausible. There was one major gap in the logic (which Fukuyama himself acknowledged): alternatives to liberal, democratic capitalism had indeed been discredited, but this did not necessarily vindicate the order itself, nor absolve it of its contradictions and limitations. In fact, the consignment of alternatives to history's dustbin deprived the order of common enemies to unify against; as a result, the imperfections of the order inevitably became more apparent.

2.5 THOSE LEFT BEHIND: ECONOMIC LOSERS OF NEOLIBERAL GLOBALIZATION

Whether neoliberalism's benefits outweigh its disadvantages, or if it distributes gains in a just manner, are complex issues and ones which we happily need not resolve to make our argument. What is relevant here – and this is probably not terribly controversial – is that any major economic shift creates winners and losers: some will benefit more than others, and some will bear greater costs, and the neoliberal revolution is no exception. That said, the winning and losing social groups differ by context. In the developed world, the losers were mostly those who lacked the human capital necessary to adapt to new economic requirements, especially low-skilled workers in the manufacturing sector. Neoliberalism accelerated the process of deindustrialization in the developed world. As trade was liberalized, low-skilled manufacturing jobs rapidly shifted toward underdeveloped countries where unskilled labor was far cheaper. Developed countries began to transition away from manufacturing and toward high-skilled services in areas like technology and communications (Rodrik 2018). While this benefited many social sectors in both core and peripheral countries, blue-collar workers in advanced economies saw their livelihoods and communities decimated.

2.5.1 The Left behind in Developed Economies

This created powerful new social divisions in advanced economies that cut across the traditional capital–labor divide. On one side are highly educated, ethnically and racially diverse urbanites who have disproportionately benefited from globalization. On the other side are what scholars have called the losers of globalization (Teney, Lacewell, and De Wilde 2014, Kriesi et al. 2006) or (mostly in the context of Brexit studies) the "left behind" (Goodwin and Milazzo 2015, Goodwin and Heath 2016, Hobolt 2016). In the remainder of this book we use the term left behind to describe any group of individuals who suffer disproportionate economic deprivation and insecurity, and thus specific demographic profiles vary from country to country based on domestic economic, social, and policy factors. One common feature worth noting is that the left behind are almost never the most deprived in society, who we might instead call the "never ahead." Discontent appears to be heavily concentrated, at least since the Great Recession, in the stressed and insecure middle sectors, especially among those who belong to the ethnoracial majority. Poor and marginalized ethnoracial groups, despite having an even stronger claim to legitimate discontent, are typically absent from the ranks of populists and organized conspiratorial movements.[3]

In the context of globalized neoliberalism, the left behind in industrialized countries are those with no university degree (and perhaps no high school diploma) who work in low- or semi-skilled manual professions, especially manufacturing. They tend to be older members of the dominant ethnoracial group in their societies and live in much more homogenous communities outside major urban centers, in industrial cities, suburbs, or small company towns in rural areas. In their book on the UK Independence Party (UKIP), Ford and Goodwin (2014, ch. 4, para. 1) give a typical portrait of one of those left behind in an advanced economy:

Meet John. He is 64 years old and was born and raised in Nottingham, where he worked for many years as a skilled machinist in the famous Raleigh bicycle factory. John started as a line worker when he was only 15 years old. "I was never much for school, left as soon as I could. I knew Raleigh were hiring, you could walk straight into a good job in those days." John prospered at the factory and, within a few years, he was supervising a team of ten. "That was how it was back then. You didn't need certificates. Work hard, show you can learn, and you'd make your way." But in 2003, John was made redundant as the last factory was shuttered. "They said something I didn't understand about European regulations, and that we couldn't compete with the Far East. They'd work twice the hours we could, for a tenth of the money." When John turned 50, he found himself unemployed for the first time in his life. "I don't blame the company, they did their best, treated me fair, gave me a good pay-off. But when I went looking, there was no work."

---

[3] There are exceptions to this trend, including the informal sector in Latin America and the BLM movement in the United States.

John goes on to explain his frustration with the lack of opportunities for employment and the lack of concern shown for people like him by the Labour Party, once his stalwart advocate, and finally his perception that the state bends over backward to help newly arrived immigrants while leaving people like him to fend for themselves.[4] Whatever the benefits of globalization, it is undeniable that workers like John suffered, at a bare minimum, a severe disruption, one that has only gotten worse during the Great Recession era.

2.5.2 The Left behind in Developing Economies

In underdeveloped countries, the patterns of winners and losers are more complex. Some peripheral countries have done quite well under globalization, undergoing rapid industrialization and an elevation of living standards. And consumers in the developing world have often benefited from lower prices and fiscal discipline, which has occasionally given neoliberal reform broad public support (Baker 2009, Weyland 1999). However, outside of East Asia, globalization's transfer of manufacturing to the underdeveloped world has been much less beneficial. Latin America has undergone a period of deindustrialization similar to that seen in the developed world, with similar negative socioeconomic consequences. Deindustrialization has accelerated the rapid growth of the informal economy (Carr and Chen 2002), wherein workers are often poor and almost always profoundly insecure, given their lack of access to many social benefits only available to the formally employed. Rural workers have also come under pressure as commercialized, export-oriented agriculture has displaced peasants and other rural workers. Finally, austerity and privatization have decimated public payrolls. This was almost certainly an economic necessity (Latin American public sectors were notoriously bloated prior to the neoliberal era), but it did remove a major source of secure employment for the middle classes.

These dynamics have formed the basis of what we and others have called the Left Behind hypothesis: that discontent has a fundamentally economic materialist basis, and that discontented political behaviors are driven mostly by these dollars-and-cents questions. Cultural factors are seen as irrelevant by-products or side effects; prejudice neither causes nor

---

[4] This latter point demonstrates both the economic logic of discontent and also the fact that economic and cultural factors tend to intermix and become difficult to separate from one another.

motivates discontent. These arguments are hardly novel: the influence of economic concerns on behavior has been studied extensively and by multiple paradigms. Marxist and other class-based analyses of discontent have been around for decades (e.g. Adorno et al. 2019, Arendt 1973, Collier and Collier 2002, Spalding 1977, Roberts 2019). Scholars of "economic voting" or "retrospective voting" have found repeatedly that ordinary citizens often choose leaders based on their perceived economic performance (see Anderson 2007 for a thorough review of the current state of this literature). Finally, several scholars have found that exposure to foreign trade competition, especially from China, encourages democratic discontent among manual laborers (Colantone and Stanig 2018a, 2018b, Guiso et al. 2017, Rodrik 2018, Autor, Hanson, and Majlesi 2020).

2.5.3 Neoliberalism and Democracy

The uneven benefits and costs of globalization have created profound political challenges for democracy, another core feature of the global order. Whether neoliberalism reinforces or undermines democracy is a complex question (see Bunce 2001 for an excellent summary) that seems to depend a great deal on contextual variables, such as the degree of statism prior to reform (Kwon 2004). Yet even if neoliberalism has improved the chances of democratic survival, it has often fundamentally eroded democratic quality in ways that have contributed to the development of the discontented era in which we find ourselves.

For one, globalization of capital eroded the tools states use (e.g. social policy, labor policy, industrial policy) to manage problems intrinsic to capitalism like inequality and poverty. States forced to compete for access to capital and investment face enormous pressure to reduce taxes, social expenditures, and regulation, lest they lose out to states more willing to dance to the capitalists' tune. The increasing homogenization of economic and social policy under neoliberal laissez-faire capitalism had political as well as economic consequences; leftist movements that embraced the global order (e.g. Keynesians, social democrats, moderate labor parties) found it far more difficult to find solutions to their constituents' economic grievances (Kurtz 2004a, 2004b, Roberts 1998). Many of those followers found themselves increasingly alienated from democratic politics as the issues that concerned them were rendered untouchable by neoliberal competition. This sense of abandonment steadily increased as center-left and workers' parties adapted to the new realities of the global economy by turning away from their shrinking blue-collar constituents, as occurred under Tony Blair's New Labour and the Democratic Party under Bill Clinton. Instead, these parties began to court an ascending middle class that was diverse, highly educated, and concentrated in major cities. We return to this shift when we discuss cultural discontent.

Underdeveloped countries such as those in Latin America faced similar challenges, but also suffered additional damage to democracy in many circumstances. In Europe and North America, neoliberalism was implemented through democratic processes by neoliberal acolytes like Ronald Reagan and Margaret Thatcher, and centrist moderates like Tony Blair and Bill Clinton. This was not always the case in Latin America, where many workers, capitalists, and white-collar employees were entirely dependent on activist states. In a few countries, especially those that faced hyperinflationary crises, a new breed of populist was able to build large electoral coalitions around neoliberal reform projects (Weyland 1999, Baker 2009). Yet in those that did not face such crises, popular resistance to reform was typically stiff.

However, virtually all Latin American countries eventually underwent significant reform, whether their populations wanted it or not. This was due to the fallout of the Mexican default of 1982, which caused debt servicing costs to skyrocket and triggered debt crises throughout the region. As a result, most countries were forced to appeal to international organizations like the International Monetary Fund (IMF) for assistance. The IMF and other international financial organizations used this period of crisis to demand reforms far beyond those necessary to ensure fiscal sustainability: by this point, the IMF had adopted neoliberalism as the solution to the woes of the developing world, and profound economic transformation was the price of its assistance (Green 2003). Democratic niceties like checks and balances and separation of powers were rarely respected. The IMF was all too happy to exploit the excessively strong presidencies of Latin America; reform was often accomplished at least in part through executive decrees (when legislatures refused to move). And the pressure was so intense that presidents had little choice in the matter. During this era, numerous Latin American countries (e.g. Argentina, Bolivia, Peru, Venezuela) elected presidents who promised never to seek IMF bailouts, only to reverse themselves immediately upon taking office.

In short, the economic challenges of economic neoliberalism placed tremendous strain on the oldest (and arguably most crucial) part of the global order: liberal democracy. The economic interests of sectors that depended upon the state were brushed aside as the parties they relied on abandoned them for greener political (and economic) pastures. And the almost maniacal zeal of neoliberal reformers blinded them to the risks of their methods, leading them to undermine institutions (especially legislatures) that were already much too weak in the developing world. Finally, the spectacle of flip-flopping over reform seriously undermined democratic legitimacy, as politicos repeatedly broke promises made to the electorate. The ability to punish incumbents by voting them out of office is a key mechanism for forcing policy change in representative democracies, and when that mechanism repeatedly fails, it is unsurprising that many would lose faith in democratic regimes.

2.5.4 The Left behind and Democratic Discontent

We are hardly the first to note that discontent may arise from economic grievances. Lipset (1955) saw the basic demographic profile we discuss here (namely relative economic privilege but with low security due to a lack of formal education) over half a century ago. Scholars have cited versions of the Left Behind hypothesis to explain The People's Party (Hicks 1931a, 1931b), Donald Trump (Sides, Tesler, and Vavreck 2018, Ferguson et al. 2018, Hochschild 2016, Gest 2016, Thompson 2016), Brexit and the rise of UKIP (Becker, Fetzer, and Novy 2017, Colantone and Stanig 2018a, Goodwin and Heath 2016, Ford and Goodwin 2014, Goodwin and Milazzo 2015), and the PRR in Europe (Macdougall, Feddes, and Doosje 2020). Economic issues have also played prominent but more indirect roles in the Chilean student protests (originally triggered over rises in public transit costs, and which included frustration over poor quality public health, education, and pensions) and in the rise of Jair Bolsonaro in Brazil, where economic declines exacerbated negative reactions to endemic corruption (Chagas-Bastos 2019). Perhaps the strongest evidence of all was provided in Chapter 1, where we showed the historical correlation between economic crises and discontented politics.

While there is considerable evidence that democratic discontent has economic roots, there are some important gaps and problems with this body of literature. First, there is not always agreement about who is left behind, nor which exact economic metrics (e.g. unemployment, growth, inequality, security) characterize those left behind. Debates also remain about whether sociotropic or egotropic economic evaluations matter more for driving discontent (Colantone and Stanig 2018a, Dettrey 2013, Kinder and Kiewiet 1981).

The most significant of these challenges is that many of the discontented movements we discuss do not organize predominantly around economic concerns but rather around cultural grievances. For every scholar that has argued for the Left Behind hypothesis, there is at least one researcher touting findings that economic concerns are irrelevant, and that what truly matters is the backlash against multiculturalism that has followed neoliberal economic globalization. These issues are compounded by divisions in the field and the understanding of the scope of explanations. As comparativists try to explain more general phenomena, they tend to downplay idiosyncratic contextual factors in order to compare across cases. Those that focus on single-country studies put more emphasis on the context and often object to this parsing down of cases; when these scholars meet, they often end up talking past each other.

2.6 THOSE FROM SOMEWHERE: MULTICULTURALISM AND CULTURAL DISCONTENT

Multiculturalism is not as foundational to the global order as either capitalism or democracy, and is relatively newer, having its origins in the social movements that arose around the world in the 1960s. Multiculturalism is an amorphous concept, but is generally defined as the political and legal recognition of minority cultural groups (Taylor 1994). In a departure from liberal pluralism, which holds that states should not interfere with cultural issues and simply allow subcultures to mix and interact, with a common culture emerging through synthesis, multiculturalism encourages minority groups to maintain their cultural and linguistic traditions. The state is expected to recognize and facilitate this maintenance of cultural distinctions and to actively combat group inequalities. Although it stretches the concept a bit, the term can (for the purposes of this book) be expanded to include recognition of minorities defined by sexual orientation and gender identity as well as culture.

Although not a part of the order from its inception, the rise of multiculturalism has been intimately connected to its development. Many of the social changes wrought by the shift from industry to high-skilled services (e.g. greater levels of educational attainment, meritocracy, acceptance of high-skilled immigration, urbanization) have led to the revitalization and diversification of urban centers. As laid out in Allport's classic intergroup contact hypothesis, social contact between disparate groups in society tends to reduce prejudicial attitudes (Allport, Clark, and Pettigrew 1954). This extends into a variety of areas, including indirect contact (Wright et al. 1997), and has received robust support even in more modern research (see Pettigrew et al. (2007) for a review).

This suggests that societies should see a lowering of prejudicial attitudes within the population as urbanization and postindustrial economics proceed, due to increased intergroup contact. And rising living standards drastically reduced the need of citizens around the world to spend all their time and energy simply trying to ensure their survival. As Inglehart and Welzel (2005) argue in their seminal study of culture and democracy, as people feel their survival is assured, they begin to care about nonmaterial goods, a set of concerns the authors call postmaterialist values. These values include self-expression (the desire to be true to oneself and to be recognized as a unique individual) as well as an erosion of traditionalism and a willingness to challenge established authorities.

Recent events have made clear that multiculturalism is not so broadly accepted as it once seemed. As Inglehart and Welzel (2005) argued, the shift from materialism to postmaterialism occurs from different set points (determined by national culture and by individual variation); not everyone embraces postmaterialist values at the same rate. Within nations, an urban–rural divide has emerged where intergroup contact and rising living standards has boosted multiculturalism in urban areas, while rural areas remained dominated by traditionalists and cultural conservatives. Anderson (2006) argued that the erosion of national identities due to globalization provokes profound anxiety among some citizens, and that this could easily be channeled into support for the PRR. More recently, Goodhart (2017) has argued that social conflict in many developed countries has come to revolve around cosmopolitan (those from anywhere) and place-based (those from somewhere) identities.

Examples of discomfort with multiculturalism are easy enough to find even outside the system-challenging political movements with which we concern ourselves. In October 2010, the German Chancellor Angela Merkel told young members of her party that the multicultural "approach has failed, utterly failed" (Weaver 2010). This sentiment was repeated by the then UK Prime Minister David Cameron and French President Sarkozy[5] (Heneghan 2011). A book by a senior official at Germany's central bank describing the "harm" of multiculturalism topped *Der Spiegel*'s bestseller list in 2010.

Multiculturalism's emphasis on diversity and so-called "identity politics" has also not been without cost. This is as good a place as any to express our dissatisfaction with many of the terms applied to the

---

[5] It should be noted that many activists and scholars of immigrant integration contest that multiculturalism was never actually tried in France. See Malik (2015) for a discussion.

multicultural left, with identity politics being among the chief offenders. Whatever a rationalist might say, group identity is a core feature of social psychology, and virtually all political behavior is influenced by the social groups with which one identifies (Tajfel et al. 1979); the notion that only left-wing multiculturalists practice it is nonsense. Yet it is true that multiculturalists emphasize and embrace the role of social identity in politics far more the socialist left (who embrace class but reject cultural identities as forms of false consciousness), centrist liberals (given their commitment to individualism), and traditionalist monoculturalists (who stress the importance of a single, national culture for the maintenance of social cohesion and order).

2.6.1 Conceptualizing Cultural Discontent

Before analyzing the interplay of multiculturalism, the backlash against it, and democratic discontent, there are conceptual problems that need resolution. First, ethnocentrism, racism, and the like are typically thought of as relatively fixed beliefs that are acquired through socialization, rather than attitudes that change over time. For example, racial resentment or general negative attitudes toward Black Americans (Tesler 2016, Sears and Funk 1999, Green, Palmquist, and Schickler 2004), and ethnocentrism, or a preference for one's in-group, and dislike of out-groups (Kinder and Kam 2009), have been conceptualized as stable predispositions.

However, recent work has thrown into question the extent to which these attitudes are truly unmovable. Engelhardt (2018) finds that, while racial attitudes were relatively stable in the United States in the 1990s, in recent years individual partisanship can predict changes in racial attitudes. In our own work, we find that experimental treatments related to economic anger and anxiety can lead to changes in self-reported ethnocentrism (Utych, Navarre, and Rhodes-Purdy 2021). While the general stability of these attitudes violates one of our core criteria and poses immediate challenges should we wish to explain the why such ideas respond to context, we do see some evidence that these attitudes are potentially moveable, or at least capable of being activated under certain circumstances. Second, we have here a version of the same problem we faced with discontent: a proliferation of specific concepts (racial resentment, nativism, Islamophobia, homophobia, xenophobia, etc.), with less recognition of the underlying similarities between them. To facilitate analysis of the sense of resentment and alienation underlying these attitudes, we developed a concept called cultural discontent (Rhodes-Purdy, Navarre, and Utych 2021b), which we define as the perception that one's values and identities are not respected in one's own society. Those values and identities are likely quite static, but perceptions of how society values them can change. This definition satisfies both our need for dynamism and our preference for ideological neutrality, which we discuss shortly. We use ten original measures that can apply to any of the ideologies to which democratic discontent may graft itself, from far left to FR and all points in between. There is growing evidence that the people on the extreme right are not the only ones who feel disconnected from their culture; leftists and marginalized groups can experience a sense of discontent, especially when the FR is in power. We do not wish to draw any moral equivalence between the understandable distress that marginalized groups feel when confronted with systematic bias against them and the frustrated entitlement of the FR, but we wish to determine whether they have the same impact on populist attitudes and thus require an ideologically neutral measure. As cultural discontent is an original concept, we include the questions used to measure it below. Each question has a pro- and con-trait version; respondents were randomly assigned to one or the other, question by question, so that each respondent received a random mix of pro- and con-trait items. The lists below includes only the pro-trait items.

Value marginalization:

- My values are not respected in this country.
- I often see my beliefs and values disrespectfully portrayed on television.
- People with values like mine are treated poorly in this society.
- The decisions our government makes usually violate my values and beliefs.
- Institutions in this country disrespect values that are important to me.

Identity marginalization:

- People like me are marginalized in this country.
- I am typically not treated as fairly as I deserve.
- Regardless of who is in political power, things are pretty bad for people like me.
- Society is generally pretty unfair to people like me.
- The political system is not set up to benefit people like me.

We conceptualize cultural discontent as having a single dimension, but with questions clustering into two groups: those asking about values and those asking about identities ("people like me"). These clusters are not truly unique dimensions as they both measure the same latent concept.

This situation creates serious challenges when using confirmatory factor analysis (CFA) to construct indices, as CFA tends to be biased in favor of multidimensionality. Furthermore, the two dimensions are highly correlated (the exact figure varies from study to study, but r typically exceeds 0.8), making it nearly impossible to include both dimensions in analyses due to severe multicollinearity. We resolve this problem in different ways in different studies. In most studies, we use a single summary measure of cultural discontent combining the two indices into a single index.[6]

Reconceptualized in this way, the Backlash hypothesis works as follows: traditionalists (mostly older, less educated rural dwellers who are cis-gendered members of culturally privileged racial, ethnic, religious, and sexual orientation groups), after decades in which their values, mores, and identities were seen as synonymous with those of the nations in which they reside, have seen their cultural dominance challenged and undermined. They have given way to more diverse, liberal, and multicultural conceptions of nationhood; as this happens, values once lauded have now come to be seen as old-fashioned at best, and racist, chauvinistic, or fascistic at worst. Additionally, these attitudes may not be created or changed per se but simply activated or made more salient. As one feels their ethnic or national in-group is in decline, they may be more willing to act on their negative attitudes toward out-groups, or be more willing to *reveal* these attitudes, as they perceive them as more important to their own identity.

Although cultural discontent is typically considered a right-wing phenomenon, this is not necessarily so. Historically, left-wing political movements tended to focus on economic concerns: inspired by Marxist and socialist principles of social equality and the Marxist consignment of culture as an epiphenomenon of the economic base, left-wing movements often ignored or minimized concerns about values and identities. But there is no a priori reason why leftists and progressives cannot concern themselves with culture and cultural power. Indeed, there are obvious examples: the New Left movement that arose in the 1960s combined economic and political concerns with a firm commitment to ending traditional patterns of exclusion based on race, ethnicity, sexual orientation, and gender identity. And progressives have broadly

---

[6] The one exception is for the PSAS-US, where we used a technique called bifactor CFA (Reise, Moore, and Haviland 2010). In this technique, we specify a two-factor CFA as in previous models, but we add an additional element: a single factor that loads on all indicators. This produces a single cultural discontent index that influences both value and identity questions, while taking the clustering described earlier into account for greater precisions.

embraced concepts like structural or systematic racism, patriarchy, and heteronormativity that see marginalization as interwoven into the sociopolitical fabric, rather than as individual pathologies.

The current multiculturalist consensus against which right-wing revanchists contend has its beginnings in these struggles. But as of late, the tide has turned. Multiculturalism has been put on the defensive, beset by the traditionalist backlash.[7] In environments where right-wing cultural movements have become prominent or even come to power (as they did under Donald Trump in the United States), we might well expect discontent to erupt among the left, breaking the right's monopoly on feeling like a stranger in one's own land. Left-wing cultural discontent may manifest as:

- Left-wing authoritarianism, a combination of anti-conventionalism, revolutionary aggression, and top-down censorship (Costello et al. 2021).
- Intolerance of conservative religion.
- Hostility and bias toward members of the majority group perceived to be especially retrograde (e.g. rural and blue-collar white people).

Once again, we do not wish to imply any moral or even full conceptual symmetry between right- and left-wing cultural discontent. While these ideations share some characteristics (a sense of cultural dislocation, a tendency to paint the other side with a broad brush, unchecked hostility, etc.), there are fundamental distinctions that cannot be ignored. Specifically, one cannot equate the excessive zeal of people struggling against centuries of injustice with the fervent desires of those who wish to perpetuate such injustices. Left-wing cultural discontent may lead to the adoption of antidemocratic tactics as a means to an end, but right-wing discontent is intrinsically authoritarian and illiberal in both means *and* ends, and thus infinitely more dangerous.

2.6.2 Conclusions on the Backlash Hypothesis

Like the Left Behind hypothesis, the Backlash hypothesis has problems. First, the most thorough treatment of the topic has been criticized on

---

[7] We see the various permutations of conservative cultural backlash (e.g. nativism, ethnocentrism, racial resentment, xenophobia) as having roots in cultural discontent, combined with conservative or right-wing ideological and social beliefs. As such, we do not go into detail about the distinctions between these concepts in this chapter: we discuss them when we discuss operationalization of cultural discontent in the empirical chapters, where those issues are much more relevant.

empirical grounds. Schäfer (2021) argues that the generational conflict cited in *Cultural Backlash*, Norris and Inglehart's book on the topic and probably the most prominent elucidation of the hypothesis, is much weaker than the book claims, and in some areas (continental Europe for example) elides the fact that younger people are, in fact, much more likely to support populist and radical right parties.

These empirical problems are mirrored when we evaluate the evidence at multiple levels of analysis. While the Backlash hypothesis seems to win when measured at the micro level with public opinion surveys, results incorporating meso-level cultural effects have not been so strong. When studying attitudes toward immigrants, for example, Filindra (2019) finds that changes in actual migration levels do not matter much in determining hostile state policy toward immigrants. While increases in immigrant populations may have effects on attitudes toward immigration (Ybarra, Sanchez, and Sanchez 2016), there is reason to expect this influences different citizens in different ways. Indeed, for Democrats in the United States, living in areas with higher levels of immigration actually predicts *decreased* support for immigration restrictions, while these effects are relatively small or nonexistent for Republicans (Hawley 2011). Georgiadou, Rori, and Roumanias (2018) find that immigration levels do matter, but their effect is matched or exceeded by economic concerns like inequality and unemployment.

Another major problem with the Backlash hypothesis is its ideological bias: only right-wing conservatives can experience backlash as defined in most works on the subject, as it is diametrically opposed to and in rebellion against the multicultural tide. Yet multiculturalism itself began as a form of discontent, with the stifling conformity and rigid racial and gender norms of the postwar era coming under attack by the nascent New Left, itself a discontented political movement that at times embraced populism, conspiracism, regime antipathy, and contention. The rise of the BLM movement in the United States, as well as the strident defense of multiculturalism made by rising left-wing populists like Alexandria Ocasio-Cortez, suggest we that the cultural element of the 1960s New Left was not a one-off. Even works that explicitly recognize the possibility of left-wing cultural discontent (Inglehart and Norris 2019) do not fully explore the obvious mixture of economic and cultural grievances such movements evince, and fail to analyze the implications this may have for a culturally focused theory of discontent. Our concept of cultural discontent helps overcome these limitations, as it is conceptually and, based on existing evidence, empirically neutral in ideological terms; it tends to manifest most strongly based on which side of the multicultural/monocultural debate is in power (Navarre, Rhodes-Purdy, and Utych 2020).

Finally, and perhaps most damning, the various versions of the Backlash hypothesis rely on mechanisms (generational conflict, changes in authoritarian values in the population, etc.) that share a relatively languid pace. As such, they fit poorly with the dynamic nature of discontent, which surges and subsides much too rapidly to be explained by slower factors. And there is no clear reason under the Backlash hypothesis for the historical pattern we presented earlier, where discontent of all stripes emerges after an economic crises. We have little doubt that Backlash hypothesis dynamics are an important part of the explanation of the age of discontent. But on its own, this hypothesis leaves far too many questions unanswered.

2.7 CONCLUSIONS

In this chapter, we established our conceptual schema, and reviewed existing arguments about the causes of various forms of discontent. The result, sadly, is a bit of a morass: the siloing of literatures by topic (e.g. populism, the FR, conspiracism) means that findings pertaining to one form of discontent often fail to influence or inform studies of other forms. As such, there are some major avoidable gaps in the literature: little work has been done on the influence of cultural discontent on regime support, or of contextual factors on conspiracism, and so on. Yet out of this quagmire we do find some common threads: specifically, the debate over economic and cultural origins appears repeatedly.

Even here, though, we have less consensus than we might like. This debate is as unsettled as it is ubiquitous. If it were merely a matter of finding the correct measures, methodologies, and analytical techniques, we could make short work of the problem; indeed, it would vitiate any need for this book. This is not the case; there is simply far too much work, much of it of the highest methodological rigor, and yet still producing irreconcilably conflicting results. Resolving these contradictions is the major purpose of the remainder of this book. To transition to this task, we point to a glimmer of hope found in the conflicting findings of the Left Behind and Backlash hypothesis literatures. While both economic and cultural variables have support in the literature, each does better at a different level. Economic causes tend to hold pride of place when analyses are conducted at the meso level, that is, when aggregate trends are analyzed with geographical locales as the level of analysis. Cultural factors do not fare so well here but excel at the micro level: when pitted against discontented economic attitudes, cultural factors consistently dominate.

There are several possible explanations for this: perhaps some ecological fallacy is at work, creating a role for economic factors that is illusory. When we go to the source (namely to the discontented individual), if culture matters so much more consistently, shouldn't we simply accept that and move on? We do not believe things are so simple. Instead, we see a complex interplay of economics and culture leading to discontent, which we lay out in Chapter 3.

3

Affective Political Economy

The Economic Origins of Democratic Discontent

We concluded Chapter 2 by alluding to the possibility that economic and cultural discontent are linked, and that the combination of the two may explain our discontented era. While the link may be intuitive, culture and economics operate on very different logics and assumptions about what motivates human behavior (Lichbach and Zuckerman 2009). Economic arguments, while not necessarily rationalist in the strictest sense, generally assume that attitudes and behavior are motivated by material self-interest. Cultural approaches, on the other hand, emphasize ideational motivations like identity and norms. We cannot link the two without finding some sort of ligament to connect them and reconcile the vast gulf in psychological and behavioral models.

In this chapter, we explain how the era since the Great Recession became an age of discontent that continues to this day. As we argued earlier in this book, discontent is the product of both long-term processes of disillusionment and alienation from democratic politics, along with more immediate triggers that allow discontent to erupt. Economic threats, long simmering due to globalization and set to a boil by the financial crisis of 2008, are the root cause of the dark turn in democratic politics seen in recent years. Although economic discontent sometimes translated directly into democratic discontent (giving rise to movements like Occupy Wall Street and boosting leaders like Bernie Sanders and parties like Podemos in Spain), the crisis occurred at the height of neoliberal globalization, with all its attendant constraints. Namely, left-wing policy solutions were still mostly off the table, and left-wing parties had mostly finished disincorporating their working-class bases. Given this, there was little left-wing organizational structure in most countries that could convert economic discontent into a meaningful challenge against the neoliberal policies that had gave birth to the crisis.

In their absence, the emotional trauma of economic devastation was left looking for outlets, which FR movements were all too happy to provide. Latent prejudices and resentments over the rapid rise of multiculturalism were activated as people transferred their resentment and anxiety to cultural concerns. In the following passages, we give an overview of how the Great Recession and subsequent economic challenges (such as the collapse of the commodities boom in the developing world) triggered intense unpleasant emotional reactions. We then analyze how those emotions, especially resentment and anxiety, can be expected to increase various forms of cultural and democratic discontent described in Chapter 2. We conclude by pointing out that, while we have economic crises at the core of our argument, the specific ways that trends played out in each country were profoundly shaped by local conditions. Finally, we show how failures of democracy, particularly those related to citizen voice, can intensify the effect of negative emotions on various aspects of discontent.

3.1 SURVEYING THE WRECKAGE: THE CONSEQUENCES OF THE GREAT RECESSION(S)

It is difficult to overstate the damage wrought by the economic crises that plagued the 2010s. Consequences varied depending on the dynamics of each crisis (the Great Recession, the eurozone crisis, and the collapse of the commodities boom), as well as political responses and the sociopolitical situation in each country. In the United States, the collapse was followed by a steady but agonizingly slow, and unequal, recovery. Unemployment rates more than doubled, from less than 5 percent to 10 percent at the height of the crisis; rates did not fall below 5 percent until five years later.[1] The wealth of the middle class, tied up as it was in home prices that collapsed as the housing bubble burst, cratered. And an entire generation of the US population delayed major milestones, such as moving away from parents, entering career tracks, purchasing homes, as well as marriage and having children (Lamberti 2019; although on this subject some of the authors of this book can personally attest).

Ironically, things were even worse outside of the country that instigated the era of economic crises. The rigidity of the US political system and the (arguably misplaced) priorities of the incoming Obama

---

[1] Source: US Bureau of Labor Statistics, www.bls.gov/.

administration did not allow for a sufficiently massive fiscal stimulus to avert the prolonged slowdown that followed the financial crisis. Yet, the USA did at least take its cues from the Keynesian playbook. In Europe, even the limited stimulus spending that buoyed the US economy to some degree was off the table. The European Central Bank (ECB), with its stringent anti-inflationary mandate, did not entertain stimulus plans, and the very nature of the euro system limited the monetary tools available to national leaders to address the crisis. As the crisis unfolded, it became clear that some of the weaker economies of southern Europe (Portugal, Italy, Spain, and Greece) were in for a rough ride; all experienced extreme budget shortfalls as state revenue collapsed along with the economy.

Instead of pursuing even the modest fiscal stimulus enacted in the United States, the ECB required strict deficit and government debt limits, conditioning bailouts for the so-called PIIGS (the countries mentioned earlier, plus Ireland) on the recipients' willingness to enact painful austerity measures in the middle of the worst recession in living memory. The results were predictable: Europe's recovery was even slower and more painful than in the United States (Herndon, Ash, and Pollin 2014, International Monetary Fund 2012).

The underdeveloped countries in the Americas escaped the Great Recession relatively unscathed. This was due less to smart policy decisions (although those played a role in some cases like Chile and Uruguay) and more to catching a new wave to replace that wave that had just receded. The continuing strong economic performance of China generated considerable demand for the primary products in which Latin American countries specialize. Nevertheless, the good times could only last so long, and China's growth finally stumbled. Demand for primary products dried up with it, and economic trouble finally came for the most disadvantaged areas of the region.

Latin American states faced challenges that bear some resemblance to those faced by the PIIGS in Europe. While they were not constrained by the limits of a shared monetary policy, they did face heavy pressures emanating from the last economic crisis they endured. In the 1980s, Latin America suffered the so-called lost decade, a period wherein growth slowed to a crawl, unemployment and hyperinflation ran rampant, and nascent democratic regimes seemed powerless to staunch the bleeding. Their only option was to go hat in hand to the IMF and other international organizations for help escaping the crises: as we discussed in Chapter 2, the price of this aid was a rapid conversion from statist economics to neoliberalism (Green 2003). Although the IMF has moderated its stance since the lost decade, neoliberal restructuring and lingering issues with debt meant that Latin American states were still constrained in their ability to use state action to turn the economic tide once the commodities boom began to fail.

3.2 APE: EMOTIONS AND ECONOMIC TURMOIL

Given the economic difficulties since the Great Recession, it should not be surprising that discontent with political systems surged. Yet when we survey the movements that mobilized discontent, surprisingly few are primarily concerned with the global economic system that allowed the crisis to happen. Instead, these movements lash out at minorities or immigrants, including asylum seekers who were too busy trying to escape violence and devastation in their own countries to play any role in the calamities that befell the West. Why did so many of these movements target the marginalized and vulnerable people who had nothing whatsoever to do with the crisis, rather than the financial elites and neoliberal politicians who actually caused it?

Here emotions enter the fray. The cultural focus of so much discontent makes little sense when viewed through the lens of material self-interest that underlies the economic arguments we summarized in Chapter 2. Nor is it immediately clear why value- and identity-oriented individuals would respond to economic crises. We can resolve this impasse by ignoring both these models of human behavior; instead, we rely on established theories and findings from psychology to craft our model of motivation. We emphasize specifically the importance of emotions, which are prone to transfer from their source to other elements of the social environment (Forgas 1995, Anderson 1983). As such, they have strong potential to connect disparate domains of human experience, like economics, culture, and politics. We call our approach APE, given its focus on economic origins of social phenomena, with emotions serving as the bridge between economics and social attitudes.

3.2.1 Emotional Frameworks: Approach-Avoidance, Appraisal, and Neural Process Theories

Theories on emotions fall into three distinct camps. These theories include approach-avoidance theories, appraisal theories, and neural process theories. There is significant variation within these theories, both in terms of *how* emotions develop and in terms of *which* emotions are relevant. Some argue for the importance of only directional emotional judgments;

that is, evaluations of things as either positive or negative (Fishbein and Ajzen 1975). Others provide nuance between types of emotions, such as the negative emotions of anger and anxiety (Marcus, Neuman, and MacKuen 2000, Albertson and Gadarian 2015). Other efforts to divide basic emotions into categories range from a relatively parsimonious six basic emotions (Ekman and Friesen 1971) to the profligate (e.g. the twenty-seven unique human emotions in Cowen and Keltner (2017)).

3.2.1.1 *Approach-Avoidance Theories*

Approach-avoidance theories are how scholars classically viewed emotions, as either having a positive (approach) or negative (avoidance) affective response (Fishbein and Ajzen 1975). Here, there is no focus on discrete emotions, but rather positive or negative reactions to events (Eagly and Chaiken 1993). Perhaps the most prominent and widely used directional theory of emotion is the theory of affect as information transfer (Schwarz and Clore 1983). This theory posits that individuals make judgments about events around them, and then transfer these moods onto a host of other things relevant to their lives. Various seemingly minor and irrelevant events, such as the weather, sports results, and movies influence how individuals rate their satisfaction with their lives in general (Schwarz et al. 1987, Forgas and Moylan 1987, Forgas and Bower 1987, Achen and Bartels 2017, Healy, Malhotra, and Mo 2010).

The approach-appraisal framework has some important insights, especially the transferability of affect, or what we call (in simpler language) *emotional spillover*. Emotional spillover occurs when feelings triggered by a specific circumstance influence a person's attitudes and behavior in another, unrelated circumstance. There may be a conscious element here: a negative event in one circumstance may lead a person to conclude that their social environment is hopeless, for example. Yet the key argument here is that these thoughts are not the connecting force: they are simply post hoc explanations of the unconscious influence of emotions

That said, the approach has some critical shortcomings, limiting its relevance for our theory. First, later evaluations of some of these works have cast doubt on the empirical support for mood transference in specific instances involving nonpolitical events like shark attacks (Fowler and Hall 2018). Most importantly, approach-appraisal theories would predict that negative affect caused by the Great Recession should be transferred to ethnic and racial minorities relatively evenly. However, we see very different responses from different members of the ethnoracial majority. Those on the right showed increased disdain for immigrants, refugees, and the like after the Great Recession, while those on the far left grew increasingly strident in their *defense* of these groups. Since we expect, and observe, different types of people reacting differently to this crisis, we cannot say these reactions are explained solely by negative affect. Given this, we turn to theories of discrete, rather than generalized, emotional response.

3.2.1.2 Appraisal Theories

Appraisal theories focus on how conscious evaluations of context called appraisals influence emotional responses. There is variation in the literature on the number and type of appraisal dimensions, but they typically focus on elements such as the certainty of the situation, cognitive effort, situational attribution, potential for control, and motivations for reward and punishment (Smith and Ellsworth 1985, Lazarus 1991, Roseman 1996). Specific combinations of appraisals tend to provoke specific discrete emotional responses: for example, anger is evoked through appraisals of external responsibility for a negative event and is distinct from other negative emotions such as anxiety (Smith and Ellsworth 1985, Lerner and Keltner 2000). Appraisal theories, thus, argue that different negative emotions are caused by different appraisals, suggesting each negative emotion may operate differently.

Like approach-avoidance theories, appraisal theories have shortcomings that render them unsuitable for our purposes. The most damning for our purposes is that appraisal theory treats emotional response as an inherently conscious process. This limits the possibility of the transference elucidated by approach-avoidance theories, which makes it ill-suited for our approach.

3.2.1.3 AIT

Because of these flaws, we turn to neural process theories of emotion. These theories fit well with our goals – they have strong grounding in both psychology and neurobiology, provide a distinct set of appraisals and emotions to examine, and do not require that these appraisals be done in a conscious manner. AIT is a neural process approach that radically reconceptualizes what emotions are. AIT argues that humans profoundly misunderstand a significant portion of their psychological make-up because we are only aware of extreme activations, where emotions commandeer motivation and behavior so completely that the conscious mind takes notice.

An appropriate metaphor might be a computer antivirus program: emotions constantly scan the environment and adjust behavior accordingly, typically with no intervention by the "system operator" (in this case, the conscious mind). Most emotional influences on behavior are so subtle and so fast that the conscious mind is not aware of the intervention. This, in fact, is the point of emotions in AIT: they allow behavioral adaptation to the environment that is automatic, thus saving tremendous cognitive capacity. Put another way, a sign of how completely most people misunderstand emotions is the fact that we speak of being "angry" or "not angry" as though these binaries were possible. In fact, we are always angry, anxious, and enthusiastic, in the sense that these systems are always there below the surface of the mind, doing their work and only rarely disturbing cognition enough for us to notice.

AIT recognizes three emotional "systems": enthusiasm, anxiety, and resentment. The three systems motivate different behaviors and produce cognitive changes depending on environmental triggers (Marcus and MacKuen 1993). Enthusiasm searches for opportunities for reward and pleasure and encourages people to pursue those opportunities. By contrast, anxiety and resentment are negative emotions that motivate individuals to extinguish them (Gross 2013). Anxiety detects unfamiliar elements of the environment. When something unfamiliar is detected, anxiety inhibits motivation and triggers an information search, as the anxious person rapidly gathers data to escape anxiety. This emotion also tends to reduce reliance on preexisting notions and biases.

Resentment scans the environment for signs that social rules and norms are being violated. Like enthusiasm, resentment is a "dispositional" system, which promotes greater reliance on existing beliefs and prejudices. It also motivates people to engage in confrontational or even aggressive behavior against the perceived offender. This need to punish is perhaps not as fundamental as anxiety and enthusiasm. It is the only system that relates exclusively to human social behavior, and thus likely evolved much later than the other two. Nevertheless, it still has deep psychological roots that tend to override conscious motivation; the punishment drive has analogues in other social animals and tends to be prioritized even over one's own self-interest (Goldberg, Lerner, and Tetlock 1999, Gollwitzer and Bushman 2012, van Prooijen 2017).

The key insight provided by AIT for our theory is simple: the motivational and cognitive changes provoked by emotions are not tied to the stimuli that engender those feelings. As such, emotions as conceptualized by AIT offer a promising bridge between different elements of the political environment via emotional spillover: resentment and anxiety aroused in one context will influence an individual's behavior toward other aspects of the environment, even if no link exists between the two.

3.2.2 Resentment, Anxiety, and Economic Discontent

Most readers will require little convincing that economic discontent can trigger powerful emotional reactions; anyone who has ever experienced an economic disappointment or setback can probably personally attest to this point. Perhaps the intuitive nature of this relationship can explain why so little research has been done on this topic: we have found few analyses of the emotional consequences of economic discontent.[2] We can rely on some simple deductions, reinforced by evidence provided throughout this book, to fill this gap.

Economic crises tend to produce tremendous uncertainty throughout society, even among those who do not directly suffer their consequences. People may not suffer any actual losses but still spend years worrying about losing jobs, careers, homes, health care, and educational opportunities for themselves and their families and friends. These worries are always a part of economic crises, but the Great Recession was, given the historical moment in which it occurred, an especially potent anxiety generator. The neoliberal era that culminated in the crisis was defined by a gradual shift of economic risk from broad diffusion throughout society to concentration on individuals (Hacker 2008; see also Chapter 5). This contention is further supported by Bermeo and Bartels (2014), who find that support for the discontented populist movements did not increase much in societies with strong welfare states, and by Roberts (2019), who argues that strong welfare states foreclose the possibility of economic populism. In most societies in the neoliberal global order, however, ordinary people were largely forced to confront the dangers of the new era alone. Rovira Kaltwasser (2015) makes this connection explicitly. Drawing on Lipset (1963) and Taggart (2000), he notes that the emergence of populism across the global is linked to a "*sense* of crisis and moral collapse" that is not dependent on "objective" measures of status or security, but rather subjective impressions (Rovira Kaltwasser 2015, 202).

The Great Recession was also ideally suited for generating resentment. The global economy did not collapse because of political instability, war, famine, or some other instance of *force majeure*. The financial crisis occurred because specific actors, fueled by greed and protected for a time from the consequences of their avarice by the financial system's use of complex investment vehicles, took risks that were, at least in hindsight,

---

[2] The strong rationalist assumptions common in economics probably also contribute to this lacuna. The general hesitance of political science to grapple with emotions is another likely suspect.

obviously ill advised. And national and international governing bodies allowed it to happen. Obviously, the real story is more complex, but the crisis lends itself to simple, moralistic narratives in a way that many previous crises did not. Yet even crises where the villains are not nearly so obvious can provoke a great deal of social outrage. Citizens may blame businesses for layoffs and governments for failing to protect them, to name just two potential targets of blame.

Resentment manifests when a threat is identified, and particularly when that threat transgresses deeply held morals and norms (Busby, Gubler, and Hawkins 2019). In addition to resentment generated at those who caused the crisis, this moral dimension played out in debates over state responses to it. Constrained by globalization and the weakness of left-wing parties that had disincorporated workers, states mostly failed to provide the kind of broad-based support the recession demanded (Roberts 2015, Dalton 2013). As such, bitter feelings have emerged as some believe help was going to the wrong people. Leftists (such as those associated with Occupy Wall Street and Bernie Sanders) accused the government of bailing out banks while leaving ordinary people high and dry. Those on the right argued that liberal multiculturalists were only interested in helping young people, people of color, and immigrants, ignoring the plight of the white majority; the Tea Party, Trump, UKIP, and VOX in Spain all made versions of this claim. It would be astounding if, given widespread conflict over the fairness and righteousness of state responses to such a calamitous economic collapse, we did not see waves of anger sweep through citizenries around the world.

We need not rely on supposition or assumption here; in subsequent chapters we provide evidence from numerous surveys and experiments that economic turmoil does produce resentment and anxiety at high levels. For now, we need only note that the relationship is very plausible; indeed, it is implausible to argue that economic troubles would *not* produce these emotions. What is not as obvious is *which* of these two emotions is most important for generating discontent.

3.2.3 Fear or Loathing? Resentment, Anxiety, and Discontent

When this project began, we were agnostic about which negative emotion would do most of the heavy explanatory lifting. A finding that either anxiety, resentment, or both connected economic and cultural discontent would be consistent with our approach. That said, we have entered a field where debates are in progress regarding the issue of whether anxiety or resentment (anger) is most responsible for discontented politics; however, these existing works do not use emotions to theoretically tie economics to culture, but rather view emotions as independent variables explaining discontent.

This ongoing controversy is most clearly seen in an article by Vasilopoulos et al. (2018), a subsequent rejoinder by Jost (2019), and a response by the authors of the original article (Vasilopoulos et al. 2019). We would generally not engage at this point with a debate at this level of detail in our theoretical chapter (we would prefer to let our data and analyses resolve these sorts of disputes), but the debate has theoretical relevance that needs to be discussed here. Jost's approach seems to fall within the bounds of appraisal theory; its emphasis on fear arising from perceptions of intergroup threat is consistent with appraisal theory's temporal order, where emotions follow cognition. Vasilopoulos and his colleagues, on the other hand, clearly embrace AIT, which holds that anxiety is a demotivating emotion, and thus unlikely to produce any such overt political action as supporting the FR; Jost argues in his response that fear may influence discontent through anger (i.e. fear leads to anger, anger leads to discontented politics).[3] Vasilopoulos and his co-authors dispute this, but we find it a compelling possibility, at least over a course of time. That said, as we find AIT more persuasive, better supported by empirical research in psychology, and better grounded in neurobiological research on how the brain works, we tend to agree that resentment/anger will be the primary unpleasant emotion driving democratic discontent. However, we do not neglect anxiety; it is included in all the analyses we conduct, and we remain cognizant of its theoretical role.

3.3 FEELING LIKE A STRANGER: EMOTIONS AND CULTURAL DISCONTENT

We are not the first to argue that economics may explain cultural discontent. Some works on fascism (e.g. Arendt 1973, Chambers and Kopstein 2001) and the rise of the modern FR (e.g. Mouffe 2000) have argued that when the political left cedes its responsibility to advance the interests of the working-class, fascist or FR movements have an opportunity to channel the resulting discontent toward marginalized groups and foreign enemies, leaving the true culprits (namely the capitalist elites) largely unmolested. We will also argue that left party weakness increases the

---

[3] We call this the "Yoda hypothesis."

likelihood of discontent manifesting as support for the FR. But many previous works in this area make assumptions based on Marxist theories of an intrinsic and inevitable affinity between the left and the working classes that simply has not been borne out by history; working-class individuals are complex human agents, with competing motivations and drives that may be consistent with a variety of political tendencies and ideologies depending on context. Inglehart and Norris (2017) propose a different mechanism; they argue that long-term economic insecurity has increased the authoritarian leanings of older people in developed democracies. Relatedly, Gidron and Hall (2019), Elchardus and Spruyt (2016), and Spruyt, Keppens, and Van Droogenbroeck (2016) argue that the erosion of society perceived by the left behind produces support for the PRR. Ethnographic work lends this theory some evidence; Williamson, Skocpol, and Coggin (2011), for example, find that the Tea Party supporters were not uberlibertarian zealots but rather felt that help was going to "the wrong people." Cramer (2016) makes a similar finding when explaining the rise of Tea Party–adjacent Wisconsin Governor Scott Walker, emphasizing the divide between urban and rural Wisconsinites. These works make very plausible arguments, but they cannot explain the diverging findings discussed in Chapter 2, nor the rapidity with which discontent metastasized after the Great Recession. These works tell us a great deal about discontent, and we rely on many of them in our analyses of discontented movements and leaders in specific areas.

3.3.1 Emotional Spillover and Discontented Narratives: The Link between Economics and Culture

Having reviewed different theories of human emotions and how economic crises influence them, we can begin to build our theory of how these emotions allow discontent to transfer from the economic to the cultural realm. Working within the AIT framework helps here, as emotions are not firmly tied down to the stimuli that aroused them. Instead, emotions trigger specific cognitive and behavioral tendencies: anxiety demotivates and triggers an information search, part of which is the questioning of previously held assumptions and ideas, while resentment encourages aggressive action toward threat and reliance on existing biases, prejudices, and beliefs.

This, combined with specific contextual factors within countries, explains why culturally focused discontent exploded as the Great Recession ground on. But what is the connection between unpleasant emotions and narratives that focus on villains and threats? Earlier we argued that the connection between economic discontent and unpleasant emotions was very intuitive, almost obvious; it might also appear that the link between cultural discontent and emotions is similarly straight-forward. However, we argue that emotions lead to cultural discontent, not the other way around.[4] The reader may wonder then if unpleasant emotions motivate individuals to extinguish the causes of these emotions, why would people in the grip of anxiety or anger be drawn to ideas and narratives that amplify rather than ameliorate those feelings?

Existing research has not addressed this issue in sufficient depth to provide full guidance here; emotions are understudied in the social sciences and there exist some theoretical gaps, particularly on issues of transference. As such, we must rely on studies that are not directly on point, but which (with a bit of deduction) can suggest answers. Studies of punitive aggression have shown that, unless satisfied, it will tend to bleed into all evaluations of the social environment (Goldberg, Lerner, and Tetlock 1999, Rhodes-Purdy 2021b). We argue that something similar occurs with unpleasant emotions in the political arena: individuals typically have limited information about the political world and confront a bewildering array of conflicting narratives and explanations of why things are going wrong in their societies. This was especially acute during the Great Recession, where a problem in the US housing market triggered a global economic collapse, and where states seemed helpless to staunch the bleeding, leaving publics around the world desperate for answers.

As such, we propose a solution that fits with a general theme through-out this book, namely that discontent must be imbued with meaning through the embrace of social narratives. We expect individuals will be attracted to narratives that reflect their own anxiety and resentment because such narratives help them understand why they feel the way they do, validate their emotions, and provide possible (if daunting) solutions to those problems. By elucidating causes and, perhaps most importantly, designating targets, discontented narratives allow individuals hope of escaping negative affect, if only once the villains have been vanquished. We freely admit that this is hypothetical, with little support in exist-ing research (but with no contradictory findings either); we therefore rely on our data to establish this link in our theoretical chain, testing

---

[4] Although we expect the relationship to be mutual; that is, we theorize that while negative emotions provokes cultural discontent, this discontent itself also provokes negative emotions, forming a vicious cycle.

it extensively in the empirical chapters of the book. Although we leave the details to case-focused chapters, we should note here that the role of discontented narratives is a major complicating factor in the comparative study of discontent. Although emotional spillover occurs in a relatively uniform manner across people and contexts, narratives are much more interwoven in the cultural contexts in which they develop and spread. As such, the details of *how* discontent manifests, including the specific cultural conflicts at issue, the prevalence of inclusive or exclusive forms of discontent, and whether discontent is directed through formal democratic mechanisms (i.e. elections) or into the streets as contentious politics, is highly contingent on the case-specific menu of available narratives. The cumulative nature of discontent further complicates the role of narratives. In several of our cases, we see a sequential process in which more inclusive narratives (e.g. Podemos in Spain, the movement behind the social uprising in Chile) falter or fail to effectively challenge the system, opening space for more exclusive or even radical right narratives to thrive. In other words, we cannot understand the prevalence of narratives at a given point in time without a firm grasp of contextual details, including the history of discontent within each context.

3.3.2 Resentment, Anxiety, and Cultural Discontent

With this proposition in hand, we can easily show why emotions with economic roots could engender a sense of cultural discontent. In Chapter 2, we defined cultural discontent as the perception that one's values and identities are not respected in one's own society. There is a clear affinity with resentment here. Resentment is driven by perceived normative threats, and feeling that one's deeply held values are disrespected and ignored is an extreme example of normative threat. Furthermore, resentment tends to intensify existing biases and prejudices and thus hostility to out-groups. Narratives that emphasize the unfair or unjust elevation of out-groups in the cultural hierarchy of a society are thus likely to resonate with angry individuals who are already predisposed to hostility toward marginalized groups. Furthermore, resentment increases reliance on mental habits, which will increase solidarity with one's in-group while intensifying negative stereotypes and prejudices against out-groups.

The role of anxiety is not quite so clear-cut, but we still have reason to expect it to encourage discontent. Anxiety tends to arouse people from cognitive complacency: anxious individuals may begin to question whether cultural values they hold dear are as valued by society as they may have previously assumed, thus opening them up to culturally dis-contented narratives. Furthermore, there is evidence that the information search triggered by anxiety is not neutral but tends to prioritize threat-ening information; cultural discontent would certainly qualify (Merolla and Zechmeister 2009, Albertson and Gadarian 2015, Gadarian and Albertson 2014).

That said, anxiety is also demotivating, and thus unlikely to produce immediate support for movements or leaders that evince cultural discon-tent. Furthermore, anxiety can *reduce* prejudice, as it discourages reli-ance on assumptions and preconceived notions and encourages active evaluation of new ideas. This feature cuts both ways: it might lead some individuals to question their prejudices, but it could also open the minds of individuals who typically took the dominant political, cultural, and social order for granted, making them more accepting of radical new sto-ries about how their societies work and how hierarchies are (or should be) structured. This is particularly true of individuals with authoritarian per-sonalities, whose conventionalism may lull them into complacency as groups they perceive as inferior gain ground (Altemeyer 1981, 1996). Among these individuals, authoritarian tendencies may be so profoundly rooted that anxiety's opening influence cannot touch its attendant preju-dices but may open them to the idea that established authorities have turned against them.

In short, we see a clear and straightforward role for resentment in generated discontent, and a more ambiguous role for anxiety. We fur-thermore do not discount the possibility of a sequential relationship, with anxiety predicting resentment, and from there leading to cultural discon-tent, as Jost (2019) argues. We also accept the possibility that anxiety may influence democratic discontent in ways that do not hold true for cultural discontent, where the erosion of prejudicial thinking may not be as relevant. All things considered, we expect resentment to do most of the heavy lifting in connecting economics to culture, and culture to politics.

3.3.3 Connecting Cultural and Democratic Discontent

With the theoretical links between economics, emotions, and culture elu-cidated, the cultural orientation of discontent in the era of the Great Recession starts to make sense. The severity of the crisis, the inadequacy of state responses to it, and fierce disputes over which social groups received the relatively paltry assistance offered in its wake, created an ideal situation for cultural discontent to thrive. Driven by anxiety and resentment, people across the globe began to rebel against establishment politics that, in their eyes, ignored and undervalued them.

There can be little doubt that conflicts over cultural issues and populist ideas go hand in hand: the rise of the PRR in Europe and more recently in the Americas is a testament to this fact. This affinity can be clearly shown by comparing the definitions of cultural discontent and populism as we present them in this book. Recall that populism holds that political elites have betrayed the people and are no longer serving as their agents or delegates but instead serving their own agenda. This narrative lends itself readily to cultural discontent: what greater betrayal could there be than elites who violate dearly held values and ignore the "true people" of the nation in favor of those who are unworthy? Indeed, conceived in this way, cultural discontent practically requires a populist political stance: how could the "proper" social order be so profoundly undermined, so totally divorced from the values and identities of "the people," *unless* political elites had turned traitor?[5]

Individuals who imagine themselves to comprise a unified "people" who feel that their values and beliefs are marginalized ask an obvious question: if democracy is about the rule of the people, how can the people's values and identities be so thoroughly marginalized?[6] Of course, there are rational but complex answers here: the unity of the people is imaginary, with real conflicts and debates running through it; the "majority" is often at most a plurality, especially as societies diversify; solidarity among the majority often rests on dehumanizing assumptions about the moral and political worth of rising "minorities"; tradition is no guarantee of superiority, thus new cultural ideas and values may in fact be more appealing to those who are not so threatened by their novelty; and political elites may simply respond to these new values more than older, more parochial concerns. Yet these explanations, which often cast those most prone to cultural discontent (especially its right-wing variant) in the role of the malcontented revanchist, are unlikely to appeal to or be embraced by cultural conservatives.

---

[5] This presupposes a basic belief in the ideal of democracy: that some relationship of trust between elites and the people either has existed in the past or can and should exist. The extreme right (i.e. fascists) also manifests cultural discontent but, given the open hostility to democracy prevalent in this corner of the FR, populism makes little sense.

[6] We focus here on the cultural discontent of dominant groups. There is certainly considerable reason to expect discontent from underprivileged groups, but that discontent seems to differ in kind, as there are likely a host of important reasons why racial and ethnic, religious, or other minorities may rightly be discontented with society. We broach this topic briefly in Chapter 9.

Leftists are by no means immune to these dynamics. With the FR threatening the multicultural consensus, and with the failure of progressive movements to forcefully challenge neoliberalism even as its failures were laid bare by the Great Recession, many progressives were forced to cast about for explanations of why their values and ideas seem so utterly impotent. These cultural issues are new to left-wing varieties of populism, which typically seek to be inclusive and elide cultural divisions, focusing instead on the unified opposition of the people to economic elites and their pawns in government, as slogans such as "we are the 99 percent" show (Kazin 1998, Mudde and Rovira Kaltwasser 2013a). Left populist movements have typically been ambivalent at best about cultural issues, preferring to ignore them or actually embracing cultural conservatism while retaining progressive positions on economics and politics (Hofstadter 1955). Yet, as we argue later in this book, concerns about the waning power of multiculturalism have become a core feature of contemporary left-wing populism, especially in situations where the PRR comes to power (Jardina, Kalmoe, and Gross 2021), and thus cultural discontent and its influence are by no means confined to any one side of the ideological spectrum.

Just as cultural discontent can lead to changes in attitudes, we also expect it to alter behavior. Individuals frequently embrace populist leaders and movements as vehicles for their cultural discontent; yet in some situations this channel may not be available. Supply-side issues, such as firm barriers to entry by new parties or political outsiders, may render the success of populist movements unable to effectively challenge the dominant political order. Some societies also have deeply rooted anti-populism as part of their identities, as was the case in Chile until recently (Meléndez and Rovira Kaltwasser 2017). In these cases, there may be little option but to challenge the dominant order and its disrespect of one's values and identity in a more direct fashion, namely by going out into the streets. Although not addressing cultural discontent specifically, a substantial body of scholarship attests to the fact that a failure of the democratic system to channel and respond to demands predicts contentious behavior (Crow 2010, Muller and Opp 1986, Opp, Burow-Auffarth, and Heinrichs 1981, Rhodes-Purdy 2012). That democracy is not listening is strongly implied by the very nature of cultural discontent; we therefore expect cultural discontent to be a major component of many (though perhaps not all) eruptions of contentious politics.

3.4 DEMOCRATIC VOICE AND THE
MODERATION OF DISCONTENT

Every country we study responded to the economic turmoil of the Great Recession era in its own way, as the array of manifestations of discontent we have so far discussed can attest. The foundational relationship of this book – the connection between economic, cultural, and democratic discontent, mediated by emotions – is relatively universal. Yet if this is the case, then why such a diversity of outcomes? Simply put, the relationship is consistent across contexts but is also shaped by local conditions.

The source of this diversity lies in the inchoate nature of discontent and its need to be fused and fleshed out through social narratives. This process creates major challenges for anyone attempting to craft anything like a "general theory" of discontent because, unlike the more universal relationships we have described thus far, narratives are deeply intertwined with the details of specific contexts. Factors that can determine which narratives rise above others include recent political history, existing cultural conflicts, the preexisting biases and prejudices held by individuals, and party system dynamics, to name only a few. We cannot ignore the role of narratives nor the factors that favor some while disfavoring others: narratives affect whether discontent is inclusive or exclusive (i.e. they merge with prejudice to become the PRR), the specific behaviors used to express discontent (e.g. support for populist leaders or parties, contentious politics), among other important factors.

Yet a general theory that attempted to incorporate narratives would be so complex and likely miss so many important details as to be unmanageable at best or misleading at worst. Given this, we make no attempt to craft a comprehensive conceptual schema here; instead, we elucidate the narrative environment for each case in our country-focused chapters, with one exception: the role of democratic voice.

3.4.1 Weak and Strong Voice

As we go through our country studies in later chapters, we find one factor that shapes, intensifies, and directs the relationships we described in this chapter in virtually all contexts: democratic voice. The concept of voice is taken from the seminal work by Hirschman (1970). An economist, Hirschman challenged the standard economic account of consumers reacting to dissatisfaction with firms by simply "exiting," or ceasing to do business with the firm in question. He argued that consumers often felt loyalty to firms with which they had longstanding relationships and might choose to pressure the firm to correct or change its behavior rather than simply leaving.

Hirschman then applied this logic to states, but he failed to fully explore the unique role of voice in democracies. Democratic regimes differ from firms and other regime types in that voice is institutionalized: those at the bottom of the hierarchy (ordinary citizens) have binding mechanisms to punish those at the top (political elites) through voting and other means, even if the strength of those mechanisms varies among democracies and over time. We discuss two forms of democratic voice in this work: responsiveness (weak voice) and participation (strong voice).[7] Responsiveness exists when political elites are seen as receptive to the demands of citizens and likely to try to satisfy those demands whenever possible. Weak voice allows citizens to feel a sense of control over politics, but that control is indirect and depends on the goodwill of political leaders. As such, it tends to be both shallower and less reliable than strong voice, the form of voice on which we focus in this book.

Strong voice (Rhodes-Purdy 2017a, 2017c, 2021c) is defined as the institutionally determined capability of ordinary citizens to influence political decisions. Although sources of strong voice vary across countries, key sources of voice include few barriers or filters between voters and elites,[8] deeply rooted political parties, and vibrantly stable party systems (Pérez Bentancur, Piñeiro Rodríguez, and Rosenblatt 2020, Rosenblatt 2018), and, in some cases, mechanisms for participatory or direct democracy. We analyze strong voice holistically; we do not code individual institutional variants, as institutional effects on strong voice (and on virtually every other outcome) vary considerably depending on other institutions and practices. Instead, we analyze each country we study in this book with an eye toward the system as a whole. We also measure perceptions of strong voice at the individual level, as for individual attitudes, perceptions of strong voice matter more than the reality. We operationalize these perceptions as "perceived strong voice" (PSV), which measures the extent to which an individual feels they can influence the political process based on the characteristics of the process itself.

---

[7] Both forms of voice have similarities to the concept of external political efficacy (Craig, Niemi, and Silver 1990, Niemi, Craig, and Mattei 1991). Efficacy can be conceived as a satisficing combination of responsiveness and strong voice (i.e. external efficacy will be the value of whichever form of voice is stronger).

[8] Such filters include bicameralism, electoral college systems, and other veto points and players that make majoritarian rule more difficult.

3.4.2 How Voice Alters Our Framework

We expect perceptions of strong voice to moderate our relationships between economics, emotions, culture, and politics in several ways. An extensive body of social psychology research in the field of organizational justice (e.g. Thibaut and Walker 1975, Lind and Tyler 1988, McFarlin and Sweeney 1992, Brockner et al. 1994, Lind 2001, van den Bos, Lind, and Wilke 2001, Cropanzano and Ambrose 2002, Lind and van den Bos 2002) has found that individuals embedded in hierarchical organizations (such as business firms, justice systems, and states) consider *how* decisions are made, as well as the content of decisions, when evaluating the organizations to which they are subject. In democracies, where the ultimate sovereignty of the people is a foundational principle, the ability of ordinary citizens to influence the political process is essential for establishing that the institutions and processes of the state are just. As such, we expect PSV to have a direct negative influence on most forms of democratic discontent, perhaps balancing the influence of economic or cultural problems.

Yet the influence of strong voice and PSV goes deeper. PSV is a political and situational variant of a critical psychological drive, namely the desire to exert control over one's environment (Bandura 1977, 1982, White 1959, Angyal 1941, DeCharms 1968). A lack of control tends to produce greater negative emotionality in response to negative outcomes than would manifest if the same outcomes occurred in a situation in which people felt some sense of control (Orpen 1994, Walker 2001, Qin et al. 2015). In the political realm, this has two implications which have been supported by prior research. First, scholars have found that perceptions of procedural injustice generally (Dahlberg and Linde 2016, Magalhães 2016, Magalhães and Aguiar-Conraria 2018) and low PSV specifically (Rhodes-Purdy 2017a, 2017c) tend to intensify negative responses to economic problems. Second, individuals do not evaluate economic performance in an unbiased way, as the extensive literature on economic voting has shown (Anderson 2007). PSV has been shown to influence evaluations of the economy directly; people with low PSV will evaluate specific economic outcomes and general economic situations much more negatively than will people with high PSV, even when evaluating identical economic outcomes (Rhodes-Purdy 2021c).

While these works deal primarily with regime support and satisfaction with democracy, we hypothesize that similar relationships will pertain to democratic discontent more generally. Specifically, we expect individuals with low PSV to react much more strongly to negative economic outcomes, both directly and indirectly via cultural attitudes. As a result, countries that provide substantial mechanisms for citizens to exercise strong voice will be better able to ride out economic downturns. Conversely, elitist democracies that provide little voice to citizens may find themselves besieged over the most modest of economic failures.

Why include voice when we just explained why we would not include other contextual factors such as party systems, cultural dynamics, and so on? Unlike these other factors, we find that voice is important in virtually all contexts and at nearly every step of our story. As a person moves from economic to cultural to political discontent, they evaluate competing discontented narratives. In later chapters, we argue that if citizens perceive themselves to have voice, they will more likely adopt narratives that support action and the system, while those that feel they are unheard and powerless will adopt narratives that are more anti-system.

3.5 CONCLUSIONS

The theory we developed over this chapter and Chapter 2 is complicated, but we can summarize it quite succinctly: economics are the roots, culture the branch, and emotions the trunk connecting the two. For the remainder of this book, we test the framework using experiments and surveys, and apply it to explain outcomes in real-world cases. At no point have we argued that analyses holding up cultural factors are wrong, or that they missed some key element of economics that neatly dispatches the role of values and identities in the surge of discontent we see in our core cases, nor will we do so anywhere else in this book. Instead, economic turmoil lurks about the margins of social dynamics, constantly increasing the pressure on a polity's imperfections and weakest points, increasing the aggregate levels of outrage and paranoia among the citizenry. Often, those weak points are found in inequities and prejudices between cultural groups. Sometimes, as in Chile, the vulnerable spots are political, rather than cultural. But the dynamics are the same: economics inflame, intensify, and exacerbate, while some other factor gets its hands dirty.

We spend the remainder of this book supporting this framework with evidence from experiments, surveys, and case analyses. Details vary depending on method and location, but the core story is like a bad film franchise, producing sequel after sequel while always telling the same essential story. We show how insecurity, inequality, poverty, and deprivation test the mettle of democratic states throughout Europe and the Americas. Some come through this process relatively unscathed, with democracy emerging bloodied but unbowed. In others, namely the core cases on which we focus, discontent provoked a full-blown rupture, damaging or disrupting politics as usual, and introducing anti-system parties into the electoral competition.

4

Affective Political Economy and Political Discontent

An Experimental Analysis

Famed scholar of right-wing authoritarianism Bob Altemeyer once opened the methods section of a book by stating his surprise that the reader chose to read the section, while playfully implying that most readers should probably have better things to do.[1] We will be neither so bold nor so glib, but Altemeyer does nicely summarize a conundrum of presenting statistical results in social science books. Our ability to make convincing arguments, especially on topics such as ours where considerable controversy exists, depends on collecting and presenting conclusive evidence, which often requires a high degree of technical sophistication. On the other hand, excessive technical detail can render a work inaccessible to broad swathes of its potential audience, thus limiting the relevance and impact of our arguments.

In this chapter we attempt to split the difference. We present the results of several experiments designed and implemented to test the core causal claims of the theory we developed in Chapters 2 and 3. To keep the material as approachable as possible, we use a narrative approach: we identify several hypothetical voters who we follow through the steps of our theory, communicating experimental results at each stage of the process. Results are presented as simply as possible, using graphs and charts for the most part, rather than complex data tables. Ancillary details (including full tables of results, results from measurement models, and balance statistics showing that all experiments were demographically balanced) are available in online replication materials stored by Harvard Dataverse.[2]

---

[1] Portions of this chapter have been previously published in: Rhodes-Purdy, Navarre, and Utych (2021b), Utych, Navarre, and Rhodes-Purdy (2021), Rhodes-Purdy, Navarre, and Utych (2021a), Navarre, Rhodes-Purdy, and Utych (2021).

[2] https://dataverse.harvard.edu/dataverse/ageofdiscontent.

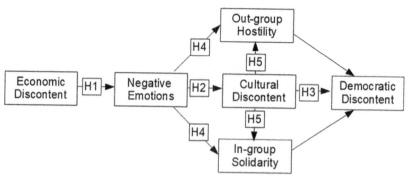

FIGURE 4.1 Theory flowchart with hypotheses.

Ours is not a simple story: it involves multiple layers of mediation and moderation, and several different manifestations of discontent. To give readers a clear guide of how the hypotheses tested in this chapter correspond to the steps of our theory, we provide a modified version of our theory flow chart, with hypotheses marked, in Figure 4.1.

4.1 PRESENTING EXPERIMENTAL ANALYSES: A NARRATIVE APPROACH

To explain the process for becoming discontented during an economic crisis we follow three hypothetical individuals: Left Leaner, Right Leaner, and Tuned Out. We use experimental evidence to analyze when their reactions mirror each other, and when and why their behavior diverges. Neither Left nor Right Leaner are necessarily committed partisans or ideologues, although they may be. What defines them is the fact that they are embedded in social and narrative networks that clearly favor one side of the ideological spectrum. Left Leaner is likely an educated urbanite, as are most of their social contacts and social media feeds. Most of their news sources are either nonpartisan or left-leaning. They probably have positive (if not necessarily well developed) views of multiculturalism and fairly negative views of cultural conservatism, although at the beginning of the process these views may not have much impact on their daily life.

Right Leaner is the mirror image; they probably live in a rural or exurban area, watch Fox News or other conservative media, socialize with social conservatives, and have latent negative stereotypes and attitudes toward immigrants, minorities, and social progressives. That said, Right Leaner does not see themselves as prejudiced or biased. They would likely counter such charges by arguing that they "do not see color," even as their social and political views are shaped by negative stereotypes of minority-coded "welfare queens" and "job-stealing" immigrants.

Tuned Out is something of a wild card; they are disengaged from politics, do not follow political news, have inchoate attitudes about political issues and actors, and generally have few attachments to any political leaders or movements. In a more typical social context, Tuned Out would probably remain a resolute nonvoter. Their attitudes and behaviors will be the most difficult to predict as they will be shaped by idiosyncratic factors and random chance to a greater extent than for the Leaners.

Since we use data from survey experiments to explain outcomes, we first need to address the shortcomings of experimental methods and how we dealt with them. When designing experiments, there is an intrinsic tension between carefully constructing treatments that will trigger the desired response and *only* that response (internal validity), and accurately simulating real-world dynamics, in all their complexity and interconnectivity (external validity). The challenge is especially acute for us because our theory is sequential, and experiments are typically structured as discrete events. Additionally, representative probability samples for experiments are often prohibitively expensive. Researchers with more modest budgets often use convenience samples, such as those provided by outlets like Amazon .com's Mechanical Turk (the Mturk platform). Mturk samples are more representative than the student samples on which psychology and other experimental behavior fields have long relied, but they still skew younger, more educated, more male, and more liberal than the population at large.

Taken together, these issues all raise the question: can we make firm inferences about relationships in the real world based on imperfect simulations presented to a group of people who differ significantly from the population we are studying? Recent history suggests we ignore this question at our peril; the replication crisis in psychology, where experimental results long relied upon have crumbled when other analysts attempt to reproduce the same effects in different samples, is perhaps the best example.

While perfect solutions to these issues do not exist, we have attempted to mitigate them to the best of our ability (and budget). To address sampling issues, we use a variety of platforms, multiple surveys, and, for our most crucial analysis, both probability and convenience samples. We find that both types of samples (Forthright and Mturk, respectively) produce similar findings. We address internal validity problem by using different types of treatments (e.g. video vs. written exercises). In later chapters, we address external validity using observation data to corroborate the relationships revealed by experimental data.

TABLE 4.1 *List of studies*

Number	Name	Fielding date	n	Hyp. tested	Description
Study 1	Mturk Populism	October 2019	997	H1–H3	Writing exercises for economic and cultural discontent, populism
Study 2	Forthright Populism	March 2019	801	H1–H4	Video treatments for economic and cultural discontent, populism
Study 3	Mturk Prejudice	February 2020	478	H4	Writing exercises for economic resentment, anxiety, and neutral
Study 4	Lucid Prejudice	April 2021	376	H5	Writing exercise for cultural discontent

Overall, we have replicated these results across different samples, at different points in time, and using different treatments, and received strikingly similar results. Taken together, the results are far stronger than any single set would be alone; the likelihood that so many different methods and approaches within methods would converge on data patterns suggested by our theory due to chance is practically nil. In order to help the reader follow the multiple replications discussed in Section 4.2, we have included a table of all the experiments referenced, including sampling method, size, dates, treatments, and hypotheses tested (Table 4.1).

4.2 THE CRISIS BEGINS: ECONOMICS, EMOTIONS, AND CULTURAL DISCONTENT

Our analytical story begins when an economic crisis erupts. The specific harms that befall the Leaners and Tuned Out, or at least people in their social environment, will vary depending on the details of the crisis. But we generally expect them to be inundated with stories of turmoil, loss, and fear about the future as unemployment spikes and people begin losing homes, businesses, and savings. As crises are typically not well understood until long after they conclude, a great deal of free-floating uncertainty pervades the social environment. Moreover, we expect narratives about who is responsible for the crisis to proliferate: tales of the greed of the financial sector and government incompetence begin circulating widely. This leads us to our first hypothesis:

H1: Economic discontent causes negative emotions, specifically resentment and anxiety.

We expect all our hypothetical citizens to have similar emotional responses at this point in the process. Although they may differ in which negative emotion predominates, we expect most people to feel both.

To test this hypothesis (as well as others), we designed two studies to simulate exposure to economic turmoil. We used different treatment modes in each study. Study 1 used a written exercise that asked respondents to remember a time the economy made them feel angry (Economic Discontent – Resentment) or anxious (Economic Discontent – Anxiety). The writing exercise allowed us to use respondents' own experiences as the simulation, taking them back to a time when they actually experienced the social environment we describe. Study 2 also included both resentment and anxiety treatments but used a video depicting a family suffering from the effects of the Great Recession. The family in question suffered unemployment, the loss of their home, and a major decline in their standard of living. We used text placards and music to direct respondents toward either anxiety or resentment. Videos tend to pack a bit more emotional punch, although their effects can vary more between respondents due to idiosyncratic reactions to the specific content of the video.

4.2.1 Measuring Emotional Responses

Emotions are among the most difficult concepts to measure that we address in this book. Numerous methods have been devised to help respondents accurately report their emotional states, but all have serious shortcomings and difficulties, chief among them the extreme difficulty of measuring discrete emotions like anxiety and resentment that share the same valence (i.e. are both unpleasant).

One of the most commonly used measures of emotions is the Positive and Negative Affect Schedule (PANAS) (Watson, Clark, and Tellegen 1988), which asks respondents to rate the extent to which they feel various emotions on a five-point scale. The PANAS, however, was not designed to measure discrete emotions like anxiety or resentment, but simply a negative or positive affect, and the measures of anxiety and

TABLE 4.2 *List of emotions on the PANAS-M*

Resentment	Anxiety	Negative affect	Enthusiasm
Angry	Anxious	Distressed	Enthusiastic
Mad	Afraid	Disturbed	Hopeful
Furious	Worried	Upset	Proud
Outraged	Nervous		
Hostile			

resentment produced using the standard PANAS are extremely highly correlated (r is typically between 0.8 and 0.9). This leads to serious issues when including these measures in statistical analysis and makes it quite difficult to reliably estimate the effects of each emotion, as both resentment and anxiety measures are contaminated by the other negative emotion. To overcome this, we developed a modified version of the PANAS, the PANAS-M. The PANAS-M, instead of asking respondents to rate the degree to which they feel a battery of emotions, first asks respondents if they felt or did not feel the following (Table 4.2).

Respondents were then presented the standard PANAS questions, with the same five-point scale, for all emotions they indicated they felt. Emotions they checked as "did not feel" were coded zero, which led to a six-point scale of emotional response. We then used CFA to generate scales for anxiety and resentment.[3] This produces measures of anxiety and resentment that are significantly less correlated than using the PANAS, and which respond to emotional triggers in a way that suggests they are more valid than the PANAS measures (Rhodes-Purdy, Navarre, and Utych 2021a). The lessened correlation between them also helps make estimates of their effects more accurate.

4.2.2 Economic Discontent and Emotions (H1)

With these measures in hand, we can test our contention that our hypothetical citizens will respond with anxiety and resentment when exposed

---

[3] See the online replication materials for more details and results of the CFA for Study 1. The negative affect factor is used simply to help isolate the effect of valence from the discrete emotions, which can occasionally reduce the correlation of resentment and anxiety, although subsequent studies have indicated this effect is minimal and thus including the negative affect factor is not necessary. Additionally, readers should be aware that what we call "resentment" is equivalent to "anger" or "aversion" as used in works on AIT. We use the term resentment for reasons outlined in Chapter 3.

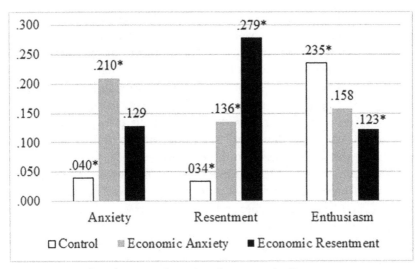

FIGURE 4.2 Predicted means of emotions by economic discontent treatments.

to the economic turmoil that typically emerges during a crisis. We do so by regressing the treatments from Study 1 on our emotional measures. Figure 4.2 shows the predicted means of anxiety, resentment, and enthusiasm by treatment.

These means show that the treatments were effective in triggering the intended negative emotion. The anxiety treatment produced nearly twice as much anxiety as resentment; the reverse is true for the resentment treatment. The effects on enthusiasm are relevant as well; the resentment treatment had a slightly larger influence on enthusiasm than the anxiety treatment, pushing it significantly below the grand mean for the sample. Finally, we should note that although the negative emotion economic treatments produced the predicted discrepancies between anxiety and resentment, both treatments significantly increased both resentment and anxiety. Simply put, our proposition that our hypothetical citizens would begin to suffer sustained and significant negative emotions is well supported.

4.2.3 Emotional Spillover: Emotions and Cultural Discontent (H2)

As the emotional effects of the economic crisis continue, the first signs of emotional spillover will begin to emerge. Even as their emotional responses are similar, our hypothetical citizens start to evince subtle differences in the narratives regarding the economic crisis that will eventually produce significant divergence. Left Leaner focuses their ire on financial elites and corporations, and the way in which the alliance between it and cultural conservatives protects neoliberalism at the expense of "the people." Right Leaner, on the other hand, blames poor people (often presented in racialized terms) and immigrants for leaching off the state and driving up job-killing taxes. In short, as resentment sets in, each Leaner digs deeper into their own predispositions and biases, blaming "the other" for their troubles and those of their country. If the crisis drags on or if the recovery falters, these blame narratives become more extreme. Resentment turns into seething rage; the "others" are not just obstacles to recovery but have "taken over" the country. Left Leaner consumes and internalizes resentful narratives that equality, solidarity, and simple decency have been supplanted by neoliberal greed and nativism; Right Leaner undergoes a similar process, only they see themselves as marginalized by an economically privileged urban aristocracy who favor minorities and immigrants over "people like them." Tuned Out is harder to predict; their reactions will, as always, depend on contingencies like social networks and media consumption, although the most likely result is a much vaguer sense that "people like me" are being ignored and undervalued. This leads to our second hypothesis:

H2: Anxiety and/or resentment cause cultural discontent.

We test this hypothetical response using Study 1 and Study 2. We report only the results of Study 1 here.[4] To begin, we regressed our economic discontent treatments on our measures of cultural discontent (see Section 2.6.2). Predicted means of each dependent variable by treatment are presented in Figure 4.3; starred data labels indicate a significant difference from the grand mean.

As predicted, cultural discontent (regardless of measure used) was significantly influenced by the economic resentment treatment. The economic anxiety treatment did not significantly influence cultural discontent, although predicted means were larger than for the control treatment. This is consistent with our earlier description of how Left and Right Leaner react to their ongoing anxiety and anger over the state of the economy by adopting culturally discontented narratives and internalizing their message.

---

[4] See the appendix to Rhodes-Purdy, Navarre, and Utych (2021b) for a replication using data from Study 2.

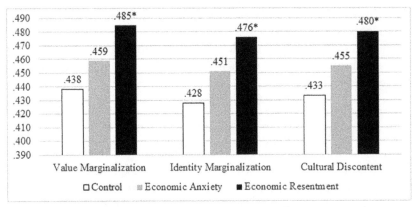

FIGURE 4.3 Predicted mean of cultural discontent by economic discontent treatments.

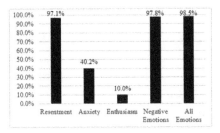

FIGURE 4.4 Percent of economic resentment treatment effect mediated by emotions.

Of course, that interpretation assumes that emotions are the causal mechanism. The difference across emotional variants of the economic treatments suggests this, but we can explore this further by looking at the change in treatment effects when different combinations of emotions are included in the model as independent variables. This mediation analysis, conducted per Breen, Karlson, and Holm (2013), allows us to include multiple mediating factors. Mediation allows us to estimate the percentage of the Economic Resentment treatment's effect on cultural discontent that flows through each emotion and combination of emotions. Results are presented in Figure 4.4.

The results are consistent with both H2 and the general trend so far established that resentment, rather than anxiety, is the primary link between economic and cultural attitudes. Including resentment alone reduces the effect of the resentment economic discontent treatment by a staggering 97.1 percent, or essentially the entire treatment effect.

Including the other emotions does only slightly better, mediating an additional 1.4 percent.[5] Although enthusiasm has a significant and negative effect on cultural discontent, it does not appear to be relevant for the economics/culture connection, as its inclusion only accounts for 0.7 percent of the treatment effect.

4.2.4 Slouching toward Politics: From Cultural to Democratic Discontent

To review, all three hypothetical citizens are now experiencing significant cultural discontent. The Leaners each have internalized specific narratives about who the belligerents are in this new culture war, and each identifies the other as a member of the opposing side. Tuned Out is not immune, although their personal narrative may appear inchoate or even scrambled. To get a sense of this person, one might look to media personalities in the USA, like Bill Maher or Joe Rogan, who rail against political correctness and the "woke mob" but also seem drawn to leftist figures like Bernie Sanders with little in the way of a unifying thread beyond a general sense of alienation from the national culture. But regardless of whether this discontent is vague or specific, as it deepens, we expect both Leaners and Tuned Out to alter their attitudes toward politics. While the Leaners may gravitate toward stronger ideologues who *share* their own ideology, Tuned Out seems likely to gravitate toward those who are challenging the system generally, regardless of ideology (as evidenced by Rogan's seemingly simultaneous enthusiasm for the candidacies of both Sanders and Trump).

4.3 CULTURAL AND DEMOCRATIC DISCONTENT (H3)

Cultural discontent presents an opportunity for political outsiders and entrepreneurs. Parties, movements, and leaders who, for whatever reason, cannot or will not pursue their claims through mainstream political channels can easily weave cultural issues into narratives that tie cultural discontent to critiques of the political system and elites. The marginalization of your group, such narratives argue, is not the product of impersonal social or historical forces but arises from the deliberate acts of elites who are arrayed against you, and of a moribund political system that allows this to happen.

---

[5] The mediation percentages for the emotions individually are larger than the difference calculated for multiple emotions due to the correlation between emotions.

Both Leaners are gradually drawn to narratives that criticize the system, but "the system" is an empty signifier. As such, each Leaner gravitates toward specific discontented narratives that hew close to their preexisting worldviews. Tuned Out rejoins the fray here. It is unlikely that they embraced comprehensive cultural narratives, instead picking up bits and pieces of narratives that reflect their own idiosyncrasies and preconceptions. However, discontented narratives will appeal a great deal to them. Tuned Out is the most likely to bounce between discontented movements, for example by supporting Bernie Sanders in the Democratic primary and then voting for Donald Trump in the general election. This leads to our next hypothesis:

H3: Cultural discontent causes democratic discontent.

As we have discussed so far, democratic discontent can manifest in different ways, depending upon how "the system" is conceived: in personal terms (the political elite) or institutionally (the regime). In some circumstances, discontented narratives can become floridly elaborate and so distrustful of all established knowledge that they evolve into full-blown conspiracy theories. We discuss the factors that can influence these manifestations in later chapters, but here we test the influence of cultural discontent on all three forms of democratic discontent.

4.3.1 Cultural Discontent and Populism

We test H3 as it relates to populism using Study 1. This study included a treatment intended to evoke a sense of cultural discontent. The treatment asked respondents to "think about a time in your life when you felt that you or people with values and beliefs like yours did not belong in this country," which they then wrote about for 60–90 seconds. We regressed three measures of populism on this treatment: anti-elitism, people-centrism, and the multiplicative index combining the two as recommended by Wuttke, Schimpf, and Schoen (2020) and Castanho Silva et al. (2018). As a manipulation check, we also include three measures of cultural discontent: value and identity marginalization (the two clusters discussed earlier) and an index combining the two by taking their mean. The results are presented in Figure 4.5: bars represent the estimated treatment effects with 95 percent confidence intervals.

As our theory suggests, cultural discontent significantly influenced all three dimensions of populism. The influence seems most pronounced on anti-elitism. This is consistent with findings throughout that have two

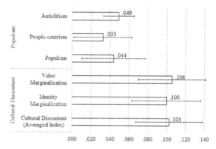

FIGURE 4.5 Effects of cultural discontent treatment on populism dimensions with manipulation checks.

important implications for the study of populism. First, anti-elitism seems to be more of a true "attitude" than people-centrism, and as such is more responsive to experimental treatments and contextual factories generally. Second, anti-elitism appears to be the "dark side" of populism, that is, it is most strongly associated with negative consequences for politics and society. In later sections, we show that anti-elitism also alters how people-centrism influences behavior: it appears to reduce any antiauthoritarian effects people-centrism has.

4.3.2 Cultural Discontent, Regime Antipathy, and Conspiracism

Experimental treatments are intended to simulate real-world phenomena, but we can never perfectly recreate the experiences we believe explain attitudes and behavior. Therefore, a single experiment is always suspect; effects of treatments might be due to some idiosyncratic element of the design, rather than the phenomena being simulated, or even due to random sampling fluctuations. As such, replication of experiments is always advisable. In this section, we test H1, H2, and H3 in a slightly different way, using data from 1,001 adult US residents recruited by the Forthright panel (Study 2 – Forthright Populism). In this study, we use videos to induce economic and cultural discontent. Cultural discontent was extremely difficult to induce via video evenly across respondents: what liberals find discontenting may very well please conservatives, and vice versa. We finally chose a video featuring Trump advisor Steve Bannon discussing immigration and cultural change. We reasoned that conservatives would find it discontenting because it dwells on cultural changes conservatives typically oppose, while liberals would find it discontenting because someone so close to the president was making such statements.

Study 2 included measures of populism and of two other types of political discontent: conspiracism (measured with the Bruder et al. (2013) scale) and regime antipathy, measured using three indicators taken from the Americas Barometer study: respect for regime institutions, pride in the political system, and confidence in the political system. Conspiracism was influenced by economic anxiety (coefficient = 0.068, standard error (SE) = 0.021, p = 0.001), economic resentment (coefficient = 0.044, SE = 0.021, p = 0.040), and cultural discontent (coefficient = 0.054, SE = 0.021, p = 0.009), while regime antipathy was influenced only by the economic resentment treatment (coefficient = 0.044, SE = 0.022, p = 0.047).

In short, we find consistent evidence that populism and conspiracism are driven by cultural discontent, as hypothesized. The results for regime antipathy were not significant, suggesting it may be a more durable attitude. We have found over numerous pilots and experiments that regime support/antipathy tends to be highly resistant to experimental manipulation.

4.3.3 Zooming Out: An Analytical Review

At this point, we have argued for a step-by-step process, where hypothetical voters go from economic to cultural to democratic discontent, and each step in that process has been supported by experimental evidence. The most important steps are supported by multiple experiments, using different treatment modes and different sample methods. That said, we risk losing the forest for the trees here. The contribution of this book is not simply in the elucidation of the sequence of discontent, but rather that economic discontent is the *root* cause of democratic discontent, even though its influence flows through several layers of mediation.

Testing the importance of economic discontent, therefore, requires a step beyond supporting the sequence; we also wish to get a sense of the total effect economic discontent has on cultural and especially democratic discontent. To that end, we used structural equation modeling (SEM) path analysis on the data from Study 2 to simultaneously estimate the following regressions: resentment and anxiety were regressed on the treatments, cultural discontent on the emotions, and political discontent measures (populism, conspiracism, and regime antipathy) on cultural discontent and the emotions. Path SEM is useful here because it allows us to estimate the total effect that economic discontent treatments had on these other variables, that is, the cumulative causal effect throughout each step in our sequence. Results are presented in Figure 4.6, which

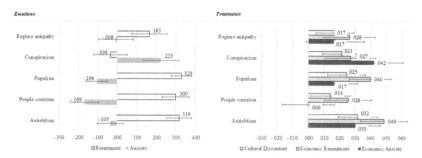

FIGURE 4.6 Total effects of economic and cultural discontent treatments and emotions on political discontent.

includes both total effects of emotions (to get more leverage on the question of which emotion is most important) and the total effect of the discontent treatments.

These figures clarify and reinforce earlier findings. Perhaps most important, resentment emerges as by far the most critical emotion for influencing discontent. The effects of the economic resentment treatment are larger on most forms of political discontent, and the effect of our measure of resentment itself is far larger than anxiety. Anxiety, in fact, had a negative influence on most forms of discontent, with one exception: conspiracism.

Conspiracism seems to be more strongly influenced by anxiety, with no or even a negative effect of resentment. This fits with the paranoia and hypersensitivity to threat that are intrinsic to conspiratorial ideation. We address the unique emotional dynamics of conspiracism in Chapter 9, where we argue that conspiracism often emerges as leaders who rely on politically discontented individuals for support falter or fail. Conspiracism serves as a coping mechanism (ironically, given the often terrifying details of conspiratorial narratives) that provides an escape hatch from irresolvable anxiety. When social threats are omnipresent and even populist or regime antagonistic leaders and movements fail to resolve the situation, conspiracy theories provide explanations and enemies. The thought that an all-powerful cabal has thwarted even a charismatic populist is actually comforting compared to the notion that social problems are simply unsolvable. Conspiracism may indeed be especially appealing to people like Tuned Out, who is distrustful of political elites of all stripes. Tuned Out is less informed about politics and inclined to believe in the corruption of political leaders, allowing their anxiety about the political world to foster these conspiratorial beliefs.

4.3.4 Discussion of Results

Typically, when discussing results of analyses, it is not strictly accurate to say that results "support" or "prove" hypotheses; rather, we only say that results are consistent with them or not. Taken together, however, we feel comfortable saying that our results presented thus far provide strong evidence for our theoretical framework. We have experimentally tested each step in our theory in multiple ways, and the results are remarkably consistent, both with one another and with our theoretical expectations.

The results also clarify some lingering ambiguities we could not resolve theoretically. First, we have shed some light on the nature of populism, specifically how its constitutive dimensions interact with one another. Hatred of elites appears to be the driving factor in dynamic populism, that is, anti-elitism is the dimension that responds most readily to contextual factors. Later in the book (Chapters 5–7), we find that it also tends to be the driver of support for populist leaders. Finally, through observational analyses included in later chapters (Chapters 5–7), we find that anti-elitism fundamentally alters the causal nature of its partner dimension (people-centrism) by negating its inhibiting effect on authoritarian and aggressive tendencies. We leave this discussion until after these analyses have been presented.

4.4 CULTURAL DISCONTENT AND PREJUDICE: THE APE OF INTERGROUP ATTITUDES (H4 AND H5)

In Section 4.3, we traced the evolution of our hypothetical citizens' attitudes toward the political system. Yet the changes and shifts in our citizens' views are by no means limited to the political system. Throughout our discussion we alluded to the different ways that resentment and anxiety shaped their views of other social groups as well. The fact that we have two parallel processes here, each triggered by economic crises and emotional responses to them, can help explain why democratic discontent and ethnonationalism tend to co-occur so frequently.

We have thus far focused on the shared trajectory the Leaners and Tuned Out followed to democratic discontent. That said, we also noted points of divergence, and those branching paths become especially crucial here. Economic discontent and emotions do not create prejudices out of thin air. Instead, they interact with existing biases and latent identities, intensifying them and increasing their salience. We use the term "prejudice" very broadly here, to refer to these intense in-group/out-group distinctions, rather than to any specific subtype (e.g. ethnocentrism, ethnonationalism).

This can lead to very different attitudinal changes depending on a person's preexisting identities. Right Leaner, for example, likely had negative attitudes toward minorities and marginalized groups prior to the crisis. Yet these attitudes were inchoate and latent, consisting of little more than a sense that people outside the white Protestant subculture to which Right Leaner belongs were fundamentally different, along with stereotypes and biases toward such individuals, such as vague associations connecting people of color with crime or violence. Right Leaner has these latent attitudes in part because most members of the ethnoracial majority share some negative attitudes toward marginalized groups (if only unconsciously), but primarily because they have existed in a conservative narrative space where these ideas are prevalent.

As the crisis unfolds, anxiety and resentment do their work. The role of anxiety is somewhat ambiguous, and there is some reason to believe it might weaken prejudice by reducing habits of mind. Yet evidence also suggests that the information search triggered by anxiety is biased in favor of threatening information (Albertson and Gadarian 2015, Gadarian and Albertson 2014). And the openness to new ideas that anxiety provokes is a double-edged sword: theoretically it might reduce prejudice, but it can also open a person to new narratives and ideas that one might have been previously hesitant to accept. Right Leaner likely would have strenuously rejected any suggestion that they were racist, bigoted, or otherwise prejudiced before the crisis began. They would probably recoil at narratives that openly targeted minorities, despite their own latent negative attitudes, if only because of an instinctual desire to avoid obviously racist narratives, or simply to avoid the social stigma of being labeled a bigot. Anxiety might well give Right Leaner pause, as prejudicial narratives emphasizing threat catch their attention, leading them to consider narratives they would have ignored under typical circumstances.

Right Leaner is highly unlikely to experience anxiety alone; they almost certainly experience resentment as well, and this latter emotion does most of the explanatory heavy lifting in our theory. Resentment increases reliance on existing biases while also increasing aggression and the need to punish perceived wrongdoers (Rhodes-Purdy 2021b). In this emotional state, Right Leaner gravitates toward narratives that reflect that aggression. We envision a step-by-step process, where anxiety opens Right Leaner to increasingly explicit ethnoracial appeals, while resentment gradually leads to acceptance of each new narrative. In other words, anxiety and resentment operate as a one-step two-step radicalization process, where the former opens the door to prejudicial narratives while the latter pushes Right Leaner through. As the process repeats, Right Leaner goes further and further into radicalized narrative spaces, away from the dog whistles and subtly of the top layers down to the depths, where ethnoracial animus is increasingly laid bare. This leads us to our next hypothesis:

> H4: Among conservatives, negative emotions caused by economic discontent cause an increase in preference for one's own ethnic group (ethnocentrism) and hostility to out-groups (hostility to unauthorized immigrants, racial resentment).

How do these dynamics play out with Left Leaner and Tuned Out? Left Leaner's intergroup attitudes will likely not respond as intensely to economic discontent simply because of the different nature of the narratives to which they are exposed. Left-wing populism (the primary mode of discontent to which Left Leaner is likely drawn) tends to emphasize the unity of "the people" against a narrowly defined political and financial elite (Mudde and Rovira Kaltwasser 2013a). This is in marked contrast to the populism that draws people like Right Leaner, which tends to obsess over both the need to purge "unpeople" as well as the hierarchical conflict. Left Leaner may well grow more hostile toward conservatives, rural dwellers, Evangelical Christians (at least in the United States) or other religious conservatives, and other right-leaning subcultures, but we do not expect (nor do we observe in our data) the same degree of intensity as we do among conservatives.

Once again, Tuned Out is the wild card. Recall that Tuned Out is defined in part by their *lack* of strong social and political opinions. As such, we cannot state with much certainty how this person's intergroup attitudes will change because it is not theoretically clear to which group or groups Tuned Out belongs. We can, however, deduce from theory that Tuned Out's responses will be highly variable and depend on small changes in initial conditions. Specifically, we can imagine two versions of Tuned Out, both of whom go searching for narratives to explain their disaffection with the status quo. Based on minor differences in personality, social environment, personal history, or even the random vagaries of social media algorithms, one version may be drawn into a left-wing discontented movement like Occupy Wall Street, while the other stumbles upon right-wing discontented narratives. Once they become psychologically attached due to shared discontent, they begin to internalize the rest of the narratives being presented as well.

4.4.1 Economic Discontent, Emotions, and Prejudice (H4)

We use data from two studies (Studies 2 and 3) to test H4. We focus here on prejudice against minorities and marginalized ethnic groups among members of the ethnoracial majority (i.e. white non-Latine individuals in the USA, where the experiments were conducted). Both studies used ethnocentrism as our proxy for prejudice. Study 2 measured ethnocentrism using three questions rating the following groups as either hardworking or lazy, intelligent or unintelligent, and trustworthy or untrustworthy: white people, Black people, Latine people, Asian Americans, and Muslims. We took the average of each rating (only among white non-Latine–identifying respondents) and deviated each response from its average to center everyone's ratings. Finally, we subtracted these centered ratings from each respondent's ratings of white people, creating a difference variable where high scores indicate substantially more positive ratings of white people than of other ethnoracial groups. This is consistent with the measure of ethnocentrism based on stereotype ratings from Kinder and Kam (2009); however, their data do not include questions about Muslims, which we have added. We also included a measure of out-group hostility, namely toward unauthorized immigrants: we asked respondents if they felt undocumented immigrants were bad for the country's economy and a drain on government spending, if illegal immigration poses a major danger to the country, and if the number of illegal immigrants crossing the border constitutes a crisis requiring drastic action. We use CFA techniques to construct all indices of prejudice used here.[6]

We then regressed both these measures on our economic treatments from Study 2. We also included a binary variable in the analysis for conservatism; respondents who identified as "conservative" or "extremely conservative" were coded 1, while all others were coded 0. We then interacted this term with the treatments.[7] As such, we get separate estimates of the treatment effects for conservatives and nonconservatives. These effects, with 95 percent confidence bars, are presented in Figure 4.7.[8]

---

[6] Results are available in the online appendix: https://dataverse.harvard.edu/dataverse/ageofdiscontent/.

[7] Ideology questions were posed prior to the experimental treatments. It is typically poor practice to interact measures taken after treatment, but as measures taken prior to treatment are by definition uncorrelated with randomly assigned treatments, such a priori observed indicators can moderate treatment effects.

[8] For a replication of the results of this experiment see Utych, Navarre, and Rhodes-Purdy (2021).

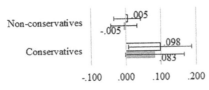

FIGURE 4.7 Effects of economic discontent treatments on intergroup attitudes by conservatism.

As expected, the treatment effects were far larger (nearly ten times as large) among conservatives as among nonconservatives. Only the effect of the resentment treatment was significant at the 0.05 level, although the difference between resentment and anxiety treatments was modest and statistically insignificant. We also repeated this analysis with the treatments interacting with a dummy for those who identify as "liberal" or "extremely liberal." As expected, none of the treatment effects were significant among liberals.

To get a better sense of the discrete emotional effects leading to ethnocentrism, we conducted another experiment (Study 3 – Mturk Prejudice) of 478 white non-Latine respondents. In this study, we measure ethnocentrism in a slightly different manner than in Study 2, only using feeling thermometers for each ethnoracial group rather than stereotype batteries. This study included one control and three writing exercise treatments. The control and first two are the same as in Study 2's economic discontent treatments: one each for resentment and anxiety. The third treatment asked respondents to think about a time when the economy was "not doing well." In other words, the third treatment can be thought of as economic discontent, emotionally neutral.

Only three of the treatment–ideology pairs were significant. As expected, the economic resentment treatment among conservatives significantly increased ethnocentrism among conservatives (coefficient = 0.118; SE = 0.033; p = 0.000), but not among nonconservatives (coefficient = −0.011; SE = 0.019; p = 0.567). The economic anxiety treatment also significantly influenced ethnocentrism among conservatives (coefficient = 0.077; SE = 0.032; p = 0.018) but not nonconservatives (coefficient = −0.006; SE = 0.020; p = 0.754). The neutral treatment, surprisingly, increased ethnocentrism among nonconservatives (coefficient = 0.042; SE = 0.019; p = 0.031) but not among conservatives (coefficient = 0.002; SE = 0.037; p = 0.967). These results are somewhat ambiguous

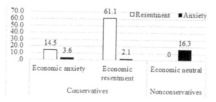

FIGURE 4.8 Percentage of treatment effect explained by emotions.

(it is not immediately clear what is going on with nonconservatives in the neutral treatment), but the results for conservatives closely match what we saw in Study 2.

However, because the written treatments produce less highly correlated emotions, we can better determine the causal mechanisms connecting economic discontent and ethnocentrism. To do so, we conducted a mediation analysis on both conservatives and nonconservatives. We calculated the percentage of the treatment effect reduced by both resentment and anxiety; results are presented in Figure 4.8.

Resentment is clearly the more important factor among conservatives when explaining the connection between economics and prejudice. Resentment mediated 14.5 percent of the anxiety treatment's effect and a significantly larger 61.1 percent of the resentment treatment's effect, rendering the treatment coefficient insignificant despite its large size. Although these results are not entirely conclusive, taken together with the results of Study 2, they strongly indicate that resentment is the primary causal mechanism among conservatives.

The results for the economically neutral treatment among nonconservatives are interesting. Here is the only place where anxiety moderated a significant portion of a treatment effect (16.3 percent). This seems odd but is in fact consistent with one possible interpretation of anxiety's role in shaping prejudice. Among liberals, who prioritize multiculturalism and inclusion of marginalized ethnicities and races, anxiety appears to act as AIT predicts, namely by reducing the influence of prior beliefs and by increasing threat perceptions.

The evidence we provide here for H4 is not as definitive as that for the link between economics and democratic discontent. Prejudicial attitudes are difficult to study experimentally for any number of reasons (e.g. social desirability bias, the relatively fixed nature of such attitudes, the tendency of ideology to alter the influence of emotions, etc.). Ethnocentrism, in particular, is seen as a relatively stable predisposition in existing literature Kinder and Kam (2009), making this a rather difficult test of how experimental treatments and emotions can move preexisting attitudes. Given all these challenges, the fact that we do get consistent findings regardless of measurement, treatment strategy, and sampling platform is powerfully suggestive. In Chapters 5–9, we reinforce these findings with observational data in multiple countries.

4.4.2 Cultural Discontent and Prejudice (H5)

Aside from the emotional influences, we also theorized that cultural discontent itself could drive negative attitudes toward out-groups and in-group solidarity. The mechanism here is straightforward. As a person feels increasingly alienated from and marginalized by the larger culture, that sense of threat will increase solidarity with one's own group while also leading one to blame members of supposedly favored groups. Right Leaner, believing that traditional values have been abandoned by the system in favor of multiculturalism, will increasingly identify with their own social group and become increasingly angry and spiteful toward groups (e.g. minorities, urbanites, the highly educated) who they feel are conspiring to keep them down. Left Leaner will similarly grow more hostile toward conservative-leaning groups as they feel cultural egalitarianism and social justice are being displaced by ethnonationalism.

To test this, we conducted an experiment with 376 self-identified white US resident adults recruited through the Lucid Theorem platform (Study 4 – Lucid Prejudice). We then randomly assigned these participants to one of two writing exercises: they were asked to write about a time they brushed their teeth (Control), or the same cultural discontent prompt used in Study 1. We then asked respondents a series of questions regarding intergroup attitudes:

- Ethnocentrism: measured by taking the difference of feeling thermometers for Black people, Latinos, Asians, Muslims, and unauthorized immigrants from the thermometer for white people, with higher scores indicating greater distance between out-group and in-group evaluations (Kinder and Kam 2009).
- Racial resentment: measured using the standard battery from the American National Election Study, agree/disagree questions about whether Black people have gotten less than they deserve, if they could overcome challenges without special favors, if the plight of Black people is due to a lack of hard work, and if slavery and its legacy is still holding Black people back (Kinder and Sanders 1996).

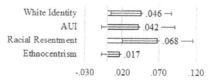

FIGURE 4.9 Cultural discontent treatment effect on intergroup attitudes.

- Attitudes toward unauthorized immigrants (AUI): a series of seven-point agree/disagree questions regarding whether undocumented immigrants are bad for the economy, whether they are a drain on government spending, whether undocumented immigration poses a danger to the country, and whether the number of unauthorized border crossings represents a national crisis.
- White identity: full scale created by Jardina (2019).

We then regressed each of these on the treatment/control variable. As we expect the relationship between discontent and intergroup attitudes to be shaped by ideology (given the growing nationalism on the right and the increasingly firm commitment to inclusive multiculturalism on the left), we specified two sets of models: one including the treatment and ideology as a control, and one in which the treatment interacted with ideology (as with all demographic questions, the ideology question was posed prior to the treatment). The results from the first set without the interaction are presented in Figure 4.9.

These results show that the cultural discontent treatment significantly increased racial resentment and white identity and had a marginally significant ($p = 0.096$) influence on AUI. It did not significantly influence ethnocentrism across the entire sample. Although these data are consistent with H6, we also get the first major surprise of our analyses here when including an interaction between ideology and the treatment. This interaction was only significant for ethnocentrism, but in the opposite direction to that expected: cultural discontent only significantly increased ethnocentrism among *liberals*, rather than among conservatives. While we cannot conclusively determine the source of this unexpected result, evidence suggests that it is due to the starting position of each group. To examine this further, Figure 4.10 presents the predicted means of ethnocentrism by treatment and ideological group (minimum and maximum scores on the ideology measure).

Here, we see that conservatives are consistently more ethnocentric than are liberals, as expected given ideological positions on race and ethnic politics in the USA. Conservatives do not respond to the treatment because,

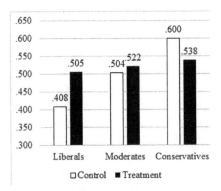

FIGURE 4.10 Predicted mean of ethnocentrism by ideology and treatment.

in a way, they have already been treated[9] by decades of dog-whistle politics and especially by four years of Trumpian ethnonationalism. This serves as a reminder that while experiments are powerful tools for causal inference, they can never fully eliminate sociopolitical context; in our earlier surveys on prejudice, taken much earlier in the Trump administration, we saw much more movement among conservatives on these variables.

4.5 CONCLUSIONS

This chapter presented a considerable amount of data and results of statistical analyses, but the patterns that emerge are nevertheless clear. First, these analyses consistently supported the role of economics in generating democratic discontent. However, the role of economic discontent is more that of a mafia don than of the street-level hoodlum: like the former, economic discontent works in the background, usually making things happen without getting its hands dirty. Not to belabor the metaphor, but the evidence presented here suggests, as our theory predicts, that the role of *capo* is played by emotions: they are the intermediary between economic grievance and cultural discontent, which does the direct causal heavy lifting for democratic discontent. This is especially true of resentment: anxiety seems to play a minor part in most of our causal story, except for conspiracism, while resentment is a much more consistent driving force.

These results also helped to illuminate why populism and prejudice so often go together. We show here, and argue throughout the remainder of the book, that this is due to convergent causality rather than any natural

[9] For more on the confounding role of pretreatment effects, see Slothuus (2016).

synergy between the two: populist discontent and various forms of negative attitudes toward marginalized out-groups share similar dynamics, being triggered by the same mediated process as democratic discontent. The anxiety and especially the resentment driven by economic trauma appears to induce a species of zero-sum ethnoracial ideas in many people. Those in the ethnoracial majority so afflicted hold tighter to the members of their social group and become more suspicious and above all more hostile to outsiders, especially those groups they see as unfairly favored in the political system.

That said, we can only conclude so much from these results. As we have stated, experiments can never fully capture the sociopolitical dynamics they are designed to study.[10] Context can always creep back into experiments: time can change the way certain variables relate to one another. The tendency of conservatives (early in Trump's administration) and then liberals (after Trump's term ended) to react differently to treatments at different time points attests to this fact. These experiments also only use samples from one country to explore what has become a worldwide phenomenon.

Nevertheless, the results presented in this chapter are essential to this book, not so much for themselves but because of the confidence they provide in our interpretation of actual cases. We will keep the findings laid out in this chapter in mind for the remainder of our story. This is especially crucial because of the somewhat occult nature of economic discontent's role in engendering democratic discontent. Because discontent lies at the back of a lengthy causal process, its role can be quite easy to miss when analyzing the real world, as FR populists drone on about immigration and race relations. And because our narrative concerns a time when most nations of the world suffered serious economic strain, even rigorous comparative methods might not fully reveal the extent to which economics impacts democratic discontent. With these results as our foundation, we can spend the remainder of this book building out our primary argument: when it comes to democratic discontent, economics matter.

---

[10] Any political phenomenon that is sufficiently uncomplicated that it can be completely simulated in a survey experiment is probably not interesting enough to be worth the trouble.

5

Frozen Parties, Failing Markets

Discontent in the United States and United Kingdom

When the financial crisis of 2008 struck, it formed the final element that would become a perfect storm for democratic discontent in the United States. The crisis unfolded in an environment where economic precarity had become the norm for large swaths of the population, including those who had previously known plenty and security. And the political system tasked to deal with the wreckage was already fraying at the seams, stretched thin and stressed from trying to fit institutions designed for an agrarian, preindustrial society onto the most economically and technologically powerful hegemon in the world. Although Donald Trump's victory shocked many, including the authors of this book,[1] in retrospect we should have seen it coming. Things were only marginally better in the United Kingdom, which witnessed a rapid increase in the electoral fortunes of the PRR, first under Nigel Farage and UKIP and later under the leadership of Boris Johnson as he took over the Conservative Party.

In this chapter, we trace the rise of both Trump and UKIP using the theory of APE we developed and tested in earlier chapters. Here, we focus on Trump, given his relatively greater success and more available data, although we point to similarities to UKIP where relevant. Despite longstanding cultural and political tensions in both countries, absent the Great Recession they would have remained nothing more than that: tensions, perhaps gradually increasing, perhaps abating over

---

[1] One of us confidently predicted before a full class that Donald Trump could never be elected in the United States, due to its institutional barriers to populists, personalists, and outsiders. Needless to say, the class after election day was one of the more interesting teaching experiences this co-author has had to endure.

time. The crisis (and the political response to it) ripped the veneer of stability and civility off both countries; yet the first attempts to mobilize discontent into actual political action fell short, failing to break through: Occupy Wall Street and especially the Tea Party managed to provoke shifts toward the extreme sides of the ideological distribution but failed to overthrow established actors or centers of power within their partisan spheres. UKIP continued in its pre-crisis boom-and-bust cycle, surging during European elections and collapsing during general elections. Trump, Farage, and Boris Johnson succeeded by doing what previous PRR leaders could not: craft a narrative about the ills of their respective countries that linked economic distress and cultural discontent to a single source, namely the losers, reprobates, and traitors in Washington DC, London, and Brussels.

5.1 BEFORE THE STORM: POLITICAL, ECONOMIC, AND CULTURAL DYNAMICS BEFORE THE CRISIS

It would be misleading to argue that the Great Recession was singularly responsible for the rise of Trump, Brexit, Farage, or Johnson. The financial crisis did not ruin ideal economies, nor did it turn perfectly healthy democracies into polarized blood sports, nor harmonious and tolerant citizenries into aggressive, xenophobic cultural warriors. The real story is subtler but nonetheless clear: both the USA and UK were uniquely vulnerable to the crisis because both had latent economic, cultural, and political tensions that had been biding their time for years.

5.1.1 The Left behind in the USA and UK

To begin, both countries had a significant population of left behind citizens. We have discussed how we define the left behind in general terms as those disproportionately harmed by economic change, and we do not wish to retread this ground here. That said, we do wish to point out some specific aspects of the left behind in the North Atlantic countries. First, we reiterate that while the left behind appellation in the North Atlantic countries encompasses people living in deindustrialized and hopelessly depressed communities (Gest 2016), in this region much of the left behind is defined by insecurity rather than poverty. Some are quite well paid and live middle-class lifestyles, complete with comfortable homes, cars, etc. Yet even among those with sizable incomes, a lack of social insurance and protection meant that the left behind were at constant risk of losing everything; in other words, while many in these countries were not living paycheck to paycheck, they could not live without a paycheck for long.

The left behind tend to cluster in economic sectors that are in decline (Goetz et al. 2019, Rothwell and Diego-Rosell 2016) or particularly exposed to foreign competition. Several scholars have found links between exposure to globalization and support for Brexit, for example (Carreras, Irepoglu Carreras, and Bowler 2019, Goodwin and Heath 2016, Becker, Fetzer, and Novy 2017, Colantone and Stanig 2018a), while Sides, Tesler, and Vavreck (2018, 2017) have found that being white and lacking university credentials was a major predictor of supporting Trump. The connection between economic and social misery and supporting Brexit can be further illustrated in a particularly ghastly correlation: between so-called "deaths of despair" such as drug overdoses and suicides and the percentage who voted for Brexit in a given area. One analysis found that an increase in drug-related deaths of 10 per 100,000 led to a 15.25 percent increase in support for Brexit (Koltai et al. 2019).

Self-employed individuals were also more likely to support Trump (Rothwell and Diego-Rosell 2016), a relationship that appears to be driven by heightened insecurity among this group. Even individuals who make comfortable livings face the prospect of economic devastation due to even temporary and modest downturns in their industry, or due to exogenous shocks like health problems or even bad consumer reviews (Schonfeld and Mazzola 2015). Along with greater insecurity comes an impoverished safety net to manage it; self-employed individuals are typically ineligible for unemployment insurance or (prior to Obamacare) subsidized health insurance. Finally, the loss of one's business can be more destructive to self-image and social position than the loss of a job. Self-employment, particularly for those of modest skills, offers the prospect of autonomy and an escape from the deep authoritarianism of firms (Anderson 2017). This escape, and the self-esteem that comes from self-reliance, is part of the reason why people take the risk of business ownership in the first place (Williams 2019).

5.1.2 The Great Risk Shift: Economic Insecurity and the Great Recession

The insecurity that defined the North Atlantic left behind was not merely a by-product of economic change but the result of deliberate policy choices. Declining real wages and income, increasing personal debt, and growing job insecurity had defined the economic systems of the USA and UK since the 1970s. This decades-long process has been given several names. Crouch (2009, 2011) describes a shift in public policy he refers to as "privatized Keynesianism." During the postwar era, the USA and UK both adopted a Keynesian capitalist model, wherein states smoothed out the business cycle by borrowing during bad times and running surpluses when times were flush (at least in theory; in practice, states frequently fail to cut back during the good times). This, in combination with a robust welfare state and widespread unionization, allowed workers to enjoy a comfortable and (more crucially) stable standard of living well into the 1970s, which large-scale capitalism needs in order to maintain a reliable consumer base (Crouch 1993, ch. 6).

As global competition intensified, the Keynesian system broke down. Corporations and wealthy individuals became increasingly unwilling to shoulder the high tax burden associated with Keynesian capitalism, arguing that these costs damaged their competitiveness with new exporters. Yet the contradiction remained: something had to smooth out the ups and downs inherent to capitalist creative destruction if the system were to survive. The workers themselves stepped in to fill this breach, albeit without realizing what they were doing. Borrowing and debt would still be the principal financial stabilization measure, but that debt would be private, rather than public. Individual workers began to self-insure against periods of wage decline, unemployment, or disabling illness through new or expanded financial products like home equity loans, lines of credit, and credit cards. Governments in the North Atlantic countries[2] shifted policy in subtle but decisive ways that encouraged private borrowing, such as low interest rates and support for housing prices and mortgage lending (Hay et al. 2008, Hay 2009).

The process that Crouch describes is only one facet of a more ubiquitous transformative process that Hacker calls the "Great Risk Shift," which he describes as "America's sweeping ideological transformation away from an all-in-the-same-boat philosophy of shared risk toward a go-it-alone vision of personal responsibility" (2008, 34). Hacker documents a staggering panorama of risks that shifted from society to individuals in the past decades: rising home foreclosures, increasing personal debt, and wilder income swings to name but a few. Hacker attributes this to the retrenchment of public welfare, but more importantly in the United States to the elimination of "mini-welfare states," that is, protections granted by corporations (often in negotiations with unions) that were backed by tax incentives (Hacker 2008, 7–8).

---

[2] Canada was a partial exception to this trend, as we discuss in Chapter 8.

The picture that emerges from the discussion in Section 5.1 is of a group of citizens desperately clinging to their lifestyles and livelihoods,[3] facing an increasingly risky world with steadily eroding protections. By the time the housing market collapsed, to paraphrase Eichengreen (2018, 114), powerful actors had spent decades rending the net under the economic trapeze.

The reactions of the left behind were different from those who had never had much to lose. Fearing the loss of jobs, incomes, homes, businesses, and social standing that comes with those things put large groups of citizens in what prospect theory calls the "domain of losses" (Kahneman and Tversky 2012, 269). The attitudinal and behavioral responses that accompany this state have been extensively studied in political science: it leads to extreme distress (as people mourn losses more than they value gains), and a much increased tolerance for risk, as they take desperate measures to escape a dire situation (Weyland 1996). Importantly, when in the domain of losses, individuals are less likely to support incumbent political leaders (Quattrone and Tversky 1988), and perhaps entire political regimes. Furthermore, the left behind (who typically belong to the ethnoracial majority) lacked strategies and coping methods that ethnic and racial minorities developed over long decades of marginalization.

5.1.3 Strong Silence: Problems of Voice and Responsiveness

US and UK democracies were ill-equipped to handle this sort of economic crisis: namely, one which called into question economic orthodoxies and demanded new ideas and bold actions. Through a variety of factors (some shared, some unique to each case) both countries faced the Great Recession with ossified party systems where virtually all major actors were firmly committed to the economic doctrine that had facilitated the crisis. Neoliberalism is more than simply a rejection of the statism of the postwar era (hence the neo), and a concomitant belief that markets are more efficient and effective economic mechanisms than states. Neoliberalism goes further, exhibiting a faith in markets (and a distrust of states) that is more religious than empirical: it holds that markets almost never fail, that states are always the problem, and that social insurance and welfare should be rigidly means-tested and available only

---

[3] The allusion to Barack Obama's infamous gaffe about clinging to "guns and religion" is intentional; we argue that there is a causal connection between these observations.

to the poorest individuals. Long before the crisis this neoliberal orthodoxy was widely embraced by the major parties in both the USA and the
UK. Although the "Third Way" ideas embodied by Tony Blair and Bill
Clinton sought to soften the harms of economic liberalization, in practice
they never seriously questioned its underlying assumptions. Much like
the Great Depression, which challenged the dominance of free-wheeling
capitalism, the Great Recession called into question the wisdom of radical liberalism. Movements and leaders quickly rose to challenge the consensus, but (very much *unlike* the Great Depression) in neither country
did any of the major political parties channel these sentiments into productive political change. Parties in the UK and the especially the USA had
little incentive to adapt, given the lack of citizen voice in both systems.

The lack of strong voice in the US system is a feature, not a bug. The
ethos underlying the US system, inspired more by classical liberalism than by
democracy, envisioned a country ruled by a natural aristocracy of educated
elites, with limited input from voters. Despite centuries of reform to this system, the basic structure remains. Governing majorities can do little, if anything, on their own. Indeed, the concept of a "governing majority" is barely
even applicable in the USA; exactly how many of the branches and chambers
must a party hold before it could be given such a label? This problem was
surmountable (mostly) in the postwar period, as the single-member district
plurality (SMDP) electoral system did its work producing two large, moderate parties (Cox 1990), making interparty compromise achievable in many
circumstances. Conservative Democrats and liberal Republicans would
work across party lines until the changing racial dynamics of the 1960s led
to the disappearance of these groups as the parties became increasingly ideologically (and sociodemographically) homogenized (Mason 2018).

Since the 1960s, the moderating effects of the SMDP system has waned.
A growing lack of cross-party competition in many, if not most, districts
shifted the nexus of electoral competition within parties, as party prima-
ries became more relevant than general elections in many districts. As a
result, parties became affectively polarized while converging on neoliberalism, all while the ability of voters to hold leaders accountable or influence
policy waned. As in Britain, the demographic decline of the white working
class eroded the social base of left parties. At the same time, new political
demands emanating from educated sectors addressing postmaterialist value
issues (e.g. feminism, anti-racism, LGBTQ rights, environmentalism) caused
a great deal of strain on parties across the developed world (Huntington
1965, Crozier, Huntington, and Watanuki 1975). A diversified electorate
became atomized and difficult to organize, while simultaneously directing

more of their energies and efforts toward nontraditional participation and away from parties (Dalton 2013, Luther and Müller-Rommel 2002).

In the USA the rigid two-party system made the problem worse. Both parties ended up with unruly coalitions, where pleasing one constituency would often alienate others. Democrats trying to satisfy culturally liberal white Americans or attempting to redress racism directed against Black Americans would risk the ire of what remained of the white working class; Republicans had to balance the economic demands of their wealthy core constituency with the cultural conservatism of their working-class Evangelical faction (Ginsberg and Shefter 1999).

Perhaps more crucially, the changing nature of the partisan coalitions led to geographic clustering, a kind of "natural gerrymander." Democrats came to rely heavily on younger, ethnically/racially diverse, highly educated urbanites, while the Republican Party found its voter base (if not its core constituency, which remained the wealthy elite) in rural areas (Scala and Johnson 2017, Gimpel et al. 2020, Eichengreen 2018, 125). As Jacobson (2013) points out, this leads to a natural "wasting" of votes in cities and safe Republican districts in rural areas. As a result, incumbents were reelected in more than 90 percent of House elections (Malbin et al. 2003) and over 80 percent in Senate elections, rates which increased from 1980–2010 (Pastine, Pastine, and Redmond 2014). By the dawn of the crisis, voters were nearly meaningless, to the point where voter preferences had virtually no influence on policy (Page, Bartels, and Seawright 2013, Gilens 2005, Gilens and Page 2014, Matsusaka 2010). This is the antithesis of strong voice; in the United States, strong silence reigned.

While the United Kingdom did not share the gravest democratic pathologies of the US system, it had its own set of defects. Unlike the Democratic party in the USA, the UK's Labour Party did not have a historical tradition of moderation and was openly democratic socialist and statist for much of its history. Serious drubbings in a series of elections began in 1979, with a period of unrest and strikes called the "winter of discontent" preceding the brutal once-in-a-generation trouncing of 1983 that continued until Tony Blair's victory in 1997. Blair was part of a new crop of Labour leaders who accepted the neoliberal consensus (albeit with a softer touch and more concern for the harms such policies could do) as they abandoned the diminishing labor movement in favor of the socially liberal educated middle sectors. While Labour moved toward the Tories on the economy, the Conservatives moved (much more tentatively) toward Labour on postmaterialist issues, gradually warming to issues like climate change and gay marriage.

In short, both the UK and the USA entered the crisis with an oligopoly of neoliberal parties. The great irony here is that, in their failure to chart a course through the crisis, these parties exemplified the kind of market failure their economic philosophy is so desperate to ignore. Oligopoly allowed moribund and mediocre parties to survive without adaptation, whereas strong competition from new or newly ascendant minor parties might have forced the issue. Terrified by the specter of their big government/big spending/big deficit reputations, the center-left had little appetite for shifting away from the consensus model even as the crisis revealed its flaws. Finally, the lack of differentiation on economic issues compelled the parties to focus more on cultural conflicts over race, gender, and sexual orientation, and to prioritize attacking and defaming the other party (Hacker and Pierson 2020). As we show later in this chapter, these democratic deficits were crucial in enabling the rise of discontented political movements in both countries.

5.2 THE NEOLIBERALS RESPOND: EARLY DAYS OF DISCONTENT

Responses to the financial crisis in both countries were, to be charitable, underwhelming. In both cases, initial responses were defined by inadequacy (under Obama in the USA) or active immiseration (in the case of the UK). Discontent flared immediately but then flailed about, doing some damage but hardly upsetting the neoliberal apple cart. The financial crisis called out for two responses, neither of which was satisfactorily pursued in either country. The first was immediate relief to citizens who lost jobs, homes, and businesses through no fault of their own. We do not wish to get bogged down in a pointless debate about whether homeowners who took out subprime loans should have known better. What is clear is that the root causes of the crisis – namely an overly permissive lending environment, a massive bubble in housing prices, and failure to adequately regulate the financial services sector – can be most clearly laid at the feet of the financial elites and the state. The housing bubble itself was in large part driven by public policy, with debt secured by housing used in place of public social insurance to smooth out the business cycle.

5.2.1 Doubling down on Neoliberalism: Immediate Responses to the Crisis

The inadequacy of the Obama administration's response quickly became apparent. Comparisons to the recent response to the Covid-19 crisis are instructive. The combined stimulus for the 2008 financial crisis (not includ-ing the Troubled Asset Management Relief Program, TARP) came to just under a trillion dollars (Kambhampati 2020); the three packages released in the wake of the Covid-19 crisis totaled 5.1 trillion dollars. Prior to the third stimulus package, total recovery spending came to 12.1 percent of GDP; the relevant figure for the 2008 crisis was 4.9 percent (Cassim et al. 2020).

The relatively miserly response in 2008–2009 resulted from the inability of major political actors to break with neoliberalism. In his own account, Obama comes off as a leader willing to try dramatic gambits but hemmed in by naysaying advisors and conservative foes within his own party (2020, chs. 10 and 11). Additionally, Obama was fighting with one hand tied behind his back: the public was already so angry about the massive amount spent on the TARP bailout for the banks that (according to Lawrence Summers, who incidentally is a nearly Platonic idea of the neoliberal Democrat) there was no chance to pass a stimulus outside the hundreds of billions of dollars range. There was also increasing dysfunction in the legislature, particularly the Senate, where the filibuster allowed a small minority of Republicans and conservative Democrats to block any legislation put forth through normal procedures that challenged economic orthodoxy.

Simply put, despite a landslide election that handed Obama and his party commanding majorities in both the legislature and the White House, the neoliberal orthodoxy held firm. After the rout in 2010, wherein Republicans recaptured the legislature, no further aid would be forthcoming. The British response was even more destructive: the Conservative Party, having convinced the electorate that the recession was driven more by government deficits than a financial collapse, pur-sued a brutal austerity policy that very likely made the recession worse than it otherwise would have been (Gamble 2015).

The second (and even more neglected) needed response was to pun-ish the guilty, especially the economic elites whose labyrinthine financial chicanery had created the collapse. Perhaps the most abysmal failure of two successive US governments was that the first "relief bill" of the cri-sis bailed out the banks, and then did nothing to punish them. Again, a comparison between 2008 and another financial crisis is instructive, namely a housing crisis in Sweden in the early 1990s. In this case, the Swedish state did not simply bail out the banks but seized them in a not-quite-nationalization, taking equity as the "price of bailing them out" and wiping out the shareholders. As Sweden's finance minister at the time put it, "for every krona we put into the bank, we wanted the same influence" (Dougherty 2008). We do not dispute that allowing banks to simply collapse in 2008 would have been among the most irresponsible decisions ever made by a modern government. Yet a more aggressive and punitive response was called for, more for political reasons than economic ones. Simply put, the punitive drive tends to grow and metastasize until satisfied, and the lack of punishment against economic elites created a seething citizenry, looking for someone, anyone, to blame.

The result of these mistakes, spread across both the Bush and Obama administrations, was a grinding, agonizingly slow slog out of the worst recession in living memory. Based on our theory, we would expect a tremendous upswelling of both resentment and anxiety as a result of these events. Sadly, there are no contemporary data available to analyze the emotional responses of citizens to the financial crisis. Yet both the experimental evidence we provide in Chapter 4, showing that economic discontent produces anxiety and resentment, as well as the general tenor of politics during the depths of the crisis, strongly suggest that emotions were running hot. The result was predictable: the wave of discontent that would engulf both the USA and the UK quickly began to gather force.

5.2.2 The Tea Party and Occupy Wall Street: Discontented Baby Steps

Although the crisis that would become the Great Recession began in 2007, it was not until the passage of the Emergency Economic Stabilization Act of 2008 (the act that established TARP) that growing resentment and discontent was imbued with meaning. The bank bailout (or at least some action to stabilize the financial sector) was an economic necessity, but to many it was also a classic example of a norm violation. The financial sector was widely perceived as responsible for the crisis by giving out ludicrous mortgages and thus crashing the economy, and yet as a punishment they were rewarded with over $800 billion of taxpayers' money, although the program eventually netted a profit for the government (Isidore 2014). Combined with the anemic stimulus package and a failure to provide effective relief for homeowners, this struck many as a severe injustice. Within a few months of TARP's passage, an online advocacy organization called Adbusters organized a "million-man march on Wall Street" to protest the political favoritism shown to banks over ordinary people. The march eventually spawned the Occupy Wall Street movement, where mostly left-leaning individuals began occupying public spaces to protest the lack of punitive action taken against the banks and the failure to aid economically distressed workers.

Arguments that the government was going too easy on the authors of the crisis were not exclusive to the left. Just a few weeks after the million-man march,[4] commentator Rick Santelli delivered a rant on the floor of the Chicago Stock exchange, decrying Obama's limited mortgage relief program. He argued that "responsible" homeowners, in trouble through no fault of their own, were being ignored while those who had taken out loans they should have known were far too large were getting bailed out, along with the hated banks (Etheridge 2009). Santelli called for a new "Tea Party" to right these wrongs. The movement that would become the Tea Party did not emerge *ex nihilo* after this rant. But Santelli gave the movement a name and crystallized the lingering resentment than many on the right felt as the recession continued and became Obama's responsibility.

From the beginning, the Tea Party movement intermingled economic grievances with Republican Party racial politics. Santelli's rant did not mention race at all, but it was made in the context of longstanding Republican cultivation of the notion that people of color and Latine people (especially unauthorized immigrants) were "welfare queens" and parasites leeching off "hardworking" (i.e. white Protestant) people (Quadagno 1994, Neubeck and Cazenave 2001). These ideas trace back to the adoption of neoliberalism under Ronald Reagan, who adapted the racial dog whistles of George Wallace and Richard Nixon to build popular support for his new economic paradigm. Under Reagan and the neoliberal Republican Party, bankers and employers were redefined as producers (a concept long deployed by US populist movements to describe ordinary working people), and the new parasites were those that relied on state support; these latter were subtly but unmistakably portrayed as people of color (Kazin 1998, ch. 10).

5.2.3 The Cultural Worldview of the PRR

At this point, we need to digress from our recounting of the evolution of the PRR and briefly discuss the cultural worldview of those who sympathize with it. This can be difficult from an academic perspective. Given the offensive rhetoric often used both by grassroots supporters and their leaders, it can be quite uncomfortable to see these individuals as they seem themselves and to describe their self-image accurately and without bias. We attempt to do so here, and we hope readers will understand that we are describing but not endorsing the self-image of those who sympathize with the ideas of the PRR. Drawing from ethnographic

---

4 Which like almost all "million-person marches" included far fewer than a million people.

works by Cramer (2016) and Gest (2016), statistically focused analyses by Abramowitz (2018) and Sides, Tesler, and Vavreck (2019), works on UKIP by Ford and Goodwin (2014), Goodwin and Milazzo (2015), and Goodwin and Heath (2016), and works on Brexit by Clarke, Goodwin, and Whiteley (2017) and Sobolewska and Ford (2020), we can deduce cultural ideas that are broadly shared by those who would become part of the grassroots Tea Party and eventually the social base of Trumpism and UKIP.

The most critical common element that arises from these books is a zero-sum view of cultural conflict. Individuals who sympathize with the PRR see intrinsic connections between the rise of a highly educated economic elite who benefit from globalization and the rise of multiculturalism. With their growing economic power, the "globalists" can impose values that actively damage the universalist values of cultural conservatives, such as the sanctity of the family (including the preservation of gender norms and roles), moral issues related to sex and procreation, and the importance of religion in public life.

Protests by PRR-sympathizing conservatives are frequently met with accusations of racism, homophobia, and other forms of prejudice. The PRR views these charges as disingenuous: such accusations are not sincere expressions of outrage but merely another cynically deployed tool to silence "real Americans." This tool is drawn from the same box as economic globalization and serves the same malign purpose, namely, to neuter the ability of the PRR to resist globalism. Additionally, criticism of left behind sympathizers of the PRR is often tinged with classism (Williams 2019), and with a view of working-class white people as morally degenerate (Gest 2016, 3–5).

It seems clear that the economic decline of the left behind is intrinsically intertwined with this sense of cultural conflict as a bloody fight to the death. The fact that those lobbing accusations of racism or bigotry are often members of relatively privileged social classes who sometimes treat working-class and rural people with thinly veiled disgust, along with the fact that the economic fortunes of those social groups that most enthusiastically embrace multiculturalism have brightened as those of the left behind have dimmed, cannot and should not be ignored.

5.2.4 The Tea Party's over: Moving toward Radical Right Populism

These growing cultural resentments proved an insurmountable challenge for the Tea Party's insurgency, as it set up a hidden conflict between the priorities of grassroots militants and Tea Party leaders. The Tea Party's raison d'être (aside from knee-jerk opposition to Obama) was militant fiscal conservatism, with cultural conservatism an important but secondary aspect of the faction's identity. This image was a reasonably accurate representation of the movement's leadership. For the most part, the leadership prioritized doctrinaire neoliberalism, pillorying government spending and using the various veto points embedded in the US political system to force spending and tax cuts, a strategy Williamson (2013) calls "austerity by gridlock." The rhetoric and policy priorities of the Tea Party's congressional leaders were more like the free market neopopulists of Latin America like Menem or Fujimori than George Wallace.

Yet the connections between economic and cultural discontent that the leadership failed to effectively make were of paramount importance to the Tea Party's grassroots militants, many of whom were rapidly embracing PRR cultural views. These dynamics played out at the national level through Tea Partiers' reactions to the Obama administration. Obama's race, biography, youth, and even his foreign-sounding name led many grassroots Tea Partiers to perceive him as a champion of the young, multiracial, educated urbanites they despised, which helped propel resentment against his administration (Abramowitz and McCoy 2018, Abramowitz 2011).

Taken together, we see a significant disconnect between Tea Party elites and grassroots supporters. The former pushed hardest on economic priorities, driven more by ideology than by discontent. As such, they failed to effectively channel the discontent seething among the base, which was both economic and cultural, frequently intermingling the two. The greatest sign of this failure was the fact that Mitt Romney, the consummate Republican moderate whose highest previous office was as governor of one of the most left-leaning states in the USA, would face Barack Obama in the 2012 presidential elections. In short, the Republican Party moved right but remained a typical conservative (if more ardently neoliberal) party. The Tea Party's most enduring legacy would be as merely a steppingstone on the road to radical right populism. In both the USA and the UK, it took two enterprising leaders – Donald Trump (USA, Republican) and Nigel Farage (UK, UKIP) to seize the day and transform their parties into genuine vehicles for the PRR.

5.3 THE PRR RISES: EXPLAINING SUPPORT FOR TRUMP

Trump managed to accomplish what the FR had previously failed to do: provoke a populist rupture, breaking through the partisan oligopoly and taking the highest office in the country. Our goal here is to explain why Trump succeeded when other would-be populists (e.g. Ted Cruz, Ron

Paul) were unable to build coalitions large enough to seize power. While
this ultimately comes down to the attitudes and behaviors of nonelites,
we cannot ignore the role that elite rhetoric plays in shaping and influencing public opinion and political behavior. With this in mind, throughout
this section we will analyze both public opinion data and Trump's rhetoric. We do not expect Trump's pitch to voters to match our complex
theory of how democratic discontent comes consistently and perfectly.
That said, if analyses of the ideas and arguments appearing frequently in
Trump's political communication is at least consistent with our approach,
it would provide further support for our argument.

5.3.1 An Overview of Support for Trump

We begin by analyzing a model of support for Trump, using data from
the PSAS-US.[5] Analyzing support for Trump specifically can be difficult,
as measures of it tend to be contaminated with support for Republicans
more generally. As such, we rely on a modified version of a strategy used
by Goetz et al. (2019), who subtracted support for Mitt Romney, a mainstream Republican and major Trump opponent, to obtain a measure of
support for Trump over mainstream Republicans. We adapt this strategy
using feeling thermometers: we subtract a respondent's score on a feeling thermometer for Romney from their placement of Trump on another
thermometer.[6] As predictors, we include the major elements of our theory (see Chapter 4 for details on measurement):

- Populist attitudes: we include both anti-elitism and people-centrism,
  as well as a multiplicative term combining the two (Wuttke, Schimpf,
  and Schoen 2020).
- Economic discontent: measured using our economic distress index.
- Cultural discontent.

Our measure of cultural discontent is deliberately nonspecific, to allow
it to measure a sense of cultural alienation without resorting to attitudes
toward specific policies, trends, or groups. However, since in this case
we are looking at support for a specific political actor, it makes sense

[5] Data were collected in February and March, 2021. Our story here concerns Trump's rise,
rather than his fall, after which these data were collected. Sadly, there are no contemporaneous datasets that include all the concepts and measures we require to test our theory.
Based on the experimental data we present, we can be confident that the relationships
established by these data have not changed a great deal over time.
[6] Results did not significantly change when using the Trump raw feeling thermometer.

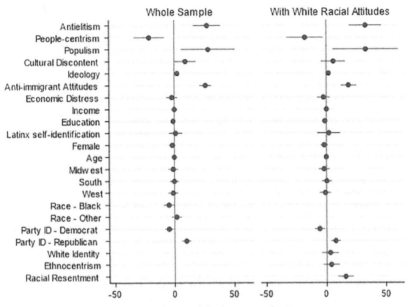

FIGURE 5.1 Tobit model of support for Trump.

to include specific manifestations of cultural discontent here. In Trump's case, we include an index of negative AUI, a major target for the former president. We also include a number of demographic controls: income, education, race, Latine self-identification, gender, age, region, party identification, and ideology.[7] We also specified a second model of support for Trump that includes several factors related to Trump's racial rhetoric: white identification, ethnocentrism, and racial resentment. As our theory holds that crises will possibly affect members of minority groups differently than members of the majority, we only include white respondents when estimating the parameters of this model. For both models, we used Tobit regression analysis. Tobit models are designed for use on variables that are not normally distributed due to censoring on the upper or lower bound (our measure is rescaled to run from 0 to 100, where 0 represents a strong preference for Romney over Trump, and 100 indicates much stronger support for Trump than for Romney, and 50 represents equal support for Trump and Romney). A chart of coefficient estimates for these models with 95 percent confidence intervals is presented in Figure 5.1.

---

[7] In most models we include only ideology, not party identification. These measures are highly correlated and thus can inflate standard errors in quantitative analyses, and our theories concern worldview rather than group attachment, making ideology the more appropriate choice.

A few elements of this chart bear special notice. One which might seem to militate against our approach is the lack of a significant effect of economic distress on support for Trump. This is, in fact, to be expected: recall that we argue economic discontent is not the immediate cause of populism or support for populist figures, but rather a root cause of cultural discontent, which is the proximate cause. We will return to this issue later. For now, the more important issue is to identify the major sources of support for Trump. We identify the following as especially important: populism, cultural discontent, and racial/identity politics. We discuss each of these in turn, in the context of Trump's rhetoric, for the remainder of this section.

5.3.2 "The System Is Rigged": Populist Attitudes and Arguments

These are special interests, folks. These are lobbyists. These are people that don't necessarily love our country. They don't have the best interests of our country at heart. We're not going to let it happen. We can't – we have to do something about it. When you see – when you see the kind of deals made in our country, a lot of those deals are made because the politicians aren't so stupid. They're making them for their benefit. We have to stop it. We have to stop it. We are now going to make it for your benefit. We're going to make the deals for the American people.[8]

Perhaps the most crucial difference between Trump and other pretenders to the populist throne was his status as a genuine political outsider. Other Republicans like Ted Cruz, Sarah Palin, Michelle Bachman, and Ron Paul had tried to seize the populist mantle with little success; as lifelong Republicans, they lacked the credibility to truly challenge the political elite. More to the point, while the Tea Party wave of Republicans that rose to prominence after 2010 might have been further to the right than their predecessors, they offered little but a more obstinate defense of the Republican Party's post-Reagan platform of Christian nationalism, dog-whistle racial politics, and neoliberalism. Despite their bombast, they also were unable to deliver on their promises, as Obama remained in office, Obamacare was still in force, and LGBTQ rights continued to advance.

Trump broke with all these conventions to varying degrees. Although he eventually governed as a reliable partner for political Evangelicals and Christian nationalists, during his campaign Trump seemed relatively unconcerned with issues like gay rights; in fact, he promised to protect

---

[8] This and all other quotes from Trump speeches are taken from the database assembled by Hawkins et al. (2019) unless otherwise noted.

LGBTQ individuals from Islamic terrorists. Appreciated by his followers for his bluntness and willingness to "say what everyone is thinking,"
Trump ripped the veneer off the Republican Party's southern strategy, no
longer bothering to hide the racial resentment and xenophobia that underlies it. And while Trump could castigate taxes, welfare, and government
regulation as well as any other Republican, he was more than happy to
throw over neoliberal priorities he felt allowed the system to take advantage of his followers, especially on the issue of trade (more on this later).

Equally crucial was Trump's unerring focus on the evil and negligence
of the political elite. Trump mentioned words and phrases related to
political elites in 85.71 percent of the speeches collected by Hawkins
et al. (2019); only Bernie Sanders, another populist outsider, mentioned
it more. Allusions to the political system being rigged appear in 61.9
percent of Trump's speeches, compared to 33.3 percent for other
Republicans.[9] More holistically, Trump's entire campaign was based
on a populist narrative. His speech at the 2016 Republican National
Convention accepting the party's nomination is a typical example:

> The most important difference between our plan and that of our opponents, is
> that our plan will put America First. Americanism, not globalism, will be our
> credo. As long as we are led by politicians who will not put America First, then
> we can be assured that other nations will not treat America with respect. This will
> all change in 2017 ... Big business, elite media and major donors are lining up
> behind the campaign of my opponent because they know she will keep our rigged
> system in place. They are throwing money at her because they have total control
> over everything she does. She is their puppet, and they pull the strings.

Evidence from our data supports the notion that these claims reso-
nated with Trump's most ardent supporters. In the models introduced
in Section 5.3.1, we included both constitutive dimensions and the multiplicative populism index because Trump support may be influenced
in nuanced or even contradictory ways by populist attitudes: specifically, the combination of anti-elitism and people-centrism may have a
unique relationship with Trump support (or discontent more generally)
while each dimension individually exerts its own effect. As we see here,

---

[9] Fifty-five speeches were analyzed from the Kirk A. Hawkins (2016) United States 2016
Presidential Campaign Speeches Dataset (available for download at http://populism.byu
.edu/). Other Republican candidates include Rubio (four speeches), Cruz (three), and
Kasich (two). The dataset includes twenty-one Trump speeches, twenty Clinton speeches,
and five Sanders speeches. Categories were created using the Topic Extraction module in
Word Stat 7, which uses factor analysis to create a topic model based on co-occurrence of
the words in sentences. This created a categorization dictionary, which was then applied
to each document.

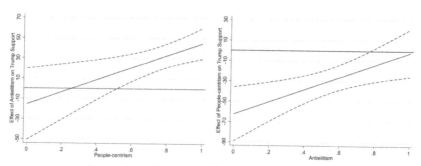

FIGURE 5.2 Interactive effect of populism dimensions on Trump support.

anti-elitism and populism are both powerful predictors of Trump support, while people-centrism has a negative effect. This can be seen in another way by presenting the effect of both dimensions, conditional on the value of the other. The horizontal line is at y = 0, or no effect; dashed lines define the 95 percent confidence interval (Figure 5.2).

Interactive effects can be difficult to interpret, so we use the simplest language possible here. To start, imagine someone with profound anti-elitist sentiments. If that person also has strong people-centric attitudes, they likely have positive attitudes toward Trump. However, if the person does not have people-centric attitudes, their anti-elitism will not lead to any appreciable increase in Trump support; without the belief that power should rest in the hands of the people, hatred of elites will not lead someone to embrace a leader making populist appeals. Although the consequences of this constellation of attitudes are not totally clear from these data, the most likely result is frustrated apathy rather than active rage.

Next, imagine a person with strong people-centric views. Absent anti-elitism, this person will actually be much *less* likely to support a populist like Trump. In this case, people-centrism operates more as a preference for direct or participatory democracy, and without antagonism toward the elite, this person will be repelled by the obvious authoritarianism and illiberalism of a figure like Trump. Add anti-elitism to the mix, however, and things change; now this person, embittered by their disgust with the elite, will no longer be repelled. People-centrism in combination with anti-elitism sets up a narrative of mortal struggle between the two sides, which justifies aggressive acts toward elites and their allies and the negation of democratic niceties that would not arise from people-centrism in isolation.

Although this interaction is complex, the important conclusion is clear enough: populism, especially its anti-elitist dimension, is profoundly associated with Trump support. We should note here that Trump's public appeals do not necessarily reflect his actual views. Trump's political communications, like those of all politicians, are an amalgam of his own views, political calculus, and the views and priorities of his advisors. For example, Trump's populism appears to become less specific and less eloquent after his break with Steve Bannon. Hawkins and Rovira Kaltwasser (2018) find that Trump was far more populist in speeches written by Bannon or Stephen Miller than by others.

5.3.3 The Great Globalist Conspiracy: Cultural Attitudes and Trumpism

> These families have no SPECIAL INTERESTS to represent them. There are no demonstrators to protest on their behalf. My opponent will never meet with them, or share in their pain. Instead, my opponent wants Sanctuary Cities. But where was sanctuary for Kate Steinle? Where was Sanctuary for the children of Mary Ann, Sabine and Jamiel? Where was sanctuary for all the other Americans who have been so brutally murdered, and who have suffered so horribly?
> –Donald Trump, speaking of people allegedly killed by unauthorized immigrants.

Populist attitudes increase support for Trump, but this leaves a great deal unexplained: if hatred of elites drove people to Trump, where does that hatred come from? Here we return to the debate between economic and cultural issues that we have addressed throughout this book. Economic distress had no direct effect on Trump support in our analysis presented earlier (something we address later), and the bulk of the public opinion research on the subject we discussed earlier points to cultural discontent, especially as manifest in conservative backlash toward multiculturalism, as the dominant (or as we argue, proximate) cause.

Cultural backlash is not an incidental part of Trumpism; rather, it lies at the core of his overall social narrative (Inglehart and Norris 2019). Trumpism is far more elaborate than the simple "we are the 99 percent" division of society favored by the populist left, and one that resists fitting into the simple people vs. elites framing of the typical ideational approach. According to Trump, politics is the struggle between two forces: globalism and America First (i.e. nationalism). With globalism – the dominant ideology of the political elite – the people are under constant assault: from criminal aliens, Islamic terrorists, violence-plagued "inner-cities" desperately in need of "law and order" (classic right-wing code for Black-on-white crime), trade deals that let corporations make billions at the expense of US workers, and so on. Throughout his political speeches, Trump draws connections between the political exclusion of the people and the denigration of their values and beliefs. This quote is illustrative:

The establishment and their media enablers wield control over this nation through means that are well known. Anyone who challenges their control is deemed a sexist, a racist, a xenophobe and morally deformed. They will attack you, they will slander you, they will seek to destroy your career and reputation. And they will lie, lie and lie even more. (Hawkins et al. 2019)

Here, Trump is tying cultural discontent to the rise of multiculturalism and shifting standards of acceptable discourse. In doing so, he evokes the idea that the cosmopolitan elite and their urbane allies are trying to destroy the national culture, using accusations of racism or other forms of prejudice. In other words, Trump makes appeals that echo what academics have called "backlash" (Inglehart and Norris 2019), feeling like a stranger in one's own land (Hochschild 2018), resentment based in rural consciousness (Cramer 2016), or the conflict between those from somewhere and those from anywhere (Goodhart 2017). Note especially the connection between the illegitimate control of elite multiculturalists and accusations of racism. To Trump and his followers, "canceling" is not a genuine expression of outrage but a power play, a cudgel against criticism and a weapon against the only effective bulwark against globalism, that is, national unity through cultural homogeneity. Our data suggest that this strategy was successful. Cultural discontent had a significant influence on Trump support in the all-sample model, but the effect was not significant in the white-only model.

Yet both these models underestimate the role of cultural discontent. We would not expect a leftist believer in multiculturalism who feels alienated in a society they feel is tinged by patriarchy, heteronormativity, and racism to then throw in with Trump. In short, we expect discontent to influence support for Trump only among those on the political right (and perhaps moderates). Among leftists, we expect the relationship to be null or even negative (this latter possibility we discuss in Chapter 9). Figure 5.3 (taken from the whole sample model) shows how the effect of cultural discontent changes as ideology changes; starred data labels indicate significant differences from the grand mean. Each bar represents a value on our seven-point ideology scale, with liberals on the left and conservatives on the right (of course).

These figures show that cultural discontent is far more powerful among conservatives than among liberals. Among liberals, discontent either reduces or barely increased support for Trump. But among conservatives,

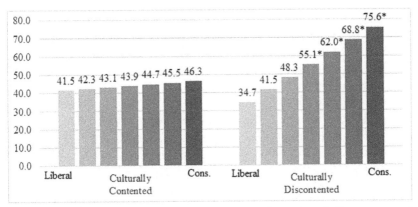

FIGURE 5.3 Predicted mean of Trump support by cultural discontent and ideology.

the effects are much more substantial; discontented extreme conservatives are nearly 30 points more supportive of Trump, as are contented conservatives.

5.3.4 Is Trump (or Trumpism) "Racist"? White Supremacy, White Nationalism, and the PRR

It is worth remembering here that Trump did not come to political prominence with an impassioned populist message. Trump's recent political trajectory began instead with a tweeted conspiracy theory, namely that President Barack Obama was born in Kenya, not Hawaii, and was thus ineligible to be president. This was no anomaly. As we alluded to earlier, perhaps the most common theme in Trump's discourse, even more than his populism, is the equation with anything unfamiliar or "foreign" (in this case, the latter term seems to include virtually anything that does not come from the white rural heartland) as evil and threatening.

Indeed, Trump's presidential campaign announcement in 2015 began with him calling Mexican immigrants "murderers" and "rapists." Jardina (2019, 230–242) provides an excellent overview of the various ways in which Trump appealed to the grievances and fears of white America. Among other things, Trump frequently evoked stereotypes about Black Americans (particularly related to crime and violence) when arguing about the decline of the USA, emphasized the threat posed by Islamic terrorism in broad terms that tended to imply that all Muslims were dangerous and promised to ban Muslim immigration, and referred to unauthorized immigrants almost exclusively as criminals who pose a grave risk to US security. Most of Trump's signature issues, such as the border wall, family separation, or the travel ban on Muslims, have clear prejudicial undertones at the very least.

More extreme forms white backlash can be seen in the rhetoric of groups supporting Trump. In the "Unite the Right" rally in Charlottesville, groups of whom Trump later spoke positively evoked the white genocide myth by crying "you will not replace us," an allusion to the Great Replacement conspiracy theory that elites encourage immigration deliberately to eliminate the white native-born population through demographics. The Proud Boys, a violent FR gang Trump would later tell to "stand back and stand by" during a debate with Joe Biden, identify unapologetically as "western chauvinists."

Nevertheless, many Trump supporters vehemently deny that he or his movement are racist or prejudiced. For example, they point to his stated concerns for African Americans (Trump often describes the poverty and misery of inner-city African Americans, mostly to point to the failures of the Democratic Party), LGBTQ individuals (always in the context of threats to this community by Islamic terrorists), and the presence of racial or ethnic minorities in his political circle. This raises the question in the title of this section: is Trump (or Trumpism) racist? This question is commonly posed but is, to be blunt, pointless. The term "racism" is so imprecise and can mean so many things to so many different people and groups as to defy scholarly analysis.

That said, we can fit Trump's racial and ethnic appeals into more specific categories. Specifically, Trump squarely fits into the concepts of ethnonationalism, specifically white nationalism, often with a distinctly rural Protestant bent. Many scholars of the FR (e.g. Golder 2016, Georgiadou, Rori, and Roumanias 2018) distinguish between two tendencies within the FR: the extreme right, which is openly authoritarian and embraces white supremacy and ethnic cleansing or even genocide against minorities and opponents, and the ethnonationalist PRR. Unlike the openly fascistic extreme right, the PRR embraces what Golder (2016) calls "ethnopluralist nationalism" in which "different cultures [are considered] to be equal, but distinct and thus incompatible. Proponents of ethnopluralism claim to celebrate cultural differences and argue that these differences must be protected from things like mass migration, cultural imperialism, and one-worldism" (Golder 2016, 480; see also Rydgren 2005). In addition, the PRR generally lacks the "blood and soil" view of culture as encoded in genes and thus immutable and fixed. Instead, members of marginalized cultural groups and immigrants are expected to assimilate into the cultural mores of the dominant group (Golder 2016).[10]

In short, whether or not Trump or his rhetoric are racist is neither here nor there. What is undeniable is that Trump has (ironically for a nationalist) imported a European-style radical right ethos, where Protestant, white, small-town culture is equated with the culture of the nation, with all who fail to fit that mold expected to conform or leave, while still allowing him to point to people like Ben Carson (who is Black)[11] or his son-in-law Jared Kushner (who is an observant Jew) as evidence of his lack of racism or anti-Semitism. The radical right welcomes those few members of minority groups who are willing to completely conform to the demands of dominant culture, while heaping hostility and scorn on the rest, who wish to simply preserve some of their cultural traditions and mores. Simply put, while Trumpism is not white supremacist (in the sense of biological superiority of white persons), it is undeniably and explicitly white nationalist.

Bringing this discussion back to our approach, one can see a clear link between cultural discontent and white nationalism. Both reflect profound concern about the relative value assigned to different cultural groups, and a combination of in-group solidarity and out-group hostility and suspicion. In a sense, in-group solidarity (white identity and ethnocentrism) and out-group hostility (racial resentment and AUI) are forms of cultural discontent, with its vague sense of alienation imbued with meaning by specification of the groups involved in the cultural conflict. To test this contention, we analyzed the influence of cultural discontent on all four concepts. As with Trump support, we allow the effect of cultural discontent to vary with ideology (discontented liberals are unlikely to have negative attitudes toward African Americans or Latine immigrants, given the prominence of anti-racism and multiculturalism in liberal thought). Predicted mean levels of intergroup attitudes by cultural discontent and ideology (left and right represent minimum and maximum values on the ideological scale respectively) are presented in Figure 5.4; starred data

---

[10] Başok and Sayer (2020) review several ways in which Trump and his allies pushed assimilationist policies, including advocating for English as the official language at both federal and state level, and eliminating bilingual education programs.

[11] An elite version of the infamous "but I have a Black friend" defense.

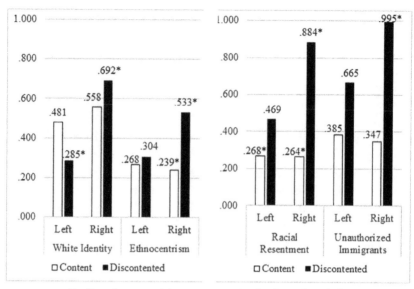

FIGURE 5.4 Predicted mean of intergroup attitudes by cultural discontent and ideology.

labels represent combinations with a mean that is significantly different from the grand mean at the 0.05 level.

For those with low levels of cultural discontent, differences in negative intergroup attitudes are minimal. Among discontented individuals, leftists tend to be somewhat *less* ethnocentric than the average person; their discontent provoked a backlash against the backlash. This finding was consistent with those of Jardina, Kalmoe, and Gross (2021), who argue that disgust with Donald Trump reduced white identity politics for those on the left.

Conservatives, however, showed dramatically increased ethnocentrism, racial resentment, and hostility to unauthorized immigrants when discontented, although discontent did not increase white identity. Cultural discontent does indirectly affect white identity by activating ideology; there is no significant difference between contented liberals and conservatives in white identification, but among the discontented, conservative white identification is almost three times as large as among liberals, who recoil from white identification when discontented. Given that some of these factors predicted Trump support in our model presented earlier, these results indicate that cultural discontent's influence on Trump support is even larger than previous analyses suggested.

5.3.5 It *Is* the Economy, Stupid! The Economic Roots of Trumpism

Free trade can be wonderful if you have smart people, but we have people that are stupid. We have people that aren't smart. And we have people that are controlled by special interests. And it's just not going to work.[12]

At first blush all this discussion of culture would seem to contradict our theory. After all, these findings match up with much of the public opinion literature on Trumpism, which has consistently found cultural issues to be a much more important antecedent of Trump support than economic woes. Yet questions linger. If culture is so important, what to make of the various studies finding meso-level effects of economic discontent? Although analyzing voting patterns can be difficult, strong evidence has emerged that a surge of low-propensity left behind voters can explain Trump's victory (Sides, Tesler, and Vavreck 2017, Morgan and Lee 2018, Goetz et al. 2019, Patenaude III 2019, Thompson 2016). These findings are consistent with earlier research in other regions showing that populists often increase the political engagement of economically marginalized citizens (Piñeiro, Rhodes-Purdy, and Rosenblatt 2016).

Furthermore, if economics matter so little, why does Trump talk about economics so much? As it turns out, Trump's political communication references the economy more than almost any other topic. His candidacy announcement speech from 2016 is infamous for his description of immigrants as criminals and rapists. However, the speech barely addresses cultural issues: the vast majority is focused on manufacturing jobs and trade (including the contention that Trump could reverse outsourcing with a few phone calls). In the speeches included in the Hawkins et al. (2019) database, Trump mentioned trade deals in 80.95 percent of his speeches, more than twice as much as Clinton (30 percent) or even Sanders, another critic of trade deals (40 percent), and much more often than he mentions immigration (61.9 percent) or the border (57.1 percent). He also mentioned manufacturing jobs more than Sanders (47.6 percent to 40 percent). These discussions of economics are nearly always tied into his broader populist narrative: the economic decline of his left behind base is not due to technology or the inexorable crush of globalization, but due to the idiocy and greed of political elites with a globalist agenda.

We never expected economics to displace culture through some methodological trick. Instead, our theory holds economic discontent to be an

---

[12] Candidacy announcement address, 2016.

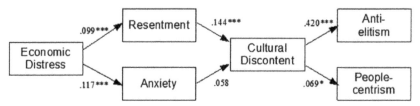

FIGURE 5.5 Path SEM model of populist attitudes. * = sig. at 0.05 level; ** = sig. at 0.01 level; *** = sig. at 0.001 level.

important root cause of these cultural conflicts, by intensifying negative emotions that cause hypersensitivity to threat (anxiety) and increased salience of preexisting prejudices and identities (resentment). In short, economic turmoil inflames cultural tensions, which then provokes populist attitudes and behavior (i.e. supporting a populist insurgent like Trump). This mediated effect of economics on populist attitudes and behavior in the United States can be seen in our survey data. We use path analysis from the SEM framework to estimate the direct, indirect, and total effects of economic discontent on populism. The model we specify is presented in Figure 5.5 (all the typical control variables were also included in each step). The numbers on the flow chart are the corresponding regression coefficients.

These results reinforce both the conclusions we drew in Chapter 4 based on experimental data and our theory of how populist attitudes are fomented during times of economic turmoil. All paths here are significant, as predicted, except for the effect of anxiety on cultural discontent. This seems to confirm findings from Chapter 4, namely that anxiety seems to play a much smaller role, if any, in translating economic discontent into cultural discontent. Cultural discontent had, as we expected, a strong influence on populism. Moving from zero to one on the cultural discontent scale produced an expected change in anti-elitism equivalent to 42 percent of the variable's scale. Cultural discontent had a more modest influence on people-centrism. As predicted by the AIT framework we have adopted for this book, resentment rather than anxiety drives cultural discontent. Finally, and as predicted, economic distress was associated with significantly higher levels of resentment and anxiety.

These effects can be further clarified by combining direct and indirect effects to produce estimates of the total effect of each variable on our populism dimensions. We use the same path model presented in the overall analysis of Trump support (whole sample), combined with the mediated model presented in the flow chart earlier in this section (Figure 5.5). For intergroup attitudes, we combine the flow chart model with our models

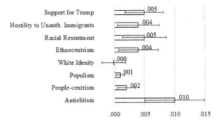

FIGURE 5.6 Total effects of economic distress on populism and intergroup attitudes.

of intergroup attitudes. In all cases, the influence of economic distress is mediated through cultural discontent (Figure 5.6).

As Figure 5.6 shows, economic discontent had a significant direct effect on both dimensions of populism, on the multiplicative populism index, and on support for Trump. These effects did not appear in the results presented earlier in this chapter because the effects of economic discontent are mediated through cultural discontent and emotions. We find similar results when analyzing intergroup attitudes: economic discontent significantly increased ethnocentrism, hostility to unauthorized immigrants, and racial resentment. Distress did not significantly impact white identity.

This, we contend, is why analysts have thus far underestimated the influence of economics on Trumpism. Economic effects are everywhere: in how people feel about their culture, how they view groups who they may mildly dislike or actively despise depending on circumstances, and on how they view their political representatives. Trump would not have been able to exploit cultural grievance and backlash so efficiently in the absence of major economic strain. With the lingering effects of the Great Recession, combined with the influence of neoliberalism, Trump's white nationalism gained an appeal they would never have had otherwise.

5.3.6 Trumpism as Failure of Democracy

Every day I wake up determined to deliver for the people I have met all across this nation that have been neglected, ignored, and abandoned ... These are the forgotten men and women of our country. People who work hard but no longer have a voice. I AM YOUR VOICE.[13]

The deficiencies of US democracy played a similar role to economic discontent: driving up outrage and fear, intensifying the tendency of that fear

---

[13] Acceptance speech at the Republican National Convention, 2016.

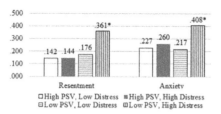

FIGURE 5.7 Predicted mean of resentment and anxiety by PSV and economic discontent.

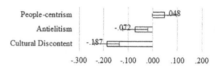

FIGURE 5.8 Effect of PSV on cultural discontent and populism.

to spill from the economic to the cultural arena, and convincing people to abandon "the system" in favor of a charismatic outsider. Trump was not the only candidate to excoriate the elite for ignoring their constituents: Bernie Sanders sounded a similar note, as had Obama eight years before, although with a more upbeat tone.

This lack of a strong voice in the United States exacerbated virtually all the economic and cultural antecedents of populism and Trumpism discussed in this chapter. To begin, the lack of voice exacerbates emotional responses to negative outcomes. As such, we would expect economic discontent to produce more resentment and anxiety among those who perceive the US political system as providing them with little influence on politics, that is, who score low on our PSV index. To test this, we include PSV and a multiplicative term with PSV and economic distress into the regression models used to predict negative emotions presented earlier. Predicted levels of emotions by PSV and economic discontent are presented in Figure 5.7.

As these results show, economic distress had no influence on negative emotions among those with high perceptions of strong voice. Only those who felt voiceless react to economic distress with resentment and anxiety. We would further expect Trump's appeal to act as the people's voice to fall on deaf ears if those people felt they could exercise voice through the political system. We therefore analyzed the influence of voice on cultural discontent and the two dimensions of populism; the results are presented in Figure 5.8.

PSV had a significant influence on cultural discontent and anti-elitism. Moving from low to high PSV decreased cultural discontent by nearly

20 percent of its range while significantly decreasing anti-elitism. PSV had a positive influence on people-centrism, although the effect was not significant. Like economic discontent, PSV dances all throughout the background of Trump's rise and eventual ascension to the presidency. A lack of strong voice intensified the resentment and anxiety the crisis produced (and also probably led to more negative evaluations of controversial policies like TARP), and increased cultural discontent and anti-elitism, two of the primary drivers behind support for Trump in our data.

5.4 ACROSS THE POND: COMPARING TRUMPISM AND UKIP

Astute readers will have noticed that the UK has been absent for a substantial part of the chapter. We return to this thread here, albeit with less detail and attention than we paid to Trumpism. There are multiple reasons why we treat the UK as a minor case here, including the absence of original data. The main reason is that the rise of the PRR in Great Britain hits so many of the same notes as its North American counterpart that an in-depth examination would likely bore the reader to tears with redundancies.[14] Instead, we highlight key similarities between Trump and the British PRR, as embodied first by Nigel Farage and UKIP and later by Boris Johnson, to demonstrate that the dynamics shown in the USA are far from anomalous.

5.4.1 Shared Trajectories: Comparing the Rise of UKIP and Trump

Much like the Tea Party in the USA, the greatest impediment to the PRR as such sentiments rose in society was a failure to reconcile elite and mass priorities. This failure was more extreme in the UK than in the USA: in the latter, the rise of the PRR was stymied by Tea Party elites' obsession with austerity and fiscal discipline, but elites sympathized with the cultural attitudes of militants, based as they were in the long-term grievance politics of the Republican Party. UKIP, however, began life as "a small band of academics and political obsessives" that had virtually nothing to say about any issue other than Britain's membership in the European Union (Ford and Goodwin 2014, loc. 334). For years, the party had a rollercoaster trajectory, peaking during European elections wherein

---

[14] For excellent and thorough treatments of this subject, see Clarke, Goodwin, and Whiteley (2017), Goodwin and Milazzo (2015), Ford and Goodwin (2014), Sobolewska and Ford (2020), Clarke, Goodwin, and Whiteley (2017).

votes were seen as a way of protesting the national government, and then floundering in national elections, where votes meant actual policy support. The party was disdained by mainstream politicos: they were a party of "fruitcakes, loonies and closet racists," as David Cameron put it (Ford and Goodwin 2014, loc. 365).

As in the USA, it took a charismatic political entrepreneur to turn things around, and similar tactics to do so. Specifically, Farage (like Trump) explicitly connected economic, cultural, and political grievances. He staked out an explicitly populist social narrative, arguing that Britain's ongoing membership in the European Union was the result of the evisceration of British sovereignty and its subsequent enslavement to a "European dream" irrationally held by bureaucrats in Brussels.[15] Farage depicts British politicians of all parties as cowards and liars, who (it is implied) knew the truth about the horrors of EU membership for ordinary Britons but were simply too afraid of being labeled as xenophobes or racists to do what was necessary. This theme is common in his pre-Brexit speeches, where he castigates both the Conservative and Liberal Democrat parties for promising and failing to deliver a referendum on membership.[16] Finally, he escaped UKIP's status as a single-issue party by tying the EU issue to rising cultural concerns, especially related to immigration. Farage often embraces welfare chauvinism when discussing immigration, arguing that financial strains on social insurance and the National Health Service (NHS) can be attributed to unproductive immigrants from other EU countries, especially those in eastern Europe.[17]

Farage also parallels Trump in charting an ethnonationalist course between the increasing social liberalism of his country's conservative party and the open and unapologetic racism and fascism of the extreme right (Sobolewska and Ford 2020, 3). As alluded to in Section 5.3, Farage endlessly flogged immigration, to the consternation of more mainstream advocates of Brexit (Clarke, Goodwin, and Whiteley 2017, 34–35), but virtually always in economic rather than cultural terms. For example, he often tied his party's opposition to immigration to the harm it does to native-born workers, rather than to cultural conflicts. Yet cultural discontent has a habit of obliquely popping up at the end of Farage's sentences. A typical gambit is for Farage to go on at length about the economic risks of unlimited immigration (typically infused with populist grievances),

[15] Speech in Canada, July 2013. From McDonnell and Ondelli (2020).
[16] Speech in Eastbourne, June 7, 2014, ibid.
[17] Speech in Cambridgeshire, May 2, 2014, ibid.

and then to quickly drop terms like "speak our language"[18] or reference a willingness to welcome immigrants who "make sure their kids integrate and become British."[19] Here again we see the ethnonationalist openness to individuals from other races and ethnicities, but only if they abandon their own culture and assimilate into that of the ethnoracial majority. Nevertheless, Farage and UKIP explicitly rejected extreme right elements in British society, spurning the quasi-fascistic British National Party and the English Defense League (a British analogue of the Proud Boys in the USA), with one UKIP activist describing the latter as "fucking nutters" (Ford and Goodwin 2014, loc. 1808).

In a final link to Trumpism's trajectory, UKIP and Farage benefited politically from the Great Recession and mainstream parties' responses to it. As with Trump, Farage explicitly connected economics, culture, and politics, in a way that reflected the process of attitude formation under emotional duress that we have analyzed in this chapter and Chapter 4. We can show that a similar process unfolded in Britain through both timing and survey data. UKIP continually boomed and busted until the Great Recession, when austerity policies embraced by all three major parties provided UKIP with a major opening (Clarke et al. 2016). Labour suffered doubly, first for having been in power when the crisis broke and second for its embrace of austerity (Campbell 2018, 333–334), while the Liberal Democrats had lost much of their anti-system luster by joining the Conservative government from 2010 to 2015 (Bartle 2018, 273). UKIP was by no means anti-neoliberal or anti-austerity, but the savage cuts made by both Labour and the Conservative/Liberal Democrat coalition in 2010 gave new salience to UKIP's signature issues: the party frequently opined that tax rises were disproportionately harmful to working-class Britons, and that such rises and cuts would be unnecessary were Britain not accepting millions of immigrants nor sending billions of pounds to Brussels every year.

Survey data from the 2010 British Election Study (Whiteley and Sanders 2014) supports this conclusion. We used a structural equation path analysis model (path SEM) to analyze the influence of economic threat (measured using prospective and retrospective economic evaluations of personal and national economic situation) on attitudes toward immigrants, measured using questions about immigrants' contribution to crime, the economy, unemployment, culture, English identity, and the

---

[18] Speech in Doncaster, September 25, 2015, ibid.
[19] Speech in Belfast, July 9, 2013, ibid.

threat of terrorism. We then regressed the influence of economic threat on immigration attitudes, and the influence of immigration attitudes and economic threat, on a feeling thermometer for UKIP. In each model, we controlled for income, gender, age, education, ideology, and race. Economic threat did not directly influence attitudes toward UKIP, but it did influence negative attitudes toward immigrants (standardized coefficient = 0.113; SE = 0.031; p = 0.000). Negative attitudes toward immigrants in turn positively affected attitudes toward UKIP (standardized coefficient = 0.186; SE = 0.035; p = 0.000). This model does not match our theory as closely as those for Trumpism, which is typical when using publicly available general topic surveys; yet the results are consistent with our experimental, observational, and qualitative findings.

5.4.2 Roads Diverge, or Do They? Populism Moves from Farage to Johnson

The major point of departure between the USA and the UK can be put down to a single event: the referendum on European Union membership in the UK (Brexit). Even as the major parties converged, David Cameron's ill-fated attempt to silence Eurosceptic forces on the right created a source of political flexibility in a political system that was otherwise ossified by the dominance of neoliberal parties. The nationalist victory at the polls upended the internationalist element of the UK political consensus by validating Euroscepticism, but it also proved a devastating blow to the relevance of UKIP, which quickly translated into an evisceration of the party's electoral support. With its signature issue now a *fait accompli*, UKIP could only watch as the Conservatives did something unusual in such a moribund party system: they adapted to the new reality, as Cameron resigned in favor of Eurosceptics Theresa May and, later, Boris Johnson, who shared with Farage both ethnonationalist and populist tendencies.

Boris Johnson seized the populist baton from Farage and proceeded to mimic Trumpism once again, albeit to a slightly diminished degree. From his purging of internationalists from the Conservative Party to the controversy over his prorogation of parliament, even to the scandal over funding of renovations to his residence, hypocritical violations of Covid-19 restrictions, and a sexual harassment scandal involving a member of his government, Johnson matched Trump beat by beat. The only exception being that the UK Conservatives eventually tired of Johnson's antics and evicted him from the premiership, while the Republican Party took only the most tentative steps away from Trump.

5.5 CONCLUSIONS

Whether due to a coincidental alignment of grievances or political canniness, Nigel Farage, Boris Johnson, and especially Donald Trump gouged quite effectively at nearly every wound and sore in their societies. Yet as our findings show, these attempts would likely have proved futile (or at least not sufficiently successful to allow outsiders with questionable qualifications to ascend high offices) without the economic devastation wrought by the Great Recession and the stifling of strong voice under ailing democracies. Emotions unleashed by economic hardship (and worsened by the ineffective and lopsidedly pro-finance government response to the crisis) intensified social grudges and prejudices.

The rise of Donald Trump in particular abounds with tragic irony; we have already mentioned some instances throughout this chapter. Perhaps the most perverse is that Trump benefited from challenging the neoliberal orthodoxy on trade. The irony comes in because Trump is the embodiment of the neoliberal ethos in many respects, excluding its internationalism. Like the philosophy that gave rise to privatized Keynesianism and the great risk shift, Trump pitched a view of the world in which all of us are profoundly, desperately alone, and where there are only two types of people (and nations): those that amorally exploit others, and those who get exploited. To the extent one can derive a consistent worldview from Trump's lifetime (if consistency is the hobgoblin of little minds, Trump might be a very stable genius after all), it is this binary division of society. This incidentally is the only way that Trump deviates significantly from populism as commonly defined in the ideational approach: his division of the world is binary, but not Manichaean. There is no moral conflict in Trump's worldview because morality is for suckers; in Trump world, there is no good and bad, only smart/tough and stupid/weak. The dog-eat-dog ethos of radical neoliberalism nods approvingly.

Deepening the irony further is Trump's appeal as an outsider, someone unencumbered by the norms and traditions of "politics as usual." Trump was hardly a commoner; he had been a wealthy man and a celebrity for decades before he entered the political fray. But Trump's consistency with politics as usual goes further. Far from some radical departure, Trump was simply the logical conclusion of the Republican Party's use of racial and cultural grievances to encourage voters to accept its neoliberal policies ("welfare queens") or to draw their attention away from their unpopular stances on economic issues, especially as the Democrats embraced neoliberalism and thus squeezed out much of the daylight between the two parties. The newest aspect of Trumpism was in synthesis: Trump finally managed to weave the two threads of late twentieth-century conservatism into something whole, a cohesive story with a foundation in white nationalism to explain all the damage and decline that characterized that same period. Eurosceptic populists in the UK largely followed suit, with similar (if somewhat less dramatic) results.

The patterns seen here will repeat as we go through the remaining case studies in this book. The political battles fought during the Great Recession were rarely waged predominantly on economic grounds. This was certainly true of Trumpism, with its focus on race, ethnicity, immigration, and gender, and we will see similar dynamics in other countries over corruption, national identity, and other noneconomic concerns. Yet economics is always there, turning up the temperature on social debates through resentment and (to a lesser extent) anxiety, driving polarization, contention, and even the threat of political violence across the world.

6

Austerity, Regionalism, and Dueling Populisms in Spain

When conducting a long-term research project, the ground has a way of shifting beneath your feet.[1] Prior to 2019, Spain had been an important case for this project: in Europe, it was a double anomaly. The rise of Podemos, a left-wing populist party that arose out of the anti-austerity movement, represented an atypical success story of left-wing populism after the Great Recession, especially in Europe where leftist ideas had long been incorporated into party systems and thus had little synergy with populist feelings of exclusion. Spain also bucked the regional trend of FR ascendance. Both the extreme right (like the Golden Dawn in Greece) and especially the PRR, embodied by movements like the National Front in France under Marie Le Pen, the Italian League (formerly the Northern League), Geert Wilders' Party for Freedom in the Netherlands, and the Alternative for Germany, had failed to take hold in Spain.

The 2019 Spanish elections forced a reconsideration. Electoral support for an FR party known as VOX surged, with the party becoming the third-largest political bloc in the country (Mendes and Dennison 2021, 753). In just a few short years, Spain went from a country where two parties held a firm oligopoly on national politics to one in which insurgent parties were an undeniable political force. After taking a moment to shake our heads in bewilderment, we began asking the obvious questions: why did a stable? party system face such strong challenges from both flanks? Why did Spain's apparent immunity to FR politics suddenly wane?

[1] Portions of the PSAS analyses in this chapter have been previously published in Rhodes-Purdy, Navarre, and Utych (2021b).

The rise of the PRR[2] under VOX presents a unique challenge to us because, although VOX also dwells at length on the typical cultural backlash canards like immigration and gender politics, we can point to a very specific precipitating event that led to the rapid expansion of its electoral appeal: the 2017 referendum for Catalonian independence. VOX's strident rejection of regional autonomy gained new salience for nationalist voters after the referendum. In other words, the rise of VOX had a readily identifiable trigger that was cultural and political, but not (at least on the surface) remotely economic. As such, this chapter presents something of a crucible for our theory: can an ongoing economic crisis help explain the political activation of Spanish nationalism?

We argue that nationalist demands for a unitary state were a case-specific manifestation of conservative cultural discontent. The importance of a unified state to the Spanish FR is inextricably linked with the importance of cultural homogeneity common among those with PRR views. VOX supporters also viewed the increased cultural assertiveness of Catalonia as an affront to the legacy of Spain's military regime, which they venerated. And just like racial resentment, nativism, and white ethnocentrism in the United States and the United Kingdom, nationalist fervor was enabled by emotional reactions to the European iteration of the Great Recession.

Spain thus shows that APE can explain manifestations of cultural and political discontent beyond the typical FR preoccupation with immigration and nativism. That said, Spain also demonstrates how the economic crises of the 2010s acted as critical junctures,[3] with the relationships specified by APE interacting with local conditions and historical process to create unique outcomes. Given the strong taboo against FR politics (a legacy of the brutal Francoist military regime that ruled the country for much of the twentieth century), Spain represents a "least likely" case of PRR breakthrough; instead, we would expect an inclusive, left-wing populism to emerge as the dominant vehicle for discontent, which is of course the path on which the country appeared to be when we began this project. If Podemos had successfully negotiated a path between the anti-austerity revolt and international pressure for budget discipline, VOX

---

[2] As we consider discontent broadly, the debated position of VOX as either a classical extreme right party or a new PRR party is not terribly important for us, as the party clearly mobilized citizen dissatisfaction with politics, as we show later. We refer to them throughout as a PRR party because they do rely on populist critiques of the Spanish political system, even if it is not the sole or even primary basis of their appeal.

[3] Thanks to Lisa Zanotti for encouraging us to emphasize this point.

would not have been able to rise as quickly or as forcefully as it did.[4] By discrediting the possibility of inclusive discontent, Podemos helped open a door for the PRR that would have otherwise remained barred.

6.1 INTERNATIONAL TECHNOCRACY AND THE GREAT RECESSION IN SOUTHERN EUROPE

A full recounting of the eurozone crisis is beyond the scope of this book, but we do wish to highlight a few important themes and parallels between Spain and our other cases. The 2008 financial crisis revealed a host of economic problems and pathologies in European countries, especially in the less developed parts of the eurozone (Kamin and DeMarco 2012). In Spain, these included a serious domestic housing bubble and declining competitiveness due to increasing wages that could not be compensated for by devaluation of a (nonexistent) national currency (Knight 2012). Spain entered a recession in 2008, as its credit rating was cut by Standard and Poor (Reuters 2012), eventually requiring a €99 billion bailout from the ECB. The country began a tentative recovery in 2011, but that recovery was undermined by the ongoing eurozone crisis as well as the recessionary effects of austerity. GDP per capita did not reach its nadir until 2015, having decreased by nearly 10,000 constant current US dollars since the onset of the crisis, from 35,336 to 25,732.

6.1.1 Left of What? Political Reactions to the Economic Crisis

At the time of the crisis, the center-left Socialist Workers' Party of Spain (PSOE) had held the country's premiership for most of the democratic period. Like Labour in the UK and the Democratic Party in the USA, the PSOE had embraced Third Way neoliberalism and struggled to adapt to the new circumstances wrought by the crisis. By 2010, when the first recessionary period ended, unemployment had risen to 19 percent and the public deficit had exploded. Yet the PSOE government led by José Luis Rodríguez Zapatero dithered, deprived of the monetary tools that countries with their own currencies could use to ease the pain of a downturn, seemingly hoping that rebounding growth would solve the country's economic problems (Donadio and Fuchs 2010).

---

[4] This is not entirely speculative; see Chapter 8 for a discussion of Portugal, where a left/center-left alliance followed this path.

The PSOE finally took a more assertive stance toward the crisis in May of 2010. However, its actions were not those one would expect from a party of the left. The PSOE narrowly approved a €15 billion austerity package, focused mostly on spending cuts. These were approved with a razor thin majority because the center-right People's Party (PP) opposed the package (ironically, given its neoliberal bent), thus requiring support from the center-right Catalan nationalist party Convergence and Union (CiU) to push the package through (Dowsett 2010). The role of the Catalan nationalists will play an important role later in our story. Spanish unions, historically close allies of the PSOE, balked at the package, following through on a threat to strike soon after its passage (Minder 2010). Further austerity and liberalization policies were enacted throughout the remainder of the PSOE's mandate. In short, the PSOE abandoned any semblance of social democracy or leftist politics, embracing austerity (not that they had a great deal of choice in the matter) while casting aside allied social organizations (Escolar 2012). The party paid a heavy price: the center-right PP won the 2011 general election in a landslide.

For leftist governments during fiscal crises, heavy is the head that wears the crown. Parties like the PSOE find themselves being held responsible for the economic hardship and controversy that typically follows neoliberal structural adjustment. The PSOE paid a considerable electoral price for its willingness to bow to the demands of the troika (the European Commission, the ECB, and the IMF), which ironically benefited a center-right party that was even more unabashedly neoliberal.

6.1.2 New Boss, Same as the Old: The PP Government

Few things weigh as heavily on the legitimacy of democratic regimes as what one of the authors of this book has called the "austerity flip-flop." This occurs when opposition parties lambast the government for enacting neoliberal austerity, gain power based on that antagonism, then proceed to implement nearly identical policies themselves. This was a common dynamic in Latin America during the lost decade of the 1980s and contributed to the emergence of leftist populists like Hugo Chávez (Rhodes-Purdy 2017c, ch. 5, Roberts 2019). Something similar occurred in Span, where angry voters evicted the PSOE in favor of the PP. However, during the interim between governments the country entered a second recession, in part because the strain of austerity negated any increase in investor confidence that might have buoyed the economy.

As Spain's public balance sheet began to slide back into the red, the PP quickly implemented a series of tax hikes and budget cuts to key services like education and health, even canceling Christmas bonuses for public servants, all of which were suspiciously similar to policies they had excoriated the PSOE for implementing only a few years before and which they had promised not to pursue (Castro 2013). Another series of bank bailouts followed, with attendant conditions requiring further austerity and liberalization measures. Unemployment remained high for years, peaking at 26 percent in 2013, compared to the EU average of 11.45 percent that year, and youth unemployment was over 50 percent from November 2011 until June 2015 (compared to yearly average of 15.23 percent in 2007) and remains high to this day (OECD 2022).[5] As a result, support for the PP plummeted: within the first year, the PP leader Mariano Rajoy gained the unenviable status of "the most unpopular prime minister" in the democratic period, and voting intention for the PP dropped by half; the PSOE's support also fell (Orriols and Cordero 2018, 93).

6.1.3 Neoliberal Convergence and the Erosion of Political Support

Democracies suffer when political elites repeatedly break promises and pursue policies that voters reject, especially when transferring power from one bloc to another has no effect on these dynamics. These effects can be seen in the precipitous decline in institutional trust in Spain during the crisis, which was especially severe compared with the rest of Europe (Torcal 2014). Muro and Vidal (2017) further found that citizens, unable to punish specific actors given that both major parties eventually embraced austerity, turned their ire on all mainstream parties and the democratic system itself. In other words, when political actors on both sides of the ideological spectrum share a fundamental economic philosophy, discontent acts like a cancer, spreading from outrage against specific policies and political parties to *all* political leaders and parties. By 2013, 45 percent of the electorate chose zero out of ten scale on scales of trust in political parties, and "one-third of the electorate considered political parties and politicians the two main problems facing the country" (Orriols and Cordero 2018, 93).

Although we lack contemporaneous data on the subject, it is clear that both the devastating economic consequences and the repeated violation

---

[5] For comparison, when youth unemployment peaked with a yearly average of 55.46 percent in 2013, the rate for the EU was 24.78 percent.

of voters' trust by political leaders generated resentment and even outrage. There was plenty of ire for both the PSOE and the PP. As the PP
government dragged on, the only question was how this resentment
would manifest. In another country, this might have triggered a struggle
between the populist left and the PRR for the support of discontented citizens. APE suggests that rising cultural discontent would activate latent
prejudices, thus providing the right a chance to court culturally aggrieved
voters. In Spain, however, a strong aversion to FR politics, forged during
decades of quasi-fascist military rule under Fransico Franco, meant that
left-wing actors would have an uncontested chance to mobilize discontent against austerity.

6.2 *INDIGNADOS*, PODEMOS, AND ANTI-AUSTERITY POPULISM IN SPAIN

The pro-austerity consensus shared by both the PSOE and PP governments created an opportunity for outsiders and new entrants to repoliti-
cize the economy (Roberts 2017, 2019). Spanish citizens reacted to their
lack of voice and the failure of the system to respond to their demands. As
the austerity treadmill ran on through 2011, the PSOE and the country's
major unions agreed to raise the country's retirement age from sixty-five
to sixty-seven. This proved the last straw for the more radical unions as
well as the "ni-nis," mostly young Spaniards who were neither employed
nor students (*ni estudia ni trabaja*). On May 15, 2011, a group of protesters organized primarily by a social media group called ¡Democracia Real
YA! organized a takeover of the Puerta del Sol, the main city square in
Madrid. Eventually, somewhere between six and eight million Spaniards
would participate in the 15-M movement, and popular support for the
movement rose rapidly, with only 7 percent expressing opposition to it.[6]

While the movement had considerable support and scope, it had little
success in achieving its aims of reversing austerity and revitalizing an anti-
neoliberal left. In other circumstances, the movement may have stuck to
contentious politics, as occurred with the social uprising in Chile (see
Chapter 7). Despite being based on proportional representation, Spain's
small district magnitudes and use of a D'Hondt method – a formula used
in proportional representation (PR) systems to translate votes into seats
that tends to favor larger parties – helped preserved the duopoly of the

---

[6] Source: RTVE, www.rtve.es/noticias/20110806/mas-seis-millones-espanoles-han-partici-
pado-movimiento-15m/452598.shtml.

PSOE and the PP, with most small parties representing regionalist movements (Freire et al. 2020). However, European elections, the moderately permissive nature of even large-party-favoring variants of PR, and the erosion of support for mainstream parties provided an opening through which the *indignados*, as 15-M protesters became known, could enter the formal political system.

6.2.1 From Protest to Party

That entry occurred when Pablo Iglesias, Juan Carlos Mondero, and Iñigo Errejón, professors at Madrid's Comlutense University, founded Podemos (We Can), a leftist populist party that drew direct inspiration and praxis from theorists of the Essex school of populism studies, especially Ernesto Laclau and Chantal Mouffe (Laclau 2005, Laclau and Mouffe 1985, Laclau 1977). The party drew in activists and sympathizers of the *indignados* movement (Martínez 2015), as well as a large proportion of left-leaning citizens who had rejected the mainstream elites. Economic concerns were at the forefront of Podemos' appeal. Citizens with negative views of the economy (Marcos-Marne, Plaza-Colodro, and Freyburg 2020) or who lived in areas that were particularly exposed to competition arising from globalization (Vampa 2020) were more likely to support Podemos. The party also appealed to those whose faith in the political system had been shaken by the economic crisis. Muro and Vidal (2017), while not analyzing Podemos itself, found that discontent with national parties tended to be higher in areas with higher unemployment. Torcal (2014) also finds that a decline in support for representative institutions correlated with poor economic performance.

6.2.2 Economic, Cultural, and Political Effects on Support for Podemos

The standard narrative – one which we have largely reflected so far – is that Podemos was primarily a partisan manifestation of the anti-austerity movement, especially the *indignados* movement. Yet the party did not focus exclusively on economics. Podemos' founders were attempting to directly put the populist theories of the Essex school into practice, which involved constructing a coalition of unheard voices against a monolithic power bloc. In socially conservative Spain, this included educated cultural progressives who cared deeply about postmaterialist issues related to the environment, immigration, and LGBTQ rights. While much of

TABLE 6.1 *Top ten categories in Podemos' April 2019 manifesto*

Category	Percent of coding units
Welfare State Expansion	15.37
Market Regulation	13.13
Labor Groups: Positive	9.33
Equality: Positive	8.46
Technology and Infrastructure: Positive	7.17
Sustainability: Positive	6.74
Democracy: Positive	4.06
Environmental Protection	3.8
Human (Civil) Rights	3.54
Education Expansion	2.68
Other	25.74

Data from Comparative Manifestos Project. A coding unit is a quasi-sentence that "contains one statement or 'message'" (Werner, Lacewell, and Volkens 2015). There are 1,158 coding units in the Podemos' manifesto.

the 2019 manifesto is about the economy and related matters, there are also sections dedicated to an environmentally sustainable economy, as well as "Guarantees for Democracy," "Social Justice," and "Territorial Justice."[7] These stances are echoed when we look at the Comparative Manifestos Project coding of the party platform (Volkens et al. 2020) by issue and stance in Table 6.1.

Two other issues emerge as crucial for Podemos' support. The first is political: Podemos particularly sought to capitalize on growing disillusionment with Spain's major parties and their repeated transgressions against the popular will. Marcos-Marne, Plaza-Colodro, and Freyburg (2020, 16) found that Podemos voters have negative views of the economy, strong populist attitudes, and generally expressed attitudes reflecting "the intersection between the economic crisis and a deepening crisis of representation in democracies." Finally, conflicts over regional autonomy that grew more heated during the crisis influenced support for Podemos; Vampa (2020) cites a survey that found a third of voters who supported greater Catalonian autonomy supported Podemos. Given all this, the standard narrative of economically driven left populism, a fairly

---

[7] Party manifestos can be found via Manifesto Project Dataset, version(s) MPDS2020b and MPDSSA2020b, https://visuals.manifesto-project.wzb.eu/mpdb-shiny/cmp_dashboard_dataset/.

common narrative applied to so-called "inclusive" populist variants, does not apply quite as neatly to Podemos as one might assume. Rather than assume the primacy of economic motives for supporting Podemos, we need to directly investigate the various motivating factors that might contribute to the party's support.

6.2.3 APE and Support for Podemos

To untangle the web of factors that led individuals to support Podemos, we conducted statistical analyses using observational data from the Spanish wave of the PSAS. To measure support for Podemos, we used a 0–10 scale measuring the likelihood a person would vote for the party and a deviated version of this variable from which we subtracted the likelihood of voting for the PSOE. This deviation strategy matches what we did for Trump support in Chapter 5, and for the same reasons. Combined, this gives us a sense of the party's general appeal as well as the elements of its appeal that distinguish it from the mainstream left party.

We wish to determine if economic, political, or cultural factors best explain support for Podemos. We include the following independent variables:[8]

- *Economics*: sociotropic economic evaluation, government performance on the economy.
- *Culture*: cultural discontent, ethnocentrism, anti-immigrant attitudes, Spanish nationalism/anti-regionalism.[9]
- *Politics*: regime support, PSV, ideology.
- *Control variables*: Gender, minority self-identification, Spanish national, gender, age, education, social class.

We begin by regressing both support measures on all variables. Regression coefficients using both measures of Podemos support, with 95 percent confidence bars, are presented in Figure 6.1.

For a movement famous for protesting austerity, the results on the economic variables are surprising. Both economic measures had a positive, rather than negative, influence on support for Podemos overall, while neither influenced support for the party over the PSOE. That said, we should not read too much into these results. The survey was taken in

---

[8] For more details on index construction and measures, see Chapter 4 and the PSAS codebook, https://doi.org/10.7910/DVN/XMNLTA.

[9] This is a dichotomous measure coded "1" if the individual prefers a centralized state with no regional autonomy.

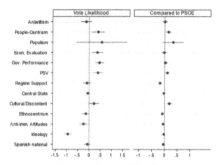

FIGURE 6.1 Antecedents of Podemos support.

March 2020 during a government which included Podemos, so this may simply be a case of biased perceptions, which is consistent with the significant result for the base measure but not for the comparative measure.

The political measures were mixed. PSV had a modest but unexpectedly positive effect on both measures; this is likely driven by the tendency of supporters of populism to feel empowered through their allegiance, an issue we discuss in Chapter 9. Regime support influenced likelihood of vote compared to the PSOE (which fits when comparing insurgent and establishment parties), and ideology had a significant effect, especially on the comparative measure. For a party that perhaps more than any other in history has deliberately tried to adapt a populist orientation, the influence of populist attitudes was surprisingly anemic. Neither anti-elitism nor populism significantly influenced either measure of support. Only people-centrism consistently increased the likelihood of supporting the party, a pattern we will see again for other leftist populists later in this book.

Cultural factors had a surprisingly consistent influence. Cultural discontent significantly increased both base and comparative support, while ethnocentrism and anti-immigrant sentiment negatively influenced comparative and base measures, respectively. Ethnocentrism negatively influenced preference for Podemos over the PSOE, and both it and anti-immigrant attitudes were associated with a lower base likelihood of voting for Podemos. The party's current base of support seems to come from those who believe power needs to be restored to ordinary Spaniards, those who do not trust the political system (without evincing the overweening hostility toward elites seen in populism), and finally those with strong postmaterialist and culturally egalitarian viewpoints, especially those who see Spain as out of sync with those values.

6.2.4 Understanding Podemos

Based on the typical narratives surrounding Podemos, one would have expected a purely economic basis of support, perhaps with populist antagonism mixed in. Instead, we see partisans with politically discontented but hardly unambiguously populist leanings, who are motivated not only by economic concerns but also by postmaterialism and disgust with conservative traditionalism.

This reflects a key point of distinction between Podemos and the *indignados* movement from which it emerged. The latter was almost myopically focused on the austerity issue, with its most ardent supporters coming from the ranks of disillusioned young people whose economic prospects had been shattered by the crisis. Podemos, on the other hand, was created by academics, inspired by scholarly discourse on populism that emphasized the need to aggregate unmet demands into a movement that could challenge neoliberal hegemony. Opposition to austerity was certainly a key part of that coalition, but so too were postmaterialist issues related to sex and gender norms, the environment, and ethnic and racial diversity. And given that Podemos' leaders were drawn from the ranks of the highly educated urbanites we have discussed throughout this book, it is not as surprising that progressive cultural issues would move to the fore as the party detached from its base in the anti-austerity protests.

Roberts (2019) explains that populists tend to politicize neglected issues and social divisions. Leftists typically politicize redistribution and statism when faced with a neoliberal consensus, while the PRR typically challenge a similar consensus on multiculturalism. This model is mostly consistent with the rise of Podemos. However, it neglects one key feature of the party's rise, namely that in contexts of widespread cultural conservativism, left populists may engage in simultaneous politicization on both axes, pursuing both anti-neoliberalism and postmaterialist progressivism. The risk here of course is that even a small incursion into cultural politicization by the left may exacerbate feelings of exclusion and marginalization among those on the right, as we later show occurred in Spain.

Ultimately, Podemos was unable to parlay its electoral successes into meaningful policy outcomes. Its best chance to do so came during the 2015 elections, in which the party had its best electoral showing (it gained sixty-nine seats, sixty-five more than it held after the previous election) and the fracturing of the right due to the rise of a new center-left party (Citizens, Cs) left the PP unable to form a government. Despite this, Podemos failed to strike a bargain with the PSOE that would have allowed a center-left government (either a coalition or a PSOE minority government supported by Podemos) to take office. We discuss this process in more detail in Chapter 8, but for the present purposes we point to the election of 2015 as a genuine critical juncture, that is, a moment in which the status quo had been destabilized, where actors were making decisions in conditions of considerable uncertainty and were thus prone to making poor decisions, and where small changes in actors' choices could potentially send their countries off on radically different political trajectories (Collier and Collier 2002). As the economy began to recover just as the PSOE and Podemos were negotiating, it provided a unique opportunity to chart a course between the troika and rising popular demands for a repudiation of neoliberalism.

The intransigence of both Podemos and PSOE led to new elections and a center-right government, meaning that anti-austerity forces would have practically no influence on how the fruits of the recovery would be utilized. As a result, there was only limited movement away from the cuts and tax increases implemented during the crisis, and little chance to soothe the resentments and anger over economic hardship that had plagued the country. Having failed to productively channel economic, cultural, and political discontent, Podemos' faltering both increased the resentment roiling Spain and also foreclosed the possibility of that resentment remaining within inclusive, leftist manifestations. In short, by trying and failing to mobilize discontent from the left side of the typical ideological spectrum, Podemos ceded the ground on the system-challenging/system-supporting axis of competition to the right, giving it an opportunity that the taboo against FR politics would otherwise have precluded. And these dynamics came to a head just as controversy over a uniquely Spanish cultural issue was about to flare up.

6.3 VOX POPULIST? AUSTERITY, NATIONALISM, AND THE RADICAL RIGHT IN SPAIN

In the simplest terms, our argument is that economic crises were the root cause of the surge in cultural discontent during the era of the Great Recession. Podemos may have been more interested in postmaterialist cultural issues than some might expect, but it still fits this argument relatively well. VOX, the radical right party that came to prominence in 2019, is a much more significant challenge for us because there is a clear and competing intervening event, namely the Catalan independence referendum of 2017, that appears to be an obvious alternative explanation. After all, the fact that a party committed to unitary Spanish nationalism gained prominence after a major attempt to destroy that unity is hardly shocking.

We push back against this facile explanation by arguing that the most relevant counterfactual here is *not* a Spain in which Catalonia never held such a referendum, but a Spain in which the economy was thriving *prior* to the referendum being held. By 2017 the Spanish economy had been in recovery for roughly two years. While the crisis had ended, the recovery was uneven, slow, and nowhere near sufficient to undo the damage of the difficult years that preceded it. GDP per capita was 28,100 in current US dollars in 2017, still well below the 2008 peak of 35,336. As we have already indicated, unemployment remained stubbornly high, especially among the young. Combined with continuing political dysfunction (including snap elections in 2016 after both major parties were unable to form a government), we see a situation that was nowhere near as dire as that which the country faced in the early 2010s but still politically and economically fraught.

It is analytically useful to imagine a situation in which a more robust recovery, or one in which the state moved more aggressively to moderate the damage of lingering economic turmoil, was well underway.[10] In such a context, would there have been enough fury at the Spanish state to justify the risks, both to Catalonia and to Catalan independence leaders personally (several were later arrested), for such a vote to even occur? If it had, would the independence forces have won the day, especially considering that pro-independence sentiment had only breached 50 percent very recently? And finally, would so many citizens outside Catalonia have been so incensed by a referendum that could have no legal force given Spanish constitutional law?

6.3.1 The Regionalist Dodge: Crisis, Austerity, and Catalan Independence

The road to the Catalan independence referendum could serve as a case study in how the brinksmanship of political elites can bring about outcomes that none of them want. Regional tensions in Spain have a long

---

[10] We need not imagine the latter, as this description matches the recovery in Portugal, as we discuss in Chapter 8.

and troubled history, including periods of violence, such as the enforcement of unity under the regime of military dictator Francisco Franco that ruled the country from 1936 until his death in 1975, and terrorism perpetrated by the Basque Homeland and Liberty (ETA) organization that peaked in the early 1990s. Franco and the Falangist movement with which he allied embraced an essentially fascistic vision of society which included intense centralizing nationalism, a core component of which was the suppression of regional identities and languages, to the point where people were strongly discouraged from giving their children Catalan or Basque names. Regionalist movements were forced underground, with some like the ETA adopting violent tactics to protest this repression. Once democracy was restored after Franco's death, however, repression ceased and tensions eased.

The roots of the modern political conflict over Catalan independence can be found in the dissolution of the Majestic Pact of 1996, a bargain struck between the PP and the center-right Catalonian nationalist coalition CiU after a general election failed to produce a clear national majority. The CiU agreed to provide support for the PP in the national parliament. In return, the PP would help the CiU maintain its power in Catalonia and devolve power to the regional government. Eventually, the pact failed, and in 2003 the CiU lost its hold on Catalonian government to a left-wing governing coalition. In 2004, the national government would follow as the PSOE returned to power.

The socialist-led government in Catalonia, attempting to goad the national government to quicker action, passed a reform to the Statue of Autonomy of Catalonia[11] that had been created in the transition to democracy in 1979. This reform would substantially increase the powers of Spain's autonomous regions. The national parliament under a PSOE government passed a pared-down version of the Catalonian Act in 2006.[12] However, the PP and other parties contested the law, and the Constitutional Court reduced the scope of the statute in 2010. Supporters of autonomy were incensed: a painstaking process that had paid close attention to the legal necessities for granting regional autonomy in response to citizen demands had been thwarted by an undemocratic body (Minder 2017). As a result, support for independence quickly rose, from 20 percent in 2010 to 49 percent in 2013 (Orriols and Cordero 2018).

---

[11] English text of the statute can be found here: https://web.archive.org/web/20140224115212/www.parlament.cat/porteso/estatut/estatut_english.pdf.

[12] English text of Organic Act 6/2006 can be found here: www.parlament.cat/document/cataleg/150259.pdf.

However, by this time the CiU had returned to power in Catalonia and the economic crisis was unfolding. The CiU, readers may recall, provided support for the PSOE's austerity policies, and they implemented similar policies in Catalonia; in fact, it was the first regional government to impose such measures. As a result, the CiU began to hemorrhage support, as voters grew angry over both its austerity measures and its lack of support for independence (Rico and Liñeira 2014). Nor was economic resentment in Catalonia limited to austerity. Catalonia is the richest region in Spain, with 16 percent of the country's population but 19 percent of Spain's GDP.[13] Tax dollars from Catalonia subsidize the rest of the country, as about 10 percent of the region's GDP is redistributed to poorer regions of Spain, a fact that became especially contentious when Catalonia had to ask for a bailout from the national government during the crisis.[14]

Independence provided the CiU with a convenient distraction from its own problems and controversies, including those related to austerity. The need for a distraction intensified in 2014 when news emerged that Jordi Pujol, the founder of Convergence, CiU leader, and president of Catalonia from 1980–2003, had for decades maintained a secret, offshore bank account that held money he inherited from his father. By shifting to a pro-independence stance, the center-right sought to embrace an increasingly popular position and to redirect attention away from its economic policies and corruption scandals. While it is difficult to untangle the causal effects of culture, corruption, political gamesmanship, and economic discontent on popular support for independence (e.g. Rico and Liñeira (2014) argue that all these factors played a role and were likely mutually reinforcing), the need for center-right elites to move the political conversation away from austerity means that it is doubtful that a referendum for independence would have been held absent the crisis. Regardless of the cause, the drive for independence had significant unintended consequences. By holding the referendum Catalonia crossed a red line for the nationalist right.

6.3.2 Dueling Nationalisms: The Right Responds to Regionalism

Between austerity and the growing assertiveness of Catalan nationalism, the pressure on the Spanish center-right and the PP grew steadily as the

---

[13] Source: BBC News, www.bbc.com/news/world-europe-29478415.
[14] Source: BBC News, www.bbc.com/news/business-18951575.

2010s wore on. Shortly after the dizzying rise and collapse of support for the PP in 2011, a group of dissident members abandoned the party to form Cs, a new center-right party that distinguished itself from its progenitor by criticizing the PP's embrace of some elements of austerity (especially tax increases) and by taking a firmer stance against Catalan nationalism. The PP's fortunes dimmed further in 2018 as a series of corruption scandals tarnished the party (Edwards 2019, Izquierdo 2014). The scandals would have been serious in any context, but economic discontent tends to enhance negative reactions to corruption (see Chapter 7), and whatever credibility the PP had maintained after its flip-flop on austerity and its perceived coddling of Catalan nationalism eroded even further.

Cs briefly mobilized resentments among moderate voters to whom Podemos did not appeal, but the emergence of Catalan independence complicated the dimensions of partisan competition. Parties now had to maneuver along both the typical economic axis as well as new axes related to postmaterialism and especially the status of Spain's regions vis-à-vis the state. Cs stumbled on this last dimension, attempting to take a middle-of-the-road position of opposing both Catalan and Spanish nationalism. This left wide open a significant space on the nationalist and socially conservative end of the cultural axis (Roberts 2019), as well as a deep well of resentment toward all aspects of the political system after five years of failure on the part of parties, both new and old, to take popular discontent and mold it into genuine political change.

6.3.3 VOX and the Cultural Ideology of the FR

VOX, a small party founded in 2013 by dissidents from the PP, was uniquely positioned to take advantage of this opportunity, as its existence was motivated directly by the regional question. VOX's leaders broke from the PP over their desire to reinstitute the Franco-era centralization of the Spanish state, while the PP had previously accommodated some level of Catalan autonomy due to its need for Catalan support for its minority government. The importance of unitary nationalism can seem strange, but it makes sense within the cultural ideology of the FR, as can be best seen in the following quote from VOX's YouTube channel:

We want the power to protect the Spanish people from their enemies, from the enemies of unity who want to break up our homeland, from the enemies of freedom/liberty who want to impose [on us their] progressive gags, from the enemies of equality who defend the privileges of the autonomous communities, and from the enemies of our sovereignty who, from their globalist positions, want to dissolve the existence of Spain in a multicultural soup.[15]

As the quote shows, the FR is defined by the belief that the cultural norms and mores of the majority should be adopted by all of society, and that the state should support the dominant culture and, in some circumstances, suppress subcultures. For the Spanish FR, this sentiment was tinged with nostalgia for the Franco era. Even if they did not embrace authoritarianism or yearn for a return to military rule, those who would eventually split with the PP to form VOX venerated the *generalissimo* and the cultural unity his regime enforced. As such, the growing clout of regional autonomy movements, and the growing acceptance of their demands by the mainstream right, was profoundly threatening.

VOX went nowhere for several years, as Cs dominated the discontented dimension on the center-right and Spanish nationalism remained a niche issue. The Catalan referendum proved a game-changing event. It brought cultural conflicts over identity to the forefront of Spanish politics (Rico and Liñeira 2014) and dramatically increased the salience of the state structure debate (Turnbull-Dugarte 2019). VOX did well for itself in the April 2019 general elections, although not as well as originally predicted. The election was devastating for the PP, which lost over half its seats. According a national paper, *El Mundo*, 1.6 million PP votes were lost to VOX, and 1.4 million to Cs (Garrido, González, and Aguirre 2019). However, once again neither political faction was able to form a government, and snap elections were called for the end of the same year.

As the November 2019 general elections approached, three events augmented the wind in VOX's sails. First, the Spanish Supreme Court approved a PSOE-sponsored plan to remove the remains of former dictator Francisco Franco from the Valley of the Fallen. Part of a longer process of removing any public display of approval for the military regime, the action incensed those on Spain's FR who continue to venerate Franco. Second, the leaders of the Catalan independence vote were sentenced, triggering protests among their supporters, furthering polarization around the issue and forcing all the major political actors in Spain's system to take firmer stances on the issue of Catalan secession. The major parties firmly opposed any moves toward independence, while Podemos supported greater regional autonomy and was open to the idea of a referendum while officially opposing secession. Finally, after trying to capture

---

[15] www.youtube.com/watch?v=zDOvL1CDZeo.

the FR in the April 2019 election, the PP moved back to the center to thwart the advance of Cs.

The result of all this maneuvering was a recovery by the PP, the rapid rise of VOX, and a staggering blow to Cs. The PP went from 66 to 89 (+23) seats, VOX from 24 to 52 (+28), and Cs from 57 to 10 (−47). According to surveys, it appears that most of the centrist Cs voters stayed at home (about a million), and of those that did not, 741,000 voted for the PP, while 648,000 went to VOX (RTVE.es 2019). On the left, PSOE lost three seats, going from 123 to 120, while Unidas Podemos went from 33 to 26. Ultimately, VOX was denied a chance to repeat the path to power it took in Andalusia, namely a coalition with the PP and other conservative factions, at the national level. Despite losing support, the PSOE and Podemos finally managed to overcome their reluctance to work together and formed a coalition government. However, it was too little and far too late: the years of recovery, which would have provided an opportunity for a leftist coalition to ensure that the recovery's boons were directed more forcefully toward those who needed it, had already passed as the economy slowed in 2018 and crashed again with the emerging Covid-19 crisis.

6.3.4 Whose VOX? Situating the Party within the European FR

At this point, a relatively simple story emerges: an FR movement that languished in obscurity for years got a new lease on life when its signature issue gained national importance thanks to a fortuitous (for VOX at least) turn of events. The role for economic discontent here seems quite minor, motivating conservative Catalan nationalists to gamble on a referendum but no more. Yet recall that we have provided considerable theory and evidence that issues like identity politics are powerfully molded by economic events through emotions. Controversies over national versus regional identities, of what it means (or should mean) to be Spanish, are not, in this sense, substantively different from other forms of cultural discontent like ethnonationalism, which we have shown to respond to economic outcomes in both experimental and observational data.

There is ample existing evidence that VOX is not so distinct from other PRR parties as its focus on unitary nationalism might imply. Mendes and Dennison (2021) and Vampa (2020) find that a high proportion of foreigners in a given polity correlated with VOX support, while Rama et al. (2021, 100; c.f. Turnbull-Dugarte 2019, Turnbull-Dugarte, Rama, and Santana 2020) find that VOX supporters were far less warmly disposed to immigrants than supporters of any other Spanish party. These findings are not unanimous. Turnbull-Dugarte, Rama, and Santana (2020) and Turnbull-Dugarte (2019), for example, find that concerns over immigration had little to no influence on support for VOX, while Torcal (2019) finds that immigration has a weak effect, with nationalism being the party's dominant appeal. There is some disagreement over whether the "populist" appellation usually included with radical right is appropriate for VOX. The party is typically considered part of the PRR wave that crested in Europe in the late 2010s (Turnbull-Dugarte, Rama and Santana 2020), and Rama et al. (2021, 130) find a small, but consistent, influence of political discontent on VOX support, but Mendes and Dennison (2021) argue that VOX's use of populist appeals are sparse and almost entirely subservient to its ethnonationalism. The trouble here is that most current works on VOX are very preliminary and thus mostly exploratory. This is understandable and useful for a new party, but it does have a high potential of obscuring more complex and indirect relationships, such as those on which our theories rest.

One common thread that does immediately emerge from studies of the party is the lack of any role for the economy: as the most thorough analysis of VOX's popular support thus far shows, when compared to its nationalism and ethnocentrism, the role of economics in VOX's popular appeals and voter support is minor (Rama et al. 2021). On the other hand, readers may recall that we found something similar regarding Trump's support in the previous chapter. Like Trump, UKIP, and much of the European radical right, VOX veers between neoliberal free marketeering and welfare chauvinism but consistently interweaves its economic and cultural messaging, as seen by the sections and issues they highlight in their party manifesto (see Table 6.2). The contrast between academic understanding of the FR and the actual praxis of these movements is growing significant: the artificial separation of economy and culture found in the former is totally at odds with the constant connections made by the latter (Table 6.3).

6.3.5 Uncovering Economics: A Statistical Analysis of Economics, Culture, and Support for Populism in Spain

To provide a theoretically driven analysis of VOX support (and also to shed more light on support for Podemos), we repeated the same analyses as we conducted in an earlier section of Podemos, including measures of both base support for VOX and the difference in support for VOX over

TABLE 6.2 *Section headers from VOX's April 2019 platform*

España, unidad y soberanía	Spain, United and Sovereign
Ley electoral y transparencia	Electoral law and transparency
Inmigración	Immigration
Lucha contra el fundamentalismo islámico	Fight against Islamic fundamentalism
Defensa, seguridad y fronteras	Defense, security, and orders
Economía y recursos	Economy and resources
Un nuevo sistema impositivo	A new system of taxation
Salud	Health
Educación	Education
Tradiciones y cultura	Traditions and culture
Vida y familia	Life and family
España por encima de los partidos políticos	Spain before political parties
Libertades y justicia	Liberties and justice
Justicia independiente y eficaz	Justice: independent and effective
Europa e internacional	Europe and the world

Party Manifesto downloaded from Manifesto Project Dataset, version(s) MPDS2020b and MPDSSA2020b https://visuals.manifesto-project.wzb.eu/mpdb-shiny/cmp_dashboard_dataset/. We should note that the VOX manifesto is extremely brief compared to traditional party manifestos and is thus perhaps not as reflective of the party's thought as it might normally be.

TABLE 6.3 *Top ten categories in VOX's April 2019 manifesto*

Category	Percent of coding units
National Way of Life: Positive	9.7
Law and Order: Positive	8.96
Traditional Morality: Positive	7.46
Welfare State Expansion	7.09
Headings	5.6
Incentives: Positive*	4.48
Centralization: Positive	4.48
Governmental and Administrative Efficiency	4.1
Immigrant Integration: Assimilation	4.1
Immigration: Negative	4.1

Data from Comparative Manifestos Project. A coding unit is a quasi-sentence that "contains one statement or 'message'" (Werner, Lacewell, and Volkens 2015). VOX's manifesto had 268 units.
* Favorable mentions of supply-side-oriented economic policies

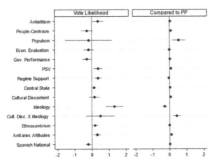

FIGURE 6.2 Antecedents of VOX support.

its mainstream rival, PP. We include a complication in these models: an interaction between cultural discontent and ideology. We do not expect value and identity marginalization to encourage voting for an FR party among those who identify with the left, so we expect any influence of discontent to manifest only among those who identify as right wing. The results are presented in Figure 6.2.

These results are consistent with the contention that VOX's primary sources of support are cultural and political rather than economic. We found no significant influence for economic factors in either model. Politically, VOX clearly appeals to those who are disgruntled with the Spanish political system; this is especially apparent when we analyze why people would more willingly vote for VOX over the mainstream conservative party. Populism as a syndrome significantly increased the likelihood of voting for VOX over PP, as did antielitism, while regime antipathy predicted the base likelihood of VOX voting. Regime support was positively associated with the base measure, likely reflecting the general deference to institutions and systems of authority common among conservatives. In short, democratic discontent did not draw individuals to VOX so much as it pushed conservative-leaning voters away from the mainstream PP and toward the insurgent conservative party.

For cultural issues, ethnocentrism and Spanish nationalism significantly increased base likelihood of voting for VOX, as did negative evaluation of immigrants. Cultural discontent increased support for VOX over the PP, and the effect becomes stronger as respondents move from left to right on the ideology measure, as Figure 6.3. shows.

Taken together, these results support the image of VOX supporters as profoundly discontented, both with politics as usual and the current cultural status quo. The importance of conflicts over values and identities becomes even more essential when analyzing the association between

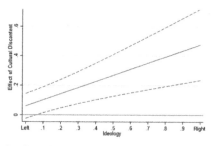

FIGURE 6.3 Effect of cultural discontent on likelihood of VOX vote over PP, by ideology

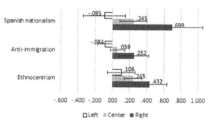

FIGURE 6.4 Predicted effects of cultural discontent on FR attitudes by ideology.

cultural discontent and FR attitudes. To show this we first regressed these attitudes on cultural discontent, again interacting it with ideology. We also include all variables in the support models except regime support.[16] We use ordinary least squares (OLS) regression for all models, including Spanish nationalism, which is a dichotomous measure. We chose OLS over logit because simulation research shows that OLS often performs more reliably in complex models such as those including interactions (Gomila 2021). The predicted effect of cultural discontent on each FR attitude, with 95 percent confidence intervals, for leftists, moderates, and rightists (min, mean, and max on the ideology measure respectively) are included in Figure 6.4.

We see the same pattern with each FR attitude: among leftists, cultural discontent negatively influenced each attitude, although not significantly so. Among conservatives, however, cultural discontent strongly affected each of the three attitudes. This reflects our contention that cultural discontent manifests very differently among the left and the right. We should also note that economic factors begin to matter here. Sociotropic

---

[16] We feel it more likely that regime support is influenced by these factors, rather than influenced by them. Including this variable did not influence any of the reported results.

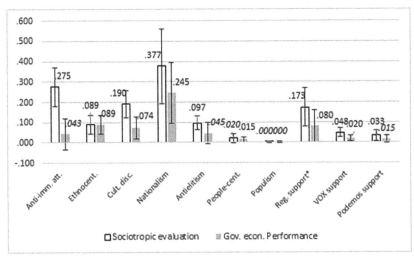

FIGURE 6.5 Path SEM of Podemos and VOX support.

economic evaluation negatively influenced ethnocentrism (Est. = –0.172; SE = 0.058; p = 0.003), anti-immigrant attitudes (Est. = –0.157; SE = 0.048; p = 0.001), and preference for a centralized state (Est. = –0.268; SE = 0.104; p = 0.010). Centralized state preference was also significantly influenced by egotropic evaluation (Est. = –0.184; SE = 0.074; p = 0.013).

The importance of economic discontent becomes even more apparent when we analyze a full mediated model. We conducted a path SEM analysis similar to that Chapter 5, with both cultural (immigration attitudes, ethnocentrism, cultural discontent) and political (populism and its constitutive dimensions, regime support) variables regressed on our economic evaluation measures, and with the comparative vote likelihood measures for both Podemos and VOX regressed on the cultural and political variables; the control variables listed earlier were included in all models. We then calculated the total effects of economic variables on the cultural and political variables, as well as support for the two parties.[17] The results are presented in Figure 6.5.

All of the measures analyzed here were significantly influenced by at least one of the measures of economic discontent except the combined

---

[17] We included the interaction between ideology and cultural discontent from our earlier model, which complicates total effect computations. To incorporate this simply, we rescaled ideology so that lower values always indicate left-wing values but so that zero indicated strong leftism in the Podemos model but indicated strong conservatism in the Vox model.

index. Both sociotropic economic evaluation and government economic performance influenced various measures. Here again, we see a substantial influence of economic discontent on cultural discontent, as well as on centralizing nationalism, as well as attitudes toward immigrants and ethnocentrism. Paradoxically, economic factors had a more consistent total effect on VOX support than Podemos support, although sociotropic economic evaluation did have a significant total effect on the latter.

6.3.6 Reviewing Our Findings

Taken together, findings pertaining to both Podemos and VOX are consistent with the expectations of APE, namely the notion that regionalism and anti-regionalism are both, at least in part, manifestations of cultural discontent. As in the United States, we find solid evidence that resentment arising from the economic trauma of the eurozone crisis stirred up these cultural conflicts, much as they did in the United States.

Finally, we find a significant role for both politics and process. Antagonism toward both the political elite and the political system significantly drove support for both discontented factions analyzed here. This fact is particularly relevant for the historical sequence we describe here. Each failed attempt to grapple with the crisis, first by the PSOE, then by the PP, and later during negotiations between the left parties, frustrated expectations and raised the level of resentment in society further, while also discrediting each actor in turn, until only the FR VOX remained untainted.

6.4 CONCLUSIONS

The primary lesson we can take from Spain is not its general consistency with those drawn from Trump and UKIP, but rather how those similarities can hide within the idiosyncrasies of each case. Discontented political attitudes do not derive from abstract principles or ideologies, although they may incorporate elements of such ideas into their social narratives. Instead, discontent reflects and is shaped by the political systems they oppose, and these particularities obscure common causal processes at work. As a result, both popular and academic narratives often make incomplete inferences regarding mass attitudes and behavior based on the marquee issues of discontented movements: Podemos castigates austerity and thus must be supported by economically oriented leftists; VOX is defined by its centralizing nationalism and so must be its militants.

Surface-level analyses can produce findings consistent with these narratives, but a deeper dive into public opinion data shows that the factors driving support for these parties are far more complex. Podemos supporters are driven more by cultural resentments than is commonly assumed, while the value and identity concerns of *voxistas* are defined not only by centralizing nationalism but also more general feelings of cultural dislocation, which is itself augmented by economic and democratic discontent.

In Spain we also see a more complex interplay between left and right in the process of cultural backlash. The model utilized by Inglehart and Norris, in which the FR rebels against a postmaterialist cultural consensus, fits well in contexts where such a consensus predominates. In cases like Spain, where cultural conservatism is much more endemic, the first move to politicize culture may come from the left, rather than the right (as we show in Chapter 7, something similar occurred in Brazil prior to the rise of Bolsonaro). Our data show that Podemos expanded beyond its origins as a partisan embodiment of the anti-austerity movement by incorporating educated cultural liberals and progressives who chafed at the country's lack of progress on postmaterialist issues. And although the protagonists of Catalan independence were conservative regionalists, their push for multiculturalism and eventually separatism triggered the current cultural conflict over regional independence. In short, backlash is not unidirectional; under some circumstances, it can carom back and forth between traditionalists and multiculturalists, amplifying as it goes.

We keep these lessons in mind as we proceed with the book. In Chapter 9 covering the Trump administration in the United States and in our conclusion (Chapter 10), we argue that this multidirectional process of cultural discontent means that democratic discontent can, once aroused by economic trauma, become a self-perpetuating vicious cycle; one which can continue to gain momentum long after the moment of crisis has passed. We also keep in mind the tendency of cultural discontent to manifest in unusual and unexpected ways as we turn to our study of Latin America in Chapter 7, where issues even further removed from the typical suite of cultural concerns than national integration take center stage.

7

Corruption, Populism, and Contentious Politics in Brazil and Chile

The post-2008 wave of discontent came late to Latin America. In a globalized economy, any serious disruption in the economic core will inevitably impact the periphery. However, in Latin America, the US financial crisis produced only a mild recession from which most countries recovered relatively quickly. Buoyed by continuing growth in Chinese demand for raw materials (Kristjanpoller, Olson, and Salazar 2016), the region experienced an economic boom while the developed world struggled. Yet all good things must end, and underneath the region's solid economic performance trouble was brewing. The commodities boom increased incomes, reduced unemployment (Álvarez, García-Marín, and Ilabaca 2021), and even led to some progress on economic inequality (López-Calva and Lustig 2010), the most intractable problem in the region. But it also reinforced some longstanding economic pathologies, such as a lack of diversification, overreliance on primary exports, and deindustrialization. Bad omens came to fruition when the boom went bust in 2014.

At this point, we have sufficiently established the core mediated relationship between economics, emotions, culture, and democratic discontent, and we do not wish to risk beating a dead horse here. Many of the discontented movements that emerged or endured during the crisis focused on familiar socioeconomic grievances, and thus the role of the commodities crisis is quite clear. As such, we only briefly mention cases (e.g. Mexico, Peru, Argentina) where discontent followed a predictable path. We instead focus here on two cases where discontent emerged in forms not typically seen in Latin America (Brazil) or in ways that differ significantly from our other cases (Chile). First, we analyze the rise of the PRR under Jair Bolsonaro in Brazil. Nativism, racism, and anti-Semitism

154

are hardly unknown in Latin America, but Bolsonaro's combination of political prejudice and populism is a recent innovation in the region. We then investigate the eruption of contentious politics in the form of the *estallido social*, or social uprising, in Chile. The Chilean protests evinced deep discontent with politics as usual, but unusually firm barriers to political outsiders and new party entry took a populist manifestation off the table, at least for a time. Eventually, the uprising wore down those barriers and allowed discontented political leaders and movements (José Antonio Kast from the right, Gabriel Boric from the left) to break through.

Comparing Chile and Brazil leads us to three specific insights. First, economic crises need not have the eschatological drama of the 2008 financial crisis to trigger widespread discontent. The commodities crisis did not involve hedge funds playing with the economy like teenagers on a joyride, nor the sudden presentiment of doom that occurred when Lehman Brothers failed, nor the contentious battles over bank bailouts and austerity. It was simply a natural and inevitable reversal of fortune of the kind that has always plagued primary goods markets. This demonstrates that our theory applies to more normal economic crises caused by market shifts rather than severe shocks to the system.

The APE theory we developed in earlier chapters held that economic discontent intensifies conflicts related to race, ethnicity, nationality, and culture; we did not, however, argue at any point that these were the *only* social conflicts that might be exacerbated by economic downturns. Chile and Brazil show that anger and anxiety borne of economic discontent turn up the heat on virtually *any* preexisting social controversy. The relevant conflicts can vary a great deal from country to country. In Brazil, the economic collapse coincided with the largest corruption scandal in the country's modern history, the *lava jato* ("car wash") affair that eventually implicated a significant proportion of the political elite in bribery and money laundering. While the scandal itself appears at first glance to be the proximate cause of Bolsonaro's ascent, we know from earlier chapters that economic discontent tends to hide in the shadows. The pattern holds here, as we find that the commodities crisis intensified anger over corruption, which is hardly a new phenomenon in Brazil and has often been tolerated during better times. In Chile, economic troubles had a similar effect on longstanding political tensions over the legacy of military rule and democratic deficits, as well as inequality and elitism.

Chile also provides our third insight: when it comes to manifestations of discontent, populism is not the only game in town. Myriad factors in Chile militated against either party-based or personalistic populism serving as an effective vehicle for democratic discontent. As a result, contentious politics has been the method of choice for disaffected Chileans to protest a system that excludes and ignores them. Chilean elites have typically made significant concessions when contentious episodes became sufficiently disruptive, including policy changes, recruitment of leaders of social movements, and ultimately agreeing to initiate a process of drafting a new constitution. Contention has been sufficiently successful in forcing Chilean elites to listen to citizens that it may have helped inoculate the public from vulnerability to charismatic populism.

Here again, events moved faster than we as writers could. The process of constitutional renewal that began as a response to the social crisis finally cracked the ironclad bounds of the Chilean political system. First, it demonstrated the fundamental weakness of the mainstream political parties, whose candidate slates for the Constitutional Convention were resoundingly defeated by independents and members of insurgent parties. Second, difficulties with the process itself generated further resentment and continued a longstanding erosion of trust in institutional political solutions to the country's problems. As a result, discontent was finally able to break into electoral politics in Chile: the 2021 election came down to a contest between a FR acolyte José Antonio Kast and Gabriel Boric, the leader of Chile's bloc of left-wing parties who, although not strictly speaking a populist, was nevertheless a political outsider and fierce critic of Chile's political and economic system. Chile's path to electoral discontent may have been especially arduous but is consistent with the processes observed in other cases. Namely, it combined a longstanding process of erosion in systemic trust and support with more sudden bursts of discontented politics, bursts that were triggered primarily by economic crises.

7.1 WHEN THE BOOM WENT BUST: THE COMMODITIES CRISIS IN LATIN AMERICA

As many readers of this book are likely less familiar with the dynamics of the commodities crisis than those of the Great Recession, it is necessary to briefly review the economic fortunes of Latin America leading up to the collapse. Latin America has a long history of dependence on primary products such as minerals, oil, and raw forestry and agricultural goods (Prebisch 1962). From midcentury to the early 1980s, most Latin American countries attempted to break this dependence through import substitution industrialization (ISI), which called for a strong developmental state that protected domestic manufacturing through tariffs and subsidies.

ISI generated considerable growth and development for a time in many countries, but eventually provoked a crisis as countries borrowed excessively to maintain economic statism (Bruton 1998). Beginning in 1982 with Mexico, country after country in the region suffered through debt and foreign exchange crises, and in some cases hyperinflationary spirals. Eventually, most Latin American countries adopted neoliberal austerity policies, either voluntarily or as imposed conditions of international bailouts, especially from the IMF. The turn from ISI to free market export-oriented development led to a decline in industrialization and a regression to dependence on commodities by the end of the 1990s (Green 2003).

7.1.1 The Commodities Crisis: Causes, Consequences, and Trajectory

Economic data from the World Bank (see Chapter 1) show that the commodities boom began in roughly 2000, with a somewhat later start for countries like Brazil that have extensive oil or natural gas resources. The boom continued throughout the aughts, with a modest and brief decline during the Great Recession, peaking in 2014, whereafter the region entered a period of recession (2014–2016) and stagnation (2018–2020), with a brief and anemic recovery in between.

The benefits of the good years did not come without cost. Increasing commodity dependence crowded out manufacturing, accelerating a process of deindustrialization that had begun during the neoliberal era. The boom also reinforced a pernicious trend of pro-cyclical spending in the region: political pressure encouraged commodity-dependent developing countries to spend more during good times, while the dictates of the global economy and the legacies of the debt crises of the 1980s demanded austerity during downturns (Ocampo 2017). These trends were particularly ominous because when it comes to commodities, what goes up must come down; commodity crises tend to decay over time in relation to manufactured goods (Erten and Ocampo 2013) and are prone to erratic boom-and-bust cycles (Ocampo 2017). History repeated itself in 2014, when Chinese growth began to falter.

7.1.2 *Informales* and Strugglers: Social Change during the Commodities Crisis

All of this took place in a context of Latin America becoming a region of "middle-class" societies: neither abjectly poor nor developed and wealthy. The combination of the boom, deindustrialization, and the decline of statism caused rapid growth in two social sectors. The first is the *informales*, or the informal sector, that is, workers who lack legal work contracts and often engage in low-skilled self-employment such as street vending (Carr and Chen 2002). The other sector is referred to by Birdsall, Lustig, and Meyer (2014) as "the strugglers": lower middle-class individuals who are not deprived but who teeter on the edge of poverty, and who will account for roughly 30 percent of the region's population in the near future. These groups differ a great deal in terms of material situation, human development, and cultural mores, but they share a common feature: profound insecurity. Informal workers may benefit from means-tested welfare policies in some states, but they often are ineligible for contributory pension programs and other social programs that depend upon legally recognized employment. The strugglers, on the other hand, are largely excluded from neoliberal welfare states. They are too well-off to qualify for means-tested programs but not wealthy enough to afford private health, education, or security services. Instead, they are forced to rely on often poor quality public services while being heavily (if indirectly) taxed to pay for programs for which they are ineligible (Birdsall, Lustig, and Meyer 2014).

In short, the commodities crisis struck societies where more than a decade of relatively consistent expansion raised expectations but hid serious vulnerabilities. Few states in the region had much capacity to soften any economic blows through countercyclical spending (e.g. stimulus). Although the commodities crisis may lack the *sturm und drang* of its North Atlantic counterpart from 2008, the fundamental dynamics were remarkably similar: an acute downturn impacting increasingly unequal and insecure societies with dysfunctional democracies. As we show throughout the remainder of this chapter, the consequences of the downturn were likewise fundamentally similar, even as local context led to significant variation in detail.

7.1.3 A Crash Course in Latin American Populism

The discontented wave we discuss in the remainder of this chapter produced both familiar manifestations of discontent and novel forms not previously seen in Latin America. To understand the uniqueness of cases like Brazil and Chile, one must first understand more mundane instances of discontent, which in Latin America nearly always present as charismatic populism. Populism in the region has typically hewed closely to models such as those proposed by Roberts (2019) and Handlin (2019).

Roberts proposes that populists emerge from voids in the policy space, that is, by embracing issue positions with which citizens sympathize but which are ignored or elided by elites. Handlin's model relies on the logic of spatial voting: by politicizing a previously nonsalient regime support–antipathy dimension, leaders with extreme positions on more typical dimensions like economics can place themselves closer to the median voter than mainstream parties and leaders by better matching voter's antipathy toward regime institutions.

These new issues tend to emerge during periods of economic transformation, thanks in large part to the additional challenges faced by underdeveloped countries during modernization. The classical wave of populism that included Juan Perón in Argentina, Getúlio Vargas in Brazil, and Lázaro Cárdenas in Mexico was provoked by the enduring influence of rural oligarchs and the resulting difficulties of completing the transition to industrial capitalism and political incorporation of the working classes (Collier and Collier 2002, Spalding 1977, Germani 1978). The exhaustion of ISI and the painful transition away from statism that followed it led directly to two subsequent waves of populism. The first occurred in countries like Argentina (Carlos Menem), Peru (Alberto Fujimori), and Brazil (Fernando Collor), where statism lingered past its welcome. Each country suffered hyperinflationary crises, which increased popular support for neoliberal reform that each of these figures were able to mobilize, alongside antipathy toward the political systems that failed to satisfactorily address the crisis (Weyland 1996, 1999). In other countries, the "Pink Tide" populists (especially Chávez in Venezuela, Morales in Bolivia, Correa in Ecuador, and Lula in Brazil[1]) mobilized discontent in the opposite direction, taking advantage of outrage over painful and undemocratically pursued neoliberal reforms.

Most of the populists who have gained or held on to power match the pattern of economically driven reaction to the status quo. Several populists or their successors (Maduro in Venezuela, Morales' Movement for Socialism party in Bolivia, and Daniel Ortega in Nicaragua) have managed to institutionalize their political dominance and have thus outlived the crises that led to their ascent, by fair means and (more often) by foul. Upstart populists during the commodities crisis match equally well. Andrés Manuel López Obrador of Mexico was elected after the left-wing

---

[1] Lula is often considered part of the Pink Tide but is generally thought of as part of the moderate faction of this wave, rather than its populist wing. We discuss this in more detail later in this chapter.

party he abandoned joined an agreement with centrist and right parties, with voters flocking to his promise to end neoliberalism once and for all (Webber 2018). Left populists in Argentina (Cristina Fernández de Kirchner and Alberto Fernández) followed the anti-neoliberal populist model pioneered by Chávez, as did Ollanta Humala and (after a brief interlude following several centrist and center-right presidencies) Pedro Castillo in Peru. On the other side of the ideological spectrum, failed left-wing reform efforts such as those in El Salvador (where crime exploded during the tenure of the leftist Farabundo Martí National Liberation Front party), as well as Ollanta's move to the center after his election in Peru, boosted the prospects of right-wing security populists like Nayib Bukele in El Salvador.

In all these cases, we see common patterns. Economic turbulence stirred up resentment against the status quo, and the populists that arise as a result are generally the negative image of the specific pre-crisis equilibrium. Failures of the left produce populism on the right, and vice versa. We also see the direct popular salience of economics, often accompanied by concerns over public safety and security among those on the right. In short, these cases are consistent with our theory, although they "cut out the middleman," with economic factors influencing democratic discontent directly, rather than as mediated by culture. As such, we do not dwell on these cases at length; they are clearly consistent with our focus on economics, and this obvious consistency offers little opportunity to learn more about discontent. Instead, we focus on the two most atypical instances of discontent during the commodities crisis, starting with the novel emergence of European-style PRR ideas and rhetoric under Jair Bolsonaro in Brazil.

7.2 THE END OF "HE STEALS, BUT HE GETS THINGS DONE": CRISIS, CORRUPTION, AND CULTURAL POLARIZATION IN BRAZIL

Explaining the rise of Bolsonaro is a surprisingly difficult task, but not because the causes are difficult to identify. The problem is that in terms of potential explanations, we are spoiled for choice, as Brazil in the late 2010s was the embodiment of Murphy's law: whatever could go wrong, did go wrong. Hunter and Power (2019) identify economic, party system, and political crises, both long simmering and acute. The crises hit particularly hard because the years preceding them were defined by brightening political and economic prospects. In addition to consistent economic growth thanks to the commodities boom, Brazilian democracy had become dominated by the Workers' Party (PT), a formerly marginal socialist party that moderated ideologically while maintaining organizational strength and ties to civil society (Hunter 2007). This made it an anomaly in Brazil, where parties are typically more invested in building clientelist networks than policy platforms, political leaders routinely switch parties as elite alliances wax and wane, and voter attachment to parties is ephemeral (Hunter 2007, Hunter and Power 2019, Samuels and Zucco 2018, Ames 2002). The PT approached both policy and politics with an eye toward practical innovation; examples include nurturing civil society and citizen engagement through participatory budgeting (Baiocchi 2001, Wampler 2007) and pragmatic but effective social policies like a major increase in the minimum wage and a groundbreaking conditional cash transfer program known as *Bolsa Família* (Sugiyama and Hunter 2013).

7.2.1 *Antipetismo* and Growing Discontent

As the commodity crisis approached, Brazil began to slide back into bad habits. Support for the PT gradually began to transmute into personalistic attachment to the party's leader, Luiz Inácio Lula da Silva, popularly known as "Lula," eroding the quality of the party's leadership bench (Hunter and Power 2019). Participatory budgeting programs did little to reform national politics (Rhodes-Purdy 2017), and the PT's increasing moderation and reliance on Lula's personal brand eroded the party's much-vaunted civic roots among the working class. And when the period of crisis began with a slowdown in 2013 and a recession in 2014, the political system had little room to engage in countercyclical fiscal policy.

Finally, the rapid growth and successful social policy under the PT produced unintended consequences once growth began to falter. The social mobility of millions of impoverished people created millions of new middle-class citizens who began to worry more about issues like education, healthcare, and transportation than about day-to-day survival. The PT's embrace of fiscal discipline and neoliberal reform meant that public services in these areas were often difficult to access and of poor quality. This led to two contradictory reasons for dissatisfaction with the PT. The middle sectors saw programs like *Bolsa Família* as an abandonment of their interests in favor of the poor; this was exacerbated by another major social policy initiative called *Minha Casa Minha Vida*, a housing program that could have helped the lower middle classes but was so poorly designed that it ultimately failed after wasting a significant amount of resources (Stefani 2021).[2] Among the left, the PT's turn from structural economic change to market-led poverty alleviation was seen as a betrayal of the party's socialist principles.

These tensions erupted in 2013, as economic growth slowed and living standards eroded due to inflation. The immediate trigger was an increase in transit fees that set off a wave of mass protests in Brazilian cities.[3] Transit fees are one of those issues that seem minor to the comfortable but have a history of causing major social disruptions: the *caracazo* protests in Venezuela that were crucial in radicalizing Hugo Chávez, for example, were also triggered by transit cost increases, as were the 2007 Transantiago protests and the *estallido social* in Chile, which we discuss later in this chapter, to name but a few. Particularly for "the strugglers," that is, those new to the middle class and still experiencing significant precarity, public transit is an absolutely essential social service, as it allows such individuals to move (relatively) freely from the urban peripheral communities in which they live to city centers where employment opportunities and services are more available. Making such services more difficult or expensive to access is far more than an inconvenience; it is a direct threat to the social status and mobility of the strugglers (Díaz Pabón and Palacio Ludeña 2021). These problems were compounded by the PT's ailing housing program, which located most housing well outside the urban core and thus increased the importance of transit services. Although the protests eventually faded as they failed to achieve any significant reform, the resentment that propelled them soon found new targets and new channels for expression.

7.2.2 The *Lava Jato* Scandal

As if these problems were not enough, the most significant corruption scandal in the country's history began to unfold as the recession began. The *lava jato* scandal expanded from an investigation into money laundering into a massive inquiry into corruption and bribery that produced thousands of arrests and ensnared a significant proportion of Brazil's political class. This endemic corruption led to a collapse of the

---

[2] Thanks to Wendy Hunter for pointing this out to us.

[3] For this account of the 2013 protests, we rely primarily one Winter (2017) and Saad-Filho (2013). Many of the specific details of these protests will seem eerily familiar when we discuss the *estallido social* in Chile later in this chapter.

party system as angry citizens turned against the political class. Lulu's successor, Dilma Rousseff, was eventually impeached for manipulating government statistics to improve the appearance of Brazil's fiscal health. Considering that many of the deputies who supported her ouster were under active investigation for much more serious offenses, the process "showed the political class at its worst" (Hunter and Power 2019, 73). Lula himself was eventually convicted for receiving a bribe and barred from running for office, thus depriving the PT of its most important electoral asset. The conviction was controversial, and Sergio Moro, the judge presiding over the case, eventually joined Bolsonaro's cabinet.

As the crises ground on, another social crisis added fuel to the fire: crime rates began to rise in 2016, due in part to the ongoing recession but also to increasing conflict between powerful gangs in the *favellas* (shanty-towns) of the largest cities and in areas that serve as key transit routes for illicit drugs (Lapper 2021, loc. 231). By 2018, violent crime had become the issue most often cited as the country's most serious problem (Chagas-Bastos 2019). By the 2018 general election, all of the traditional major parties were hemorrhaging support (Duque and Smith 2019). The PT actually fared better than the other major parties, taking a hit but maintaining its dominant status as the standard-bearer for the left. The worst losses were suffered by the establishment opposition parties, leaving the system vulnerable to a charismatic outsider.

7.2.3 The Rise of Jair Bolsonaro

If one were looking for a case with similar outcomes to the United States, it would be difficult to find a better case than Brazil. Jair Bolsonaro bears a striking resemblance to Trump in terms of policy preferences and personal style, and even had contacts with people in Trump's inner circle, especially Steve Bannon. Bolsonaro was for years viewed as little more than a colorful but offensive throwback. A former military officer and a gleeful apologist for Brazil's military regime, he spent years in Brazil's congress as a lonely voice for the FR. To the extent that he was known to the public, it was mostly for his quixotic efforts to increase military salaries and later for his vitriolic rhetoric. A brief highlight reel of Bolsonaro's most outrageous statements include his profession that an opposing member of congress was "too ugly to rape," a belief that Afro-Brazilians were unworthy of procreation, and stating that he could not love his son if he were homosexual (Lapper 2021). When casting his vote to impeach Dilma Rousseff, a former leftist guerilla during Brazil's military regime, he dedicated his vote to one of the military officers who orchestrated Rousseff's torture (Hunter and Power 2019). The politicization of these sorts of cultural issues are unusual in Latin American populism. Bolsonaro thus represents a clear break with past practices, including those of earlier Latin American right-leaning populists (Layton et al. 2021).

Untangling the various factors that allowed this isolated revanchist to rise to the highest office in Latin America's largest country is difficult, simply because all the crises (economic, political, corruption, crime) overlapped so completely. Bolsonaro capitalized on all of them, albeit to different degrees. Economically, Bolsonaro had been (surprisingly) an iconoclast, vehemently opposing the privatization and austerity measures implemented during the 1990s and which all the major political movements had accepted by the 2000s (Hunter and Power 2019, 75). Yet his economic positions during the election were ambiguous, mostly consisting of appeals to nostalgia for the economic prosperity that he argued had existed under the military regime (Lapper 2021). He made violent suppression of crime, both by police and by gun-owning private citizens, a core element of his campaign. Bolsonaro was also uniquely able to mobilize anger over corruption; on this topic he ironically benefited from his prior marginalization, as he was so unimportant that no one would bother attempting to curry his favor with bribes or kickbacks.[4] Finally, his appeals relied on "a messianic proposal for saving the country from the incompetence and corruption of traditional elites, mostly the left-wing PT" (Rennó 2020, 7).

This last quote provides the clearest picture of Bolsonaro's appeal. Like most populists, Bolsonaro gained support over other would-be standard-bearers of discontent by being the polar opposite of the political status quo. Prior to his rise, that status quo was largely defined by the preeminence of the PT and its leaders, especially Lula and Rousseff. Samuels and Zucco (2018) find that the behavior of Brazilian voters is profoundly shaped by *antipetismo*, or specific rejection of the PT, including its leaders, its policies, and virtually anything it stands for. Bolsonaro's success can be attributed in no small part to his brand as the complete antithesis of everything related to the PT, especially the party's record on crime, corruption, and social issues related to race and gender.

At a passing glance, Bolsonaro's Brazil seems a potentially difficult case for our theory. The rises in crime and corruption prior to his election

---

[4] Since coming to power, Bolsonaro has shown himself to be quite amenable to corruption, with scandals involving his children as well as his handling of the Covid-19 crisis and vaccine purchasing popping up throughout his tenure.

seem to be the proximate cause of his appeal, although backlash against recent moves by the PT toward racial equity and LGBTQ acceptance may also have played a role (Rennó 2020, Hunter and Power 2019, Lapper 2021). In comparative politics we must always be aware of the possibility of conjunctural causality (Rihoux and Ragin 2009), and perhaps Brazil represents a separate causal path to populism and extremism, where political scandals drove the rise of discontent, with little role for the economically engendered emotional backlash we suggest.

7.2.4 The APE of Anti-corruption Backlash

At this point, we once again rely on APE to argue that the lack of obvious economic influences should not be taken at face value. Economics did contribute to Bolsonaro's breakthrough, and as in our other cases, its influence was mostly indirect. The strongest evidence for this is the simple fact that while the *lava jato* scandal revealed particularly endemic and egregious behavior on the part of the Brazilian political elite, corruption was hardly unknown in Brazil. In fact, Lula and the PT had survived such scandals quite handily in the past. For example, the *mensalão* scandal of 2005, which involved the PT using funds skimmed from state companies or bribes from contractors to pay deputies in parliament to support Lula's agenda, caused a serious crisis for the PT government. Nevertheless, the party was able to recover from the episode despite an erosion of support among educated moderates, largely by appealing to the poor with programs like *Bolsa Família*. Lula was later reelected comfortably, and the PT retained its dominant position.

What changed? People do not respond to corruption with similar ire in all contexts. Numerous works have shown that corruption may be tolerated or even accepted if those responsible are seen as capable of producing economic benefits, either to individuals directly (Manzetti and Wilson 2007) or to the economy as a whole (Choi and Woo 2010). Brazil even has a specific phrase that captures this idea, which translates roughly to "he steals, but he gets things done": as long as benefits flow, a certain degree of venality is an acceptable price, especially if such vices are endemic among the political elite. In 2006, the economy was buoyed by the commodities boom, and Lula's government was pushing increasing social spending throughout to the country's poorest citizens (Desposato 2006). When *lava jato* broke during the worst recession in recent memory, citizens were far less disposed to let corruption go unchallenged.

Corruption is not typically considered a "cultural issue" nor an element of cultural backlash or discontent, and we will not attempt to stretch and strain these concepts to enable such an inclusion. We will simply note that corruption does touch on important values such as trustworthiness, honesty, and the fealty of representatives to those they represent. We therefore expect anger born of economic discontent to inflame and intensify reactions to corruption. Although we are unable to test the role of emotions directly due to a lack of available data, existing literature supports this assertion. Numerous scholars of psychology have found that anger that has arisen by one set of circumstances can make individuals more aggressive and punitive on other, unrelated social issues (Rhodes-Purdy 2021b, Goldberg, Lerner, and Tetlock 1999). Seawright (2012) has applied a similar logic to the collapse of Latin American party systems: he argues that anger over corruption leads to antipathy toward political systems and a greater tolerance for risk, which leads citizens to embrace outsiders who promise to fight against a corrupt elite. In short, while corruption is not a cultural issue of the same sort as ethnonationalism or immigration, emotional spillover from the economic realm can influence it in a similar fashion.

7.2.5 Economics, Corruption, and Democratic Discontent in Brazil: A Statistical Analysis

To test our approach as it pertains to Brazil, we rely on data from the 2018 Brazilian Election Study. As we do not have original data for Brazil, we cannot test our theory as comprehensively as we would like, but we can test certain associations that would be consistent with our approach. We used regression analysis to estimate the influence of various factors on a ten-point scale of approval of Bolsonaro, and on a CFA-constructed index of *antipetismo* using ten-point approval measures of Lula, Dilma Rousseff, and Fernando Haddad (the PT's most recent presidential candidate). The substantive variables we include in which we are interested are:

Economic discontent: five-point retrospective evaluation of the national economy.
Corruption: CFA-constructed index including questions on perceived prevalence of corruption in Brazil, severity of corruption as a social problem, whether corruption goes unpunished in Brazil, and whether corruption is a "cultural trait" in Brazil.

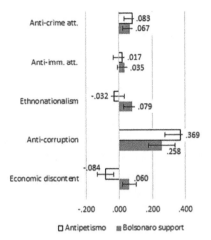

FIGURE 7.1 Analysis of support for Bolsonaro and *antipetismo*.

Ethnonationalism: CFA-constructed index of questions measuring the importance of being born in Brazil, following Brazilian customs, speaking Portuguese, and having Brazilian ancestors for being "truly Brazilian."

Anti-immigrant attitudes: CFA-constructed index using questions about whether immigrants harm Brazilian culture and whether immigrants harm the economy and increase crime.

Anti-crime attitudes: a five-point approve/disapprove measure of how the government handles the issue of crime, where higher scores indicating less favorable evaluations.

All variables were rescaled to range from zero to one for comparability. We conducted separate regressions for both Bolsonaro support and *antipetismo*; when we included the latter as a predictor of the former, the association was so strong that it was nearly impossible to detect other associations, indicating that *antipetismo* is less a cause of Bolsonaro support and more of an essential component of it. Each model also included control variables for income, education, race, age, gender, and Evangelical Christian self-identification. The results are presented in Figure 7.1.

The two factors that emerge as especially important for explaining the rise of Bolsonaro here are concern regarding corruption and crime. These two attitudes are significantly associated with both Bolsonaro support and with *antipetismo*. The role of corruption is particularly pronounced. Other factors were less consistent. Ethnonationalism appears to be a factor that uniquely increased support for Bolsonaro, rather than discontent with the PT-defined status quo. This is consistent with the notion that Bolsonaro's unique embrace of radical right cultural rhetoric is more an idiosyncratic characteristic of the populist that helped him distinguish himself as the leader most thoroughly opposed to politics as usual, rather than a major source of discontent with politics itself. The direct effect of economic discontent was also a bit puzzling; it positively influenced attitudes toward Bolsonaro but not negative attitudes toward the PT. We suspect this arises from the paucity of economic attitude indicators available in this study: we rely on a retrospective evaluation that covers the period after the PT was evicted from power and thus does not reflect evaluations of the economy under PT governance.

We clarify the role of economic discontent by regressing anti-crime attitudes and anti-corruption sentiments on economic evaluation and our control variables. Economic discontent significantly influenced concern over corruption (Est. = 0.032; SE = 0.013; p = 0.012) and crime (Est. = 0.117; SE = 0.023; p = 0.000). For corruption, only education had a more pronounced influence, while economic worries were the largest influence on anti-crime attitudes; it was nearly three times as important as education, the next largest influence.

7.2.6 Conclusions: Lessons from the Rise of Bolsonaro

In short, the evidence here suggests that support for Bolsonaro was driven partly by his embrace of ethnonationalism, but also by disgust with politics as usual. This latter was more a product of concern over corruption and crime, each of which was augmented by the difficult economic environment. Bolsonaro's support was thus a coalition of social conservatives who felt ignored and threatened by the modest cultural advances under the PT as well as those who were driven primarily by discontent. This does not mean that cultural discontent was incidental: in a situation of widespread discontent on the right and a breakdown of the traditional opposition, Bolsonaro's ability to unify hardline conservatives with less ideological but discontented citizens allowed him to rise above any other potential rivals who might have hoped to raise the populist banner.

Despite the unique circumstances and details surrounding the rise of Bolsonaro, digging beneath the surface reveals dynamics that are remarkably similar to those described in Chapters 5 and 6. The causal role of economic hardship here is once again hidden underneath other, "nosier," social conflicts, in this case mostly over crime and corruption rather than race and gender. Although we cannot directly observe a Brazil where crime rates rose, *lava jato* revealed massive corruption, but the economy continued to grow, the data here (along with our theory and the support provided for it in earlier chapters) suggest that the erosion of support for the political system and the PT in particular would have been much milder during boom times. For that matter, responses might have been more muted during the bust had the boom never happened: without the elevated expectations and expansion of the strugglers during the good years, perhaps the hardship that came later would not have stung so much.

Perhaps the strongest evidence that *lava jato* was not the whole story in Brazil is the protests of 2013, which predated the scandal. These protests show conclusively that discontent was already deeply imbrued in Brazil, as the economic boom simultaneously increased demands and expectations while failing to provide the real gains in income and the public services necessary to satisfy them. The sheer volume of issues that eventually attached themselves to the protests, including everything from LGBTQ rights to the impeachment of Dilma Rousseff and even the restoration of military rule (Saad-Filho 2013), demonstrates that discontent in Brazil was both deep and wide before the *lava jato* investigation came to public attention.

The key lesson here is that responses to social crises are highly variable: when the economy is humming along (as it was during the earlier *mensalão* scandal), even serious corruption (buying legislators' votes is arguably more damning from a democratic perspective than the kickbacks and bribery of the later scandal) can elicit little more than disgusted shrugs. Without the priming of an incipient economic crisis, the anger necessary to motivate people to challenge the status quo and to take the necessary risks simply would not exist. And the situation becomes even more complex when we realize that economic crises themselves, or to be more precise popular reactions to such crises, are likewise variable, as we see in our next case.

7.3 THIRTY YEARS, NOT THIRTY PESOS: DEMOCRATIC ELITISM, ECONOMIC EVALUATIONS, AND CONTENTIOUS POLITICS IN CHILE

The emergence of the *estallido social* (social uprising) in Chile that began in October of 2019 (Disi Pavlic 2021, Somma et al. 2021) was surprisingly similar to the transit protests that rocked Brazil in

2013.[5] We do not wish to belabor a point by harping on endlessly about similarities; as such, in this section we focus on how Chile differs from Brazil, and what these differences tell us about discontent. First, Chile's economic troubles were considerably less serious than those of Brazil, partly because Chile is, thanks to a stabilization fund dictated by law, one of the few Latin American countries capable of countercyclical spending (Fuentes 2011). Reactions *to* the economic downturn, however, were comparable to those in Brazil, which compels us to analyze why Chileans were so quick to abandon economic optimism even as the Chilean state responded appropriately and responsibly to the oncoming recession.

The second major difference lies in the outcome. In Brazil, the anger embodied in the protests slowly transferred to the emerging scandals over corruption and criminal violence, eventually contributing to the election of Bolsonaro. Despite similar levels of discontent, populism proved a non-starter in Chile until very late in the game: various actors tried to use populist messaging or behavior from time to time, with limited success until the 2021 presidential elections pitted two discontented candidates against each other. Instead, contentious politics remained the primary vehicle for discontent, a strategy that proved quite effective when it forced the right-wing Piñera administration to allow a popular vote on crafting a new constitution. Only when the constituent assembly began to falter did populist and discontented political actors begin to emerge from the political fringes. To explain these divergences, we point directly to Chile's political system, which is both formally democratic and profoundly elitist.

7.3.1 The Latest Wave: Democratic Elitism and Contentious Politics in Post-Pinochet Chile

Contentious politics has a curious feature in Chile: time after time, it catches the *intelligentsia* by surprise. This was true of the 2006 wave of protests, dubbed "the march of the penguins" after the film and the uniforms of the students who initiated it, the 2007 protests over the revamping of Transantiago, the transit system in the country's largest city, and of the *estallido social*. One would think that at some point these things would become predictable.

---

[5] The line "thirty years, not thirty pesos" refers to an increase in transit fares (pesos) and Chile's lugubrious democratization process (years). Although a widely used slogan during the social uprising, we took the phrase from the title of an article by Borzutzky and Perry (2021).

The surprise has its roots in perceptions of Chile as, in the words of President Piñera, an "oasis" of stability and good governance in a region known for neither (Navia 2019, Watson 2020, Somma et al. 2021). Since the restoration of democracy in 1990, Chile has consistently out-performed its neighbors on most political and economic metrics: it has a stable party system with peaceful exchanges of power, minimal corrup-tion, an effective state, strong economic growth, and low unemployment, and it has been a leader in the developing world on poverty reduction. Given this, why would Chileans continue to engage in disruptive and occasionally violent protest against such a successful system?

These waves of contention can be understood by recognizing the price of the country's performance and stability. Chile's current con-stitution dates back to 1980, during the darkest days of the military regime, and to the pacted transition to democracy that began in 1988 (Siavelis 2016). Like most transitions of this type, the negotiated exit of the military from politics achieved greater stability (because the sup-porters of the authoritarian regime demanded protection of their inter-ests as a condition of transition) than might have occurred if the regime had collapsed. However, such concessions often hamper democratic quality (Encarnación 2005). In the Chilean case, the result was some-thing resembling a protected or "guardian" democracy (Dahl 1989, chs. 4–5), where the core constituency of the military regime was granted a plethora of institutionalized veto points (Tsebelis 1990) throughout the new democratic regime (Rhodes-Purdy 2017c, ch. 6). This veto power for conservative forces was multifaceted, working through the National Security Council (which was dominated by the military and had extensive veto power), appointed senators with lifetime tenures who came disproportionately from the ranks of military regime sup-porters and functionaries, an electoral system that advantaged the right while discouraging popular mobilization, constitutional organic laws that required supermajorities to make even modest policy changes in areas like labor relations, health care, and education, and the judicial system (Rhodes-Purdy and Rosenblatt 2021). The result was a demo-cratic system riddled with "authoritarian enclaves" (Garretón 2003), in which even the most modest of reforms or policy shifts could only be undertaken with the consent of the conservative stewards of the mili-tary regime's legacy.

Although many of these features were modified or removed as democ-racy consolidated, the fundamental elitism of the system did not change. Maintaining and exacerbating it was the growing embrace by parties of the center-left Concertation coalition of a new form of guardianship. Although the military's role has waned over time, a new set of guardians emerged: the technocrats (*los tecnicos*) – economic experts who were given a relatively free hand to manage the economy free of political influence (Silva 1991). The Concertation parties, having grown accustomed to bargaining with the right to accomplish goals and constrained by the institutions in their ability to respond to popular demands or mobilize voters, gradually severed their connection to civil society.

7.3.2 Strong Silence, System Support, and Contentious Politics

The resulting political system delivered strong policy outcomes, yet virtually all forms of citizen voice were blocked. We have discussed the role of voice as a factor that shapes the relationship we theorize, and, given its importance, we need to expand on these issues here. Previous work has shown that policy performance and voice work in an interactive manner to shape support for and attitudes toward the political system (Rhodes-Purdy 2017a, 2017b, 2017c). Specifically, strong voice increases support directly, minimizes the negative influence of poor performance on system support, and (most importantly in the Chilean context) leads to more positive perceptions of economic outcomes. We would not expect a system like Chile, with strong performance and weak voice, to have consistently high levels of discontent. Instead, as one of the authors of this book argued several years before the *estallido social*, we would expect system support that is relatively widespread but shallow, and thus dangerously vulnerable to even modest economic problems or disappointments (Rhodes-Purdy 2017c, ch. 7).

7.3.3 Economic Discontent, Voice, and the *Estallido Social*

The social uprising began in the context of a modest but significant economic downturn due to the second phase of the commodities crisis that began in 2018, as well as a transition of power from the center-left to the right-leaning government of Sebastián Piñera, who owed his election more toward frustration with the Concertation than to enduring support (Navia and Perelló 2019). As in Brazil, a small increase in transit fares (roughly 4 percent) triggered a populace already frustrated by economic decline and the high cost of living in Chile, which is a product of neglected public sector services in health, education, and pensions that force middle-class Chileans to spend significant portions of their incomes and often go deeply into debt to maintain their comfortable lifestyle (Borzutzky and Perry 2021, Disi Pavlic 2018).

A special survey by the Center for Public Studies (CEP) shortly after the crisis began found that pensions, healthcare, and education – three areas where public services are woefully inadequate and most Chileans of any means feel compelled to buy expensive private alternatives – were the three most important social problems in the country cited by respondents as the driving force behind the social uprising (Gonzalez 2019, 6). The report also shows a rapid increase in economic pessimism: immediately following Piñera's election in 2018, 27 percent of respondents described the national economic situation as "bad" or "very bad"; a year later this had increased to 56 percent (Gonzalez 2019, 9). Yet, this report also shows how economic and political issues around the social uprising are intertwined; among the most important solutions to the crisis suggested/endorsed by respondents, the most frequent include laws allowing structural political change (40 percent), drafting a new constitution (37 percent), or participatory democracy fora (37 percent), all of which were cited more frequently than reform to public services (34 percent).

7.3.4 Statistical Analysis of Voice, Performance, and the *Estallido Social*

In short, Chileans see the poor quality of public services and high prices more as symptoms, with the actual sickness found in the political system. Deeper analysis of the CEP study on the social crisis supports this. We used CFA techniques to generate several measures of interest. For PSV, no indicators were available, but the survey did include several indicators of government responsiveness, a related concept that we discuss thoroughly in Chapter 8 (survey items: policies reflect the majority will, people like me get what they want from the political system, parties' policies reflect the majority will). We also produced CFA-constructed indices of systemic confidence (confidence in government, congress, public administration, and approval of congress), economic distress (1–10 scale questions regarding how much respondent worries about being able to pay debts, afford healthcare, afford schooling for their children (if they have children), and about finding or keeping a job), and ideology (incomes should be made more equal, state is responsible for economic well-being

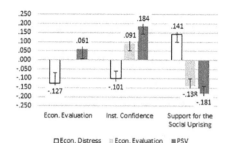

FIGURE 7.2 Analysis of economic evaluation, distress, systemic confidence, and support for the uprising.

of the public, success depends on luck and contacts).[6] We also include a measure of the current evaluation of the national economy, a five-point measure of support for the social uprising, and a yes/no measure of participation in a protest related to the uprising.

Our theory is that both economic discontent and a lack of PSV contributed to the social uprising and the lack of systemic confidence that contributed to it. We also argue that low PSV influences how people perceive and react to national economic dynamics. As such, we performed the following analyses: economic distress and economic evaluation were regressed on PSV (economic distress was also included as a predictor for economic evaluation), and systemic confidence and support for the social uprising regressed on PSV, economic distress, and economic discontent. The results are presented in Figure 7.2.

The results here are largely consistent with our theory. PSV, as expected, positively influenced national economic evaluation. Economic evaluation and PSV both positively influenced systemic confidence and negatively influences support for the social uprising, while economic distress displayed the opposite pattern, as expected. PSV and economic discontent also influenced respondents' behavior; namely, whether they had ever participated in a protest related to the uprising. We conducted a logit analysis to estimate these effects; charts of the predicted probabilities of protesting are displayed in Figure 7.3. The results were consistent with those found using ordinary regression: moving from minimum

---

[6] We use this unusual measure of ideology because the vast majority of Chileans do not identify with either an ideological tendency (72 percent) or a political party (86 percent), which is in and of itself a sign of the disgust most Chileans feel towards their political system and politics in general.

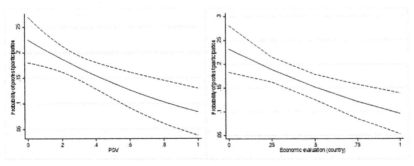

FIGURE 7.3 Logit analysis of protest behavior.

to maximum on PSV cut the probability of protesting by almost two-thirds, while moving from minimum to maximum on economic discontent (measured by economic evaluation) decimated the probability of protesting.

7.3.5 Wither Populism? Norms, Institutions, and Channels of Discontent

Given the combination of economic pressure on the middle sectors, a modest but significant recession, and a complete lack of institutional voice, the *estallido social* was the very antithesis of surprising; in fact, it was practically inevitable. What *is* surprising is the lack of any populist manifestation of that discontent even as various actors have dipped their toes into the populist pool. Marco Enríquez-Ominami, a left-leaning businessman, has attempted to run independent and third-party presidential campaigns on anti-party platforms several times, but gained little traction. The new Broad Front (FA Chile) coalition, which includes parties like Democratic Revolution that are closely associated with the student movement, came within two percentage points of making the second round of presidential elections in 2017, while José Antonio Kast, from the opposite side of the ideological spectrum, also had limited success. Yet Chileans remained surprisingly cool to the messages of these would-be populists until 2021, when Kast and the Boric (of FA Chile) both advanced to the second round, leaving the major parties behind for the first time (Aguilar and Carlin 2017).[7]

---

[7] There are signs that appetites for outsiders may be growing, partially owing to an opening of the political system due to the Constitutional Convention.

The significant delay in the emergence of populist entrepreneurs is one question on which we cannot provide a definitive answer. The data required to conduct such analysis are simply not available, and comparative analysis can only provide limited leverage on a case-specific idiosyncrasy. We do have several possible reasons why the populist channel for discontent seems to be blocked in Chile, including the strong taboo against populism that developed as a result of the trauma of the Allende government and the collapse of democracy that ended it (Meléndez and Rovira Kaltwasser 2017). The possibility of FR populism has also likely been precluded in Chile by the country's relative ethnic and racial homogeneity, and by the presence of a profoundly socially conservative but nonpopulist party, the Independent Democrat Union (UDI). Neither explanation is perfect. Taboos are endogenous, as Spain demonstrated; they can erode and wither away when underlying pressure becomes too intense to hold back. And UDI has, despite the structural advantages of the right, had little success in slowing the advance of cultural progressivism pushed by the Concertation. This is due in part to tensions within the party over its identity, which is split between a culturally revanchist, authoritarian, and Catholic nationalist old guard and a newer cadre of nouveau riche leaders who are driven by commitment to neoliberalism and are less than enthusiastic, even somewhat embarrassed, by their *Opus Dei* elders.

We consider the most important factor to be the demonstrated effectiveness of contention over populist voting in achieving policy change. Chile's major coalitions have grown closer programmatically over time despite the growing polarization of society, failing to respond to popular demands as a matter of course (Madariaga and Rovira Kaltwasser 2020). The only time the parties have made consistent concessions is in the immediate aftermath of major bouts of contention. Even as parties outside the Concertation have grown in stature, the Chilean political system has long been uniquely inhospitable to third forces. The recently repealed binomial electoral system artificially manufactured majorities for large, moderate parties more efficiently than either plurality or D'hondt PR systems. The majority runoff system for presidential elections has a concomitant effect. Taken together, there were few opportunities for a third coalition, even one with substantial popular support, to force real changes in government policy.

While Chile appeared to be a significant outlier when we began this process, by the time this book was finished Chile's invulnerability to populism had waned; the 2021 runoff election pitted PRR José Antonio Kast against Gabriel Boric, a former leader of the student movement whose platform was not explicitly populist but certainly evinced considerable discontent with Chile's political, economic, and social systems. Chile's shift from outlier to a more typical case is a reminder that discontent is a process, one where each outbreak of discontent, whatever its form, tends to wear away system support and expose the weakness of mainstream political actors. Repeated waves of protest gradually forced reforms to the system (especially the electoral system), and eventually forced the initiation of the Constitutional Convention. This new forum provided a chance to break decisively with the democratic status quo, and the collapse of mainstream parties in elections for the constituent assembly exposed the weakness of Chile's formerly dominant parties.

Optimism over the assembly might have had the same effect as earlier concessions, namely depriving populists of oxygen and preserving the core of the political system. Yet as the assembly's work dragged on, some of its members were engulfed by scandal (e.g. a major leader of the left coalition was found to have lied for about a cancer diagnosis), and the incipient Covid-19 crisis only raised increasing doubts about the ability of the convention to produce structural transformation. With faith in even the ability of a new constitution to provide meaningful change waning and the major parties shown to be giants with clay feet, outsider candidates finally got the widespread consideration they had long been denied. In short, discontent in Chile took perhaps a bit longer to evolve from contention to electoral channels than in other cases, but once barriers to outsiders were either removed or shown to be paper tigers, Chile's politics began to resemble those of other Latin American countries during the commodities crisis.

7.4 CONCLUSIONS

Although separated by six years, the bouts of discontented politics in Chile and Brazil shared remarkably similar contexts and trajectories that were consistent with APE, albeit with significant differences in the details. In a sense, both countries were victims of their own economic success: two increasingly middle-class societies successfully moved millions of people out of poverty, which ended up revealing profound failures that success had, for a time, remained hidden. In each case, economic pain caused by either recession or slowdown exposed these weaknesses while also forcing other social issues like crime, corruption, and inequality to the surface. But these should not be overstated; discontent may have arisen from similar stimuli but manifested in ways that could not have been more different.

With this in mind, we conclude this chapter by drawing attention to two factors we have not yet discussed. First, these cases paradoxically expanded our theory's reach while also highlighting some important limitations. Brazil and Chile demonstrate that social issues beyond the typical postmodern milieu of race and identity can be exacerbated and politicized during economic crises. Yet APE would not have predicted why we should see the PRR suddenly appear in a region where such ideas had never been very important, nor why Chileans would for so long forego populism in favor of repeated bouts of contentious politics. In short, APE can explain why discontent rises in specific contexts, but it is (to borrow a phrase from the ideational approach to populism) a thin-centered framework. To truly understand outcomes in specific cases, APE must be fleshed out with contextual factors, especially the flow of recent political history. Brazil embraced a leader from the PRR because the PT took tentative steps to politicize postmaterialist issues during its tenure, thus allowing Bolsonaro to construct an emotional coalition of conservative and discontented Brazilians by positioning himself as the negative image of everything associated with the PT. Chileans turned to contention because nothing else, including supporting political outsiders at the polls, could deliver the same results until recently. Even though we rely heavily on quantitative data throughout this book, in this instance we hope to emphasize the continuing importance of case-focused qualitative data and research; were we to use only one method or the other, our understanding of real-world political outcomes would be profoundly impoverished.

The second factor we must address here is that, although the subjective stimuli (economic discontent) was similar and consistent with our approach across cases, the objective economic factors were not. In short, Brazil had a crisis, Chile a relative bump in the road. Chileans reacted with fury over what was objectively a very minor economic downturn, compared to their Brazilian counterparts who confronted a genuinely devastating recession. Chileans also took great umbrage over corruption toward the end of the Bachelet administration, even though the alleged malfeasance in that case when compared to *lava jato* in Brazil amounted to using the wrong fork during the salad course. The obvious question is a sort of inversion of the typical political science puzzle: why are there such similar perceptions and reactions to such drastically different stimuli?

The key lesson here is simple: perceptions matter. Objective reality has a major influence on economic attitudes: both Brazil and Chile did suffer significant erosions in living standards, after all. Yet Chileans did not see their slowdown as minor, because it intensified outrage and frustration over all the economic and social problems that had not improved along with unemployment and poverty over the years. Chile also reveals a key insight into *why* perceptions can become so negative in response to such mild macroeconomic troubles: the failure of democracy to fulfill its promises of popular sovereignty, of giving citizens collective control over their lives. This factor explains why Chile, a case with perhaps the most modest economic downturn among the cases we study, erupted in ire nevertheless. In Chapter 8, we combine both of these lessons (i.e. the importance of qualitative analysis and the subjectivity of economic discontent) to try and explain an opposing puzzle: why some countries avoided major episodes of discontent during much more serious economic downturns.

8

The Dogs That Did Not Bark

How Canada, Portugal, and Uruguay Avoided Discontent

Considering the severity of the economic crises that struck the world during the 2010s, the surge of democratic discontent in Europe and the Americas was hardly shocking. The surprising countries were those that did *not* face major episodes of political turmoil. Such cases are rare because the crises of the 2010s spared very few countries in Europe and the Americas. But their existence provides an opportunity to analyze the conditions under which the relationship between economic turmoil and democratic discontent fails to take its usual course. In this chapter, we conduct a comparative case study of three such "negative" cases, each of which pairs with the cases covered in earlier chapters: Canada (the USA and UK), Portugal (Spain), and Uruguay (Chile and Brazil). The negative designation does not mean discontent is totally absent from these cases. Canada has long had regional FR and populist actors, Uruguay's domi-nant party lost its hold on the presidency and saw the emergence of a new socially conservative party, and an FR party managed to get a single seat in Portugal's parliament during the time period analyzed here. Yet none of these parties rose to a level of support or prominence sufficient to truly threaten the political status quo, which is what distinguishes them from our "positive" cases.

Why the difference? The simplest explanation would be that the nega-tive cases suffered less economic damage than our positive cases, but the evidence does not support this: Canada's recession was mild, but Portugal suffered one of the worst downturns in Europe. Understanding outcomes in our negative cases requires recognizing the subjectivity of economic discontent. After all, people do not turn against their political systems after careful perusal of economic reports; they do so because they fear for their livelihoods and seethe at those they blame for their troubles and those of their country. In short, discontent is in the eye of the beholder, and as macroeconomic factors do not satisfactorily explain the nonemergence of discontent in these cases, we focus instead on factors that can shape subjective perceptions of economic outcomes.

Throughout this book, we have alluded to the role that a lack of democratically guaranteed voice played in exacerbating the crises we study. Thus far, we have examined countries with party systems that were either rigid or inchoate and where ordinary citizens had little capacity to force elites to respond to their demands. In this chapter, we find a mirrored pattern. While the democratic systems in these countries were not all paragons of voice and popular empowerment, their party systems did respond to new circumstances by adapting and channeling citizen demands, especially for some departure from the status quo, while our positive cases clung to obsolete political norms and practices. All three negative cases departed from neoliberal orthodoxy in significant ways, and in each case those decisions were driven by greater political responsiveness than we saw in corresponding positive cases. Deviation from neoliberalism due to party system dynamism is the only factor all three of our negative cases share and which all our positive cases lack. Combined with our individual-level analyses presented in Chapters 4–7 and further experimental evidence presented here, all of which emphasize the role of voice in mitigating discontent, we point to this political variable as the key factor that determined whether countries would (relatively) smoothly sail through troubled waters or be sunk by discontent.

8.1 WHERE DID THE ECONOMY GO? MACROECONOMIC FACTORS AND NATIONAL OUTCOMES

Given the overriding importance of economic discontent in our theory, the most obvious place to look first for an explanation of country-level dynamics is to macroeconomic factors. While intuitive, this approach suffers from a significant problem: individuals do not evaluate economic outcomes objectively. Scholarship on economic voting (Anderson 2007, Conover and Feldman 1986, Gerber and Huber 2010) and organizational justice (Magalhães and Aguiar-Conraria 2018, Rhodes-Purdy 2021c) has shown that various factors distort individual perceptions of economic outcomes, although objective reality does have an influence on those evaluations as well (Nadeau, Lewis-Beck, and Bélanger 2012).

8.1.1 Looking for Patterns: A Preliminary Case Analysis

The fact that macroeconomic outcomes do not totally determine mass perceptions is borne out when we analyze the two most likely conditions that might explain a national-level eruption of discontent: unusually severe recessions and unusually stingy welfare spending/social insurance. The role of the former is fairly obvious (more economic trauma equals more economic discontent), while Bermeo and Bartels (2014) argue that robust social welfare and protection insulates populations from the pain of macroeconomic fluctuations. Table 8.1 includes all eight countries of interest here, coded by these two factors. We coded each country's recession as "severe" or "mild" based on the economic data presented throughout this book. Welfare state generosity was coded based on each country's position vis-à-vis the Organisation for Economic Co-operation and Development (OECD) average except for the USA, Brazil, and Uruguay. The last two are not part of the OECD, but Uruguay is famous for its robust and generous welfare state. Brazil's generosity increased during the Lula years but is still typical for Latin America. The USA was close to the OECD average but lacks the support for things like health and childcare that are common features of other advanced democracies and social programs tend to be aggressively means-tested.[1]

These data provide little insight into the economic origins of discontent; they show that discontent came for those who suffered and those who got off relatively easy, and for misers and spendthrifts alike. Severity of recession was common among our positive cases, but it was neither a necessary nor sufficient condition. Portugal avoided discontent despite suffering as much as any eurozone country, while modestly impacted Chile eventually overturned its foundational document. Welfare state strength yielded slightly better results. Although discontented countries run the gamut from stingy to generous, we observe no misers in our negative cases. And the only generous case among our positive cases – Spain – had to significantly retrench its social spending as part of its bailout proceedings. In other words, the protective influence of welfare states may be apparent here but is easily undermined by its endogeneity. When a severe crisis knocks national budgets into the red, social spending often gets slashed and thus loses its insulating properties. All told, we see some

---

[1] Coding the US as average on welfare state generosity would not change any of the conclusions drawn from the comparative analyses.

TABLE 8.1 *Table of macroeconomic factors and discontent outcomes*

Country	Recession	Welfare state	Discontent
Positive cases			
USA	Severe	Stingy	Yes
UK	Severe	Average	Yes
Spain	Severe	Generous	Yes
Brazil	Severe	Average	Yes
Chile	Mild	Stingy	Yes
Negative cases			
Canada	Mild	Average	No
Portugal	Severe	Generous	No
Uruguay	Mild	Generous	No

thin evidence in favor of Bermeo and Bartels' (2014) hypothesis that a robust welfare state can insulate societies from economic fallout, but that evidence is far from conclusive.

8.1.2 Mining an Outlier: Voice, Economic Perceptions, and Discontent in Chile

What we find in Section 8.1.1, when combined with the individual-level analyses presented in Chapters 5–7, is yet another paradox: economics clearly matter at the micro level, yet those effects are not apparent at the macro level. To unravel this paradox, we turn to the one case that breaks the pattern of mild recession leading away from discontent: Chile. At first, Chile only deepens the paradox further. Here we have a country with perhaps the mildest economic downturn of any of our cases, yet its discontent is also the most unambiguously economic of all our positive cases. The social uprising was triggered by transit fees, and survey data presented in Chapter 7 showed that concerns over public services and economic inequality were paramount in the minds of those who supported the movement. Even in cases like Spain and the USA, where anti-austerity movements and leaders became important political actors, the clarity of economic origins is complicated by the presence of powerful and culturally oriented FR movements and leaders.

The obvious question here is why Chileans rebelled against their country's economic model, despite the model's apparent success in weathering the damage of the commodities crisis? In Chapter 7, we argued that political concerns amplified and intensified anger against the model's failings: the lack of support for all but the very poorest, the need for middle-class families to go ever deeper into debt to pay for high-quality private services (and avoid their bare-bones public counterparts), and of course appalling levels of inequality even by regional standards. We keep this in mind as we begin to analyze our "negative" cases, making a simple leap of logic: if a lack of democratic responsiveness can explain excessive discontent in Chile, perhaps responsiveness can help explain the near absence of discontent in Canada, Portugal, and Uruguay?

8.1.3 Voice, Responsiveness, and Inoculation against Discontent

It would be easy to miss the political similarities across our negative cases. Although all three countries evinced dynamic political responses to their respective crises, they share little else. Within these three countries, we find presidential and parliamentary systems, PR and single-member district systems, as well as a host of economic, cultural, social, and historical differences. Yet in each case, political parties facing institutional incentives and constraints did what their peers could not: they adapted to radically altered circumstances and to satisfy public demands for a new path. We find two distinct paths toward party system dynamism in these countries. The first (in Uruguay) involves the broad provision of strong voice through what we have in prior works called "continuous democracy" (Rhodes-Purdy and Rosenblatt 2021). In continuous democracy, institutional rules guarantee citizens a direct and active role in politics on an ongoing basis (i.e. not limited to periodic elections). The second path is more mundane, relying simply on representation and accountability. In Canada and Portugal, competition between parties of the left, combined with imperatives of parliamentary politics and the dynamics of government formation, placed unusually strong pressure on left-wing parties to shake off neoliberal orthodoxy and adopt innovative responses to the crises. In each case, whatever the specific institutional mechanisms, the result was the same: responsive parties adapted to crises rather than being overwhelmed by them.

We do not argue here that the crises of the Great Recession era inaugurated a substantial and clear ideological shift away from neoliberalism or toward economic leftism among ordinary people. There is little evidence in cross-national surveys of any such shift. This is not very surprising; scholars of economic behavior have known at least since the beginning of the modern era of survey research that ideologies of ordinary citizens are often inchoate and exert only weak influence on policy preferences (Campbell, Gurin, and Miller 1954). For our purposes, we do not see citizens demanding concrete policies (although some movements did castigate specific austerity policies once they had been proposed or implemented), so much as making vague demands for "change" or "a new direction," and later responding negatively to political actors who kept to "politics as usual" and responding positively toward parties they saw as breaking with the past.

8.1.4 Voice and Discontent: Experimental Evidence

We rely primarily in this chapter on comparative analysis to demonstrate the importance of voice, but we can provide some a priori justification for our focus on this factor using experimental data collected in the United States. We conducted two experiments, both using respondents recruited via the Lucid Theorem platform, to test the influence of voice on various elements of discontent.[2]

The treatment used in these studies was a writing exercise that asked respondents to remember a time when they felt like their voice was not heard in this country, like nothing they did could have any effect on the political or social situation. In one study, we also attempted to induce greater PSV in respondents using a parallel exercise, but this treatment failed. Analyzing the written responses, this can be attributed to the fact that many respondents simply could not remember or imagine a time when their voices would be heard. As such we do not report the results of this treatment, except to say that it had no detectable influence on any dependent variable included in any study, including measures of PSV, thus indicating the treatment failed rather than a lack of relationship.

In the first such study (Lucid Voice/Regime Support) we included the two voice treatments (the negative and the failed positive) as well as a control condition (a writing exercise about brushing teeth). We then asked 1,141 US resident adults recruited via Lucid Theorem to complete one of the three exercises. After the exercise we asked a series of questions about voice (including PSV and measures of government responsiveness), regime support, and regime performance, using measures discussed earlier, which we then regressed on the treatments. Effects of

---

[2] Balance statistics and other ancillary details of the analyses are presented in the online appendix: https://dataverse.harvard.edu/dataverse/ageofdiscontent/.

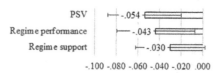

FIGURE 8.1 Effects of Negative Voice (PSV) treatment on regime support and regime performance.

the Negative Voice treatment with 95 percent confidence intervals are presented in Figure 8.1.

The treatment did have a significant, negative influence on PSV, indicating modest success at triggering a sense of political silencing. This lack of voice also significantly contributed to a decline in evaluation of regime performance and a marginally significant (p = 0.068) decline in regime support. These results suggest that voice influences regime support both directly and through the influence of voice on perceptions of regime performance (Rhodes-Purdy 2021c).

These results likely underestimate the influence of voice in some circumstances. As discussed in Chapter 3, voice is hypothesized to influence political discontent directly, but also through its ability to reduce negative reactions to undesirable political outcomes or threats. To test this possibility, we conducted another experiment (Lucid Voice/Populism) which recruited 467 US resident adults via the Lucid Theorem platform. For this experiment we have two factors, with two levels of each factor: a voice factor (the Control and Negative Voice treatment from the earlier study), and a Threat factor, which asked respondents to read a brief statement prepared by experts about the immediate future of the United States. In the "No Threat" level, this statement was optimistic:

This country has seen some difficult times lately, but things are improving rapidly. The end of the Covid-19 pandemic is on the horizon. Businesses are hiring again. It's looking more and more as though the financial damage done to individuals, businesses, and state and local governments is reversing and will continue to improve for the foreseeable future. We've been through a very dark time, but our future appears very bright.

The "Threat" level presented a parallel statement that was much more pessimistic:

This country has seen some difficult times lately, but things are only going to get worse. The end of the Covid-19 pandemic is coming but much too slowly to undo all the damage. Businesses have been very slow to hire. It's looking more and

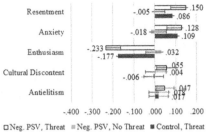

FIGURE 8.2 Effects of Negative Voice (PSV) and threat treatments on emotions, cultural discontent, and populism.

more as though the financial damage done to individuals, businesses, and state and local governments will continue to worsen for the foreseeable future. We've been through a very dark time, and there's no end in sight.

We then regressed several measures of important concepts from our theory (resentment, anxiety, enthusiasm, anti-elitism, and our combined cultural discontent measure)[3] on these treatments. Treatment effects are presented in Figure 8.2.

The sheer quantity of results and treatments here can make interpretation difficult, but the results generally confirm that the combination of low PSV and threat has a uniquely potent influence on discontent and its various antecedents. For the emotions, threat seems to be the primary direct driver: even the Control, Threat condition significantly increased both resentment and anxiety, while also significantly dampening enthusiasm. However, in each case the change was larger when Threat combined with the Negative Voice condition. This was especially pronounced for resentment, where the amount of resentment when exposed to threat nearly doubled from the control (0.086) to Negative Voice conditions (0.150). For cultural discontent and anti-elitism, on the other hand, the combination of these two factors seems to be necessary for either to exert any influence. In both cases, the Negative Voice without Threat and Threat without Negative Voice had negligible effects on these measures of discontent. When these two factors combine, however, the effect magnifies considerably and becomes statistically detectable. This fits with both our theory and with prior work showing that voice often conditions the relationships that produce various forms of discontent, which can also be seen in the results for anti-elitism

---

[3] We exclude people centrism as none of the treatments significantly affected this measure and eliminating it helped reduce the complexity of an already crowded graph.

and cultural discontent, both of which were only significantly influenced by the low PSV, Threat treatment.

Taken in tandem with results from the PSAS studies in earlier chapters, as well as results from previous studies, we have good reason to suppose that voice may explain discrepancies between economic outcomes and discontent. In the remainder of this chapter, we analyze our three negative cases with the role of voice firmly in mind. We focus on how the course of events interacted with institutions and party system dynamics to produce unusually robust voice, whether strong (Uruguay) or weak (Canada and Portugal).

8.2 STRONG VOICE AND CONTINUOUS DEMOCRACY IN URUGUAY

Of all our negative cases, Uruguay has the most comprehensive institutional mechanisms for ensuring strong voice. The country developed unusually participatory institutions and parties thanks to a unique political history. During the twentieth century, Uruguay was dominated by two forces. The first was a duopolistic party system where power was largely controlled by the center-left Colorado Party (the Colorados) and the center-right National Party (the Blancos). The second was the legacy and sociopolitical thought of José Batlle y Ordóñez, often referred to simply as Batlle, and of Batllism (*batllismo*), his ideology and political legacy. It would be difficult to overestimate Batlle's prominence in Uruguay's political history. He is seen as the founder of modern Uruguay, the leader who shaped its democracy and vaunted welfare state, creating the closest thing Latin America has to a genuine social democracy. Although the Colorados and the Blancos took the relative positions one would expect from a left- and right-leaning party respectively, neither force, nor the military regime that ruled the country from 1973 to 1985, seriously challenged the fundamental role of the Batllist welfare state (Castiglioni 2005), which had become a point of national pride for a small country in a region awash in inequality and poverty.

8.2.1 Neoliberalism and Mechanisms for Direct Democracy (MDDs)

Despite the continuing power of Batllism and the veneration of its creator's legacy, Uruguay faced enormous pressure to adopt neoliberal reforms during the 1990s, to which both Colorado and Blanco governments eventually bowed. Here Uruguay's path diverges from the rest of

Latin America, thanks in large part to its unusually robust democratic institutions. Uruguay had incorporated a variety of MDDs into its constitutional system since the 1960s, including referenda and initiatives, but they were not utilized often until the return of democracy in 1985 (Altman 2011, loc. 3716). We do not wish to overstate the importance of MDDs generally; several studies have found that such mechanisms are more effective at preserving an existing status quo than promoting policy change or innovation (Christin, Hug, and Sciarini 2002, Altman 2011, loc. 4200). Yet in the context of the neoliberal era, when political elites were often far more enthusiastic (or at least accepting) of uncertain and untested reforms than were their constituents, the conservative leaning of MDDs was more an asset than a hindrance. Through a provision allowing citizens to repeal laws passed by the Uruguayan congress via an initiative process, citizens were able to overturn certain provisions of neoliberalization, including pension reforms and some aspects of privatization (Altman 2011, loc. 3795).

In other words, MDDs allowed citizens to hold the processes of neoliberal structural reform (or at least the most objectionable elements thereof) at bay. This did not alter the fact that Uruguay's combination of strong social welfare and ISI had been under strain since midcentury, and was not sustainable in the long term (Pérez Bentancur, Piñeiro Rodríguez, and Rosenblatt 2019, 75). MDDs were, given their conservative tendencies, not well suited for crafting nor implementing solutions to the challenges created by global economic change.

8.2.2 Organizing Anti-neoliberal Resistance: The Role of the Broad Front

Even the limited institutional resource of MDDs would likely have been insufficient to guard against neoliberal erosion of democracy in Uruguay without help. Despite their growing use, the legal requirements for activating MDDs were quite stringent (Altman 2011, loc. 3724); as a result, their use essentially required the backing of social organizations or parties. In the case of Uruguay in the 1990s, the difficulty of activating MDDs could have proved a barrier to popular control over politics, but also carved out a potential role for an insurgent political movement. MDDs provided a meaningful and direct role for citizens who were fed up with establishment parties' uncritical embrace of neoliberalism, but also gave purpose and necessity to the organizations and movements outside the mainstream whose structure was necessary for MDDs to be effective.

This space in the political system was quickly filled by the Broad Front (Frente Amplio, FA). A detailed discussion of the party's history is beyond the scope of this chapter,[4] but briefly put, the party emerged from an alliance of leftist parties and dissident popular factions of both the Colorados and Blancos. After the end of military rule, many ex-militants from the country's small but determined left-wing insurgency of the 1960s and 1970s also joined the movement. Although a minor political force at first, the FA gained prominence in part through its support of the use of MDDs to resist structural adjustment, which proved crucial (Monestier 2011).

This support had substantial benefits for the FA beyond blocking economic policies it opposed. Its activism in support of MDDs "positioned the party as the single political actor on the center-left of the ideological spectrum" (Pérez Bentancur, Piñeiro Rodríguez, and Rosenblatt 2019, 77) and forged and augmented ties between the party and social movements (Bidegain and Tricot 2017). Although many factors contributed to the rise of the FA, it is fairly clear that its role in successfully opposing the least popular elements of economic liberalization aided and accelerated the party's electoral trajectory: the FA increased its vote share in the first round of presidential elections from 21.3 percent in 1984 to 44.7 percent in 2004, when the party first took control of the government.

8.2.3 The Institutional and Historical Origins of Voice

One can easily imagine a situation in which the FA, having taken the reins of power, followed the trajectory of countless other left parties in Latin America: first abandoning resistance to neoliberalism under international pressure and out of fear of having to face the electoral consequences and risks of bucking global economic orthodoxy, then following the natural tendency of party elites to increase their control over their organizations. The FA did the first to a degree, shifting away from its earlier commitment to state socialism, ISI, and other discredited alternatives. But where most center-left parties in Latin America largely bowed to the logic of neoliberalism, the FA embraced something very similar to Scandinavian-style social democracy: markets would become the primary mechanism of the economy, but they would also be overseen by a strong regulatory apparatus, moderated through a robust and universalistic welfare

---

[4] For an excellent and thorough analysis of the FA, see Pérez Bentancur, Piñeiro Rodríguez, and Rosenblatt (2019).

state with progressive taxation, and politically balanced through strong unions and social organizations.

How did the FA avoid the erosion of its leftist principles? Pérez Bentancur, Piñeiro Rodríguez, and Rosenblatt (2019) treat this question at great length, pointing to a combination of party structure and political institutions. From its inception, the FA was organized as a "mass-organic leftist party" (Pérez Bentancur, Piñeiro Rodríguez, and Rosenblatt 2019, 161), where decision-making authority flowed from base-level grassroots organizations and militants upward, rather than down from party leaders. Activists are represented at every level of the party and have a direct role in every aspect of party decision-making, from strategy to platform formation. Furthermore, party bylaws require a nine-tenths supermajority to alter this structure (Pérez Bentancur, Piñeiro Rodríguez, and Rosenblatt 2019, 186). In practice, this meant that no matter how expedient it might have been at one time or another, nor how tempting for party elites who would prefer to act unilaterally without having to justify the actions to grassroots militants, elite capture would have been virtually impossible. This foreclosed the possibility of the "iron law of oligarchy" (Michels 2001) playing out as it did with other mass-organic left parties after they achieved success, such as the PT in Brazil (Pérez Bentancur, Piñeiro Rodríguez, and Rosenblatt 2019, 55). Furthermore, party structures provide activists and members with a profound sense of voice and efficacy, promoting their loyalty during difficult periods and leading them to accept controversial or costly decisions (Pérez Bentancur, Piñeiro Rodríguez, and Rosenblatt 2018). This has helped the party maintain support during the current era, where economic decline threatened the party's platform.

Of course, this raises the question of why the FA, weighed down by the empowerment of its social base as organized labor declined and society diversified, did not simply collapse or fade into obscurity. There is, after all, a reason why virtually all other leftist mass parties in Latin America forsook ideology and converted to catchall parties during this time period: doing so was typically necessary to maintain electoral viability. On this point the FA was supported by the formal institutions of democracy, which in Uruguay are uniquely hospitable to parties with strong popular bases. Uruguayan elections have two relevant peculiarities: the fused ballot and the double simultaneous vote (DSV). Elections operate using proportional representation, but rather than voting for parties (as in closed-list PR) or ranking candidates within parties (as in open-list PR), voters select lists of candidates within parties. These lists are named factions (in the case of the FA, parties within the Broad Front's permanent coalition). Parliamentary seats are then apportioned to parties and then to lists within parties. So, if a party receives 40 percent of the vote, and a list within that party receives 20 percent of votes for the party, that list receives roughly 8 percent of the seats in the lower house. The presidency is awarded to the candidate of the most voted list in the most voted party; the fused ballot requires that citizens vote for the same list and party for both presidential and parliamentary elections.[5]

This system has two effects. It is arguably the most proportional electoral system in the democratic world, and certainly the most in Latin America. As such, it tends to privilege parties with highly committed voters rather than parties with broad but shallow appeal. Furthermore, the DSV allows factions within parties to remain unified while still maintaining their own identities and brands, while providing a transparent and legitimate electoral mechanism for settling disputes between factions. The fused ballot inhibits the worst pathologies of presidentialism by ensuring presidents have strong parliamentary support (although not necessarily governing majorities) and by tying the fate of presidential candidates to that of their parties, thus reducing the risk of personalism.

8.2.4 The FA during the Age of Discontent

In most of the other cases we have reviewed, a major factor in the hollowing out of democracy was the gradual disconnection of left-wing parties from the working class. The combination of permissive institutions and party rules allowed the FA to avoid this path. Popular-sector party militants maintain control of every aspect of the party and are well represented in its candidate lists in numbers not seen anywhere else in Latin America. As a result, the FA is an unusually effective mechanism for continuous democracy. The other major parties in Uruguay are not as participatory as the FA, but they are also well organized and responsive to the demands of their base-level militants (Rosenblatt 2018). Simply put, Uruguay is a democracy where strong voice is maximized, and as a result it consistently ranks among the highest in Latin America for satisfaction with democracy and regime support.

This is not to say that Uruguay is immune to the difficulties posed by the commodities crisis. The recession made the FA's ambitious economic reform program more difficult and led to a rise in both the deficit and

---

[5] Unless no candidate achieves a majority, in which case the top-two such candidates participate in a second-round runoff.

crime,[6] both of which have become contentious issues in recent years. In the most recent election in 2019, the FA was narrowly evicted from government in favor of the Blancos.

Potentially more troubling, a new right-wing party called Open Meeting (Cabildo Abierto, CA) entered the electoral arena in 2019, gaining 11.46 percent of the vote. Some have pointed to the CA as part of a trend in Latin America toward right-wing populism, lumping it in with Bolsonaro in Brazil (Melgar 2019). This is understandable but largely misinterprets the nature of the CA, which is certainly socially conservative and nationalistic but is neither populist nor system-opposing. The party abides by electoral rules and is a well-organized and functional vehicle for those, particularly among the poorer sectors of society, who embrace Batllism but spurn cultural liberalism (Montestier, Nocetto, and Rosenblatt 2021). The CA is in many ways an odd party, drawing support from all three major parties, including a substantial portion (24.8 percent) from the left-wing FA.[7] The party has strong support from members of Uruguay's military (its leader, Manini Ríos, is a former general), but party leaders have long had surprisingly cordial relationships with the ex-guerillas who lead the FA. The CA largely supports the Batllist welfare state and the FA's economic policies, but it strongly opposes the FA's increasing liberalism on postmaterialist issues like abortion, gay rights, and gender issues (Rosenblatt 2021).

The party's rise is a constructive example of why context matters in politics. While the CA shares the social conservatism of the radical right, it does not properly belong to that family of parties and its rise is little more than the natural outcome of a new policy cleavage in a highly open democratic system, and by granting such a movement voice, its influence is unlikely to spread beyond a relatively small group of doctrinaire social conservatives. The 2019 election certainly displayed citizen dissatisfaction with the FA government (although its candidate nearly prevailed in the presidential election, losing by only a few points in the second round). However, there is no evidence of any serious erosion of regime support, nor of surging discontent. FR parties thrive when they can unify right-leaning but mostly apolitical citizens who are disgusted with politics as usual with true believers; in Uruguay, the latter group is in very short supply.

---

[6] Source: www.bbc.com/news/world-latin-america-50138945.

[7] www.elobservador.com.uy/nota/el-24-del-electorado-de-manini-rios-voto-al-fa-en-2014-segun-cifra-201910312150.

8.2.5 Conclusion: Is Uruguay Unique or Informative?

Most readers have probably already gathered that Uruguay is an exceptional case. This is, analytically speaking, a double-edged sword: unique cases can throw relationships into sharp relief, but drawing inferences from them to more typical countries can be questionable. Many readers may wonder how much can we learn from a small country with a peculiar political history? We would contest the idea that Uruguay's participatory democracy is directly the result of its small size, nor totally determined by its history. Both contributed, but it was the combination of party rules and democratic institutions that produce strong voice. Yet for this study the question is especially relevant: if the Uruguayan standard of voice and continuous democracy is required to ameliorate discontent, then the country is analytically useless because of the improbity that any other country would meet this standard.

As we move our focus to Portugal and Canada, we see that this is not the case. These countries show that even much weaker forms of voice, engendered by much more common features of democratic institutions and political history, can be sufficient to stave off discontent. Still more heartening, this protective effect appears to hold even if the economic crisis exerting pressure on the political system is particularly severe.

8.3 TIMING IS EVERYTHING: INTRA-LEFT DIVISIONS, GOVERNMENT FORMATION, AND RESPONSIVENESS IN PORTUGAL AND CANADA

While Canada and Portugal differ in any number of ways, they share a combination of conditions that allowed them to avoid the fate of their counterparts, the USA/UK and Spain. Party systems that were moderately representative, government formation politics, and political learning through both experience and replacement of key personnel compelled the major parties of the left to move with the times, while Labour, the Democrats, and the Spanish socialists stood still. In other words, the political situation in these countries differed in only minor respects from that of their corresponding positive cases, but a combination of satisfactory (but not exceptional) representation and good timing made all the difference.

The comparison of Canada and Portugal gives us some extra leverage because their crises were so different: Canada suffered a pair of relatively modest downturns, including a recession related to the 2008 financial collapse and a slowdown triggered by the commodities crisis in 2013–2016.

Portugal, on the other hand, was one of the few eurozone countries to experience a genuine sovereign debt crisis and thus suffered one of the worst crises in the western hemisphere. That even reasonable levels of representation compelled parties to respond to citizen demands for new kinds of politics allows us to end this chapter on a heartening note, as it suggests that modest democratic reforms might yield significant returns.

8.3.1 Leftist Monopoly, Choice, and Responsiveness

Neither Portugal nor Canada can be considered paragons of representation. Through different electoral system characteristics (single-member district in Canada and D'Hondt PR with small district magnitude in Portugal), both suppress the effective number of parties and thus place limits on the choices citizens have regarding who represents them. Yet each party system manages to outclass those of its counterparts by providing multiple choices on the left side of the ideological spectrum. This is not to say that representation for right-leaning citizens does not matter, but in a context of dominant neoliberalism and a crisis of faith in that dominance, left-wing parties were far better situated to respond and adapt.

All three of our positive cases were (at least until very recently) characterized by single parties on the left. In the United States, presidentialism interacts with plurality rules to create perhaps the most ironclad two-party system in the democratic world. In the United Kingdom, the declining Liberal Party gradually lost control of the left side of the policy space to the newly ascendant Labour Party in the early twentieth century (Wilson 2011). The liberal cause was later resuscitated by the Liberal Democrat Party, which for a time served as an alternative between the state socialist platform of Labour and the Thatcherite extremism of the Conservatives, but with the economic convergence of the major parties on the neoliberal consensus the Liberal Democrat Party has struggled to justify its continuing existence except as a protest vehicle. Finally in Spain, the pacted transition toward democracy created a system that emphasized stability and governability over representation and choice. Spain's electoral system allowed more room for minor parties than the plurality systems in the USA and the UK, but regional divisions prevented this from translating into broader programmatic options for citizens. Rather than multiple left parties, regionalist parties predominated.

In contrast, both Canada and Portugal depressed the number of parties, but not so much that it precluded the existence of alternative left parties. Unlike the UK, the Canadian Liberals did not collapse under pressure from the socialist left. The Liberals instead moved to the left in the midcentury due to the rapid emergence of social democratic third parties, creating Canada's single-payer healthcare system, in addition to other social welfare initiatives, placing the party firmly in the center-left position (Maioni 1997, 415). However, because the left was dominated by a large catchall party, rather than a firmly ideological party such as pre-Blair Labour, room remained for an alternative toward the left pole. This space was filled by a succession of movements and parties of various ideologies, culminating in the rise of the social democratic New Democratic Party (NDP). Leftist insurgents, including the NDP, have been enabled by federalism, as regional elections have long provided a proving ground for new political movements and given such movements room to develop and grow before facing the gauntlet of federal elections (Maioni 1997, 413).

Circumstances were similar in Portugal, albeit with very different institutional details. A PR system similar to that of Spain inhibited the growth of minor parties, but the absence of regionally oriented parties in Portugal allowed the far left, including the Communist Party and the Left Bloc, to maintain a small but consistent presence (Fernandes, Magalhães, and Santana-Pereira 2018, 506). In addition, both the Communist Party and the Left Bloc took anti-EU/Troika stances, allowing protest to be channeled into the existing party system (Lisi 2016, Quintas da Silva 2018). In short, both Canadian and Portuguese left-leaners may choose from multiple viable left-leaning parties. Conversely, to punish the Democrats or Labour, US and UK leftists must either cross the ideological boundary or throw their votes away on long-shot third parties. This gives the mainstream "left" parties little incentive to listen to the voices of leftist citizens; instead, they tend to focus on reinforcing their position with centrist voters, or more recently with postmaterialist progressives and educated urbanites.

As a result, during economic crises monopolistic left parties have little incentive to stray from Third Way neoliberalism. This is exactly the gap that both left- and right-wing populist parties have tried to fill. On the other hand, partisan divisions within the left can promote policy responsiveness through strategic shifts in party platforms. Spatial theories of party competition tell us that parties change positions in response to the behavior of other parties, as each tries to get as close as possible to the median voter. Adams and Somer-Topcu (2009) find that parties are much more attentive to fellow travelers than to opponents. Left parties tend to move together, trying to maximize their share of their side of the spectrum, while right-wing parties do the same. As such, even small parties can encourage their larger counterparts to stray further from the political center, especially when some exogenous shock like an economic crisis drives voters closer to the ideological poles.

Although the presence of small leftist parties was an important condition in both Canada and Portugal, it was not sufficient to ensure the responsiveness necessary to avoid major discontent. Small parties are just that: small, enjoying support from only limited segments of the electorate and thus rarely can they exert the kind of influence necessary to force a systemic shift of sufficient gravity to ward off discontent. As such, dodging the bullet was not inevitable in either country. Instead, the outcomes were determined by incentives shaped by the process of government formation combined with fortuitous timing, with the agency and choices of political leaders thrown in for good measure.

8.3.2 Government Formation and Policy Innovation in Portugal

Even by the standards of most similar system designs, Portugal and Spain have some eerie similarities. Leaving to the side the institutional and historical traits they share, their paths during the first phase of the euro-zone crisis were remarkably consistent. In both cases, socialist parties were in government when their economies began to collapse. Both governments collapsed as citizens revolted against the neoliberal austerity packages the socialists had implemented, leading to center-right governments in 2011. However, winning these elections came with their own costs; the center-right parties (PP in Spain and the Social Democratic Party and Christian Social Democratic Popular Party in Portugal) were left to implement the very austerity packages they had criticized, and later forced to adopt packages of their own. As a result, the rightist parties bled support throughout their governments, although both survived their entire four-year mandates, with elections held in both countries in late 2015.

Neither election proved decisive. Both left and right had been discredited by austerity, and dissatisfaction with the conservatives led to a decline of sixty-four seats (18.3 percent) for the Spanish PP and twenty-four seats (10.4 percent) for the Portuguese conservative alliance. Yet these losses did not translate to a boost for the center-left: neither socialist party recovered from its 2011 losses. Leftist outsider parties surged, with the populist Podemos gaining sixty-five seats and the far left (Left Block (BE)) more than doubling its seat share, from eight to nineteen seats. In both countries, the largest party was center-right, while the left won more seats as a bloc. As such the rightist parties were granted the opportunity to form a government, but the PP failed to do so and the Conservative government in Portugal quickly collapsed.

The aftermath of the collapse of center-right governments proved a critical point of divergence for both Spain and Portugal. In Spain, the PSOE attempted to negotiate a support agreement with Podemos, but the populist party made their support contingent on being part of a coalition government. The PSOE preferred instead to form a minority government in which Podemos would support the party's platform but not receive any offices (Simón 2016). The negotiations became deadlocked, forcing snap elections in 2016 in which the right rebounded and was (thanks to PSOE abstention after evicting its leader) able pass an investiture vote and form a government that lasted until 2019. Both Podemos and the PSOE were blamed by many of their sympathizers for not stopping the return of the right (Zarzalejos 2016). This effectively foreclosed any possible push-back against austerity at the worst possible moment; the entire recovery period occurred under the auspices of a conservative government.

The Portuguese socialists managed to thread the needle that the Spanish socialists could not. Several factors contributed to the successful negotiations between the Socialist Party (PS) and the far left (which included the BE and the Communist/Green alliance, known as the Unitary Democratic Coalition (CDU)). Both leftist parties had suffered bruising electoral defeats after the BE joined with the right to evict a PS government in 2011, suggesting that the population would punish similar actions in the future (Fernandes, Magalhães, and Santana-Pereira 2018, 509). Earlier periods in which the left parties extracted policy concessions in exchange for not challenging PS minority governments led them to prefer such an arrangement over joining a coalition, which was the preferred choice of the PS's leadership (Lisi 2016, 554). Such tactics allowed the far left to influence policy while avoiding any responsibility for the performance of the government. Indeed, the desire to force the far left to share responsibility shaped the PS's demands that the far left join the government.

Both the moderate and far left Portuguese parties had learned through bitter experience the costs of intransigence. The rejuvenation of the PS was also a form of institutional learning, where new ideas were introduced and accepted due to the admittance of a new generation of leaders who were more open to the idea of working with the radical left (Fernandes, Magalhães, and Santana-Pereira 2018, 508). Podemos' meteoric rise gave its leaders an excessive sense of their party's capabilities. The party's leaders believed Podemos could replace the PSOE as the electoral standard-bearer of the left, something which was not shared by the leftmost parties in Portugal (Fernandes, Magalhães, and Santana-Pereira 2018, Zarzalejos 2016). This led to a lack of awareness of the potential costs of demanding more than the PSOE was willing to concede. The PSOE for its part had typically relied on regionalist parties for support during periods of minority government, but there was no precedent for negotiating with an upstart that many in the party blamed for dividing its electorate. In Portugal, the PS, by contrast, was no stranger to minority governance. The Portuguese Constitution does not require an investiture vote to form a government (Teles 1998), and as such, the PS had governed in the past with the passive acquiescence of the far left.

Nevertheless, the PS faced a major hurdle: the Portuguese president, not wishing to allow another *"geringonça"* (rickety contraption), that is, a government that was doomed to immanent collapse like the one the right had attempted to construct, demanded a binding, written support contract between the PS and the far left parties.[8] The bargain would not come cheap. The BE and its Communist and Green Party allies demanded a near total unwinding of the austerity policies that had been implemented as part of the country's bailout, a demand to which the PS was eventually forced to relent. However, the bailout agreement also gave the far left cover to accept some deviations from the agreed upon platform, especially regarding the speed of reform, as it allowed them to blame the pact and thus justified its continuing support of the government. Additionally, by supporting the PS without actually joining a coalition government, far left parties could take credit for stopping austerity without risking their "brand" (Lupu 2011) and incurring electoral consequences (Fernandes, Magalhães, and Santana-Pereira 2018).

At this point in our narrative, we must acknowledge that structural and institutional factors do not determine everything; the PS ended up walking a very thin tightrope, trying to simultaneously satisfy the demands of the Troika and their far left counterparts. There was every possibility the PS could have plunged from the tightrope into a political crisis. Instead, PS leaders got creative, finding new ways of doing both politics and policy. During the government's tenure, representatives of the PS met weekly to negotiate programs bilaterally with both the BE and the CDU. This led to a relatively strong turn away from austerity just as the country was emerging from the crisis and could thus afford to restore

[8] The term, which translates more specifically to "an unusual apparatus characterized by lack of solidarity and frequent malfunctioning," was first used derogatorily by the recently ousted conservatives to refer to the PS minority government. As the durability of the government became clearer, it was reclaimed by partisans of the left (Fernandes, Magalhães, and Santana-Pereira 2018, 503).

much of what had been slashed. Still, the continuing constraints of the bailout and the need to avoid spooking international markets encouraged innovation on the part of the PS, which offered new programs such as "progressive gratuity of school textbooks, the protection of homeowners against eviction resulting from tax debts or assuring that all citizens have family doctors and nurses assigned by the National Health Service (NHS)" (Fernandes, Magalhães and Santana-Pereira 2018, 509–510).

To briefly summarize, Portugal did not require a party with deep social roots or institutionalized channels of voice like the Uruguayan FA to stave off deterioration of system support. Nor did the PS suddenly rediscover its leftist principles. Instead, something more mundane (but still enormously consequential) occurred: the PS responded to the brutal logic of electoral competition and parliamentary politics. Against all odds the party managed to chart a course between the Scylla of some of Europe's most radical left parties and the Charybdis of the bailout agreement. It did so by overturning austerity to the extent possible and by finding innovative ways to get around the bind in which it found itself. Citizens saw a government that was responding to demands for breaking from the status quo, and rewarded the parties accordingly as the PS increased its plurality by twenty-two seats in 2019, allowing it to form a traditional minority government. The one significant attempt to capitalize on any democratic discontent was mostly a flop; the radical right populist party Chega (Enough), which was clearly modeled on VOX in both its tone and style, only gained one seat in this election.[9] The only other new party to emerge during this time was a right-leaning but pro-system liberal party that reflected modest dissatisfaction with parties on the right, rather than system-antagonistic discontent. In Spain, on the other hand, the PSOE could not abandon old ways of doing politics and Podemos refused to appreciate the consequences of its actions, leading to a right-wing government during most of the country's economic recovery. In the absence of an adaptive left, the ongoing weight of economic trauma continued to erode system support which, combined with the Catalan crisis, left the door wide open for further democratic discontent.

---

[9] As this book prepared to go to press, the agreement between the PS and the left collapsed, the Covid-19 crisis forced the PS to once again back austerity, and Chega has since gained significant ground. Despite this, the PS managed to increase its seat count in the January 2022 elections, allowing it to form a majority government without the other left parties. This is a sign of the party's success, but also raises the possibility that the PS will again drift toward the center, abandoning the responsiveness forced upon it by the need to maintain the support of the smaller left blocs.

8.3.3 The Revival of the Liberal Party of Canada

The fall and resurgence of the Canadian Liberals differed significantly from the trajectory of the PS in Portugal, but we find in Canada the same role for intra-left competition and parliamentary politics in forcing responsiveness. After spending much of the latter half of the twentieth century as a dominant force in Canadian politics, to the extent that some observers declared them as "the natural ruling party of Canada," the Liberals entered a period of decline in the 1980s. We have already discussed at length the factors leading to the decline of the left in the developed world (the decline of the working class due to globalization, pressure on welfare states, growing cultural conflicts, etc.), and Canada was no exception. The Liberals recovered somewhat in the 1990s by moderating, although not to the same degree as Labour in the UK or the US Democrats, for reasons we discuss later. Like those parties, moderation allowed the party to become competitive in the short term but diluted its brand and partisan identity, leading to a decline of support and resurgence of the Conservative Party, which took power after dethroning a Liberal minority government in 2006.

As the crisis unfolded in 2008 and Canadians returned to the polls in the midst of it, the Harper government, despite a lack of a clear plan for confronting the crisis (CBC News 2008), increased its seat count and formed a new but stronger minority government. Harper immediately attempted to pursue austerity policies, including significant spending cuts in order to eliminate an emerging budget deficit. At this point, responsiveness arising from parliamentary politics comes into play. One can imagine another scenario, not unlike that which Barack Obama faced in the last six years of his presidency, where institutions advantaged austerity-supporting political forces, thus leading to a long and drawn-out recovery, with all the democratic discontent that went along with it.

Instead, the Conservative's minority status gave parties of the left both the motivation and the institutional clout to oppose self-injurious spending cuts during an economic slowdown. Motivation was important because both the Liberals and the leftist NDP were wary of their prior reputations for fiscal irresponsibility, a theme that will recur later in this chapter. However, the issue gave the parties an opportunity to demonstrate to voters that the parties could effectively stand up to the Conservatives and thus they were willing to embrace policies at which they might have quailed had they been in government and thus responsible. Instead, the Conservatives were forced to retreat and enact stimulus policies instead under the threat of a Liberal-NDP coalition which might have brought down the Conservative government (Ellis 2016). This would have been impossible in a system with fixed terms of government without motions of confidence.

Ironically, by pulling the Conservatives back from the brink of what might have been a disastrous policy platform, the left parties probably helped shore up support for the Conservatives as the economic situation improved. The Liberals lacked a strong critique of the Conservative government and found themselves increasingly starved for oxygen, as satisfied Canadians rallied around Harper while opposition forces began to migrate to the NDP. This process reached its nadir for the Liberals in the election of 2011, when the party collapsed, losing forty-three seats and its status as the second largest party, ceding the role of official opposition to the NDP.

Staggering electoral losses such as this can occasionally be a blessing in disguise. Parties, especially elite-dominated catchall parties like those that came to dominate most democracies in the early twenty first century, are notoriously unwieldy and find adaptation to new circumstances difficult. Crushing defeats can arouse parties from complacency and give them new life. After 2011, the leader of the Liberal Party, Michael Ignatieff, resigned his position after he failed to win a seat in his own riding. This cleared the way for a rejuvenation of leadership as Justin Trudeau was elected party leader. Trudeau is a scion of a long and storied political family, but his youth, relatively recent entry to politics, and even his home riding (a small district in Quebec that had voted heavily for the NDP in 2011) positioned him to modernize the Liberals.

As the elections of 2015 approached, conventional wisdom, supported by early polling, suggested that the Liberals were headed for yet another disaster. Expectations were that these elections would inaugurate a new era of party competition in Canada, where the NDP would permanently seize the role of standard-bearer for the left. As it happened, Trudeau proved much more able and charismatic than his opponents assumed. The Liberals' downfall in 2011 gave Trudeau a great deal of latitude to take risks and stake out bold policy positions. In better times, conservative voices in the party might have prevailed and preserved the party's status quo.

But with little to lose, those in the party calling for a new direction prevailed, which was embodied in both Trudeau's election and his policy platform. Unlike both his rivals, Trudeau bucked the consensus that immediate action was necessary to bring the federal budget into balance, successfully arguing that low interest rates and a continuingly negative economic outlook made investment through borrowing, rather than austerity, the best course for the country. He also leaned into cultural issues with a newly assured progressivism, moving to the left on issues related to First Nation Peoples, LGBTQ rights, and immigration. This endeared him to many progressive Canadians who had become increasingly incensed by Harper's social conservatism (Jeffrey 2016). The gamble, assisted by both growing dissatisfaction with Harper and the NDP's inability to overcome fears of being labeled a "tax and spend" left party (McGrane 2016, loc. 1667), paid off. The Liberals more than quintupled their seats in 2015, from 36 to 184, while the Conservatives and NDP lost over a third and more than half their seats, respectively. Support did not just accrue to the Liberal Party, but also to the political system itself. A recent report by the Environics Institute, using data from the Americas Barometer, found that support for democracy in Canada was extremely robust during the Great Recession (Parkin 2021).

8.4 CONCLUSION: VARIETIES OF DEMOCRATIC RESPONSIVENESS

We should note here that the stunning reversal of fortune the Canadian Liberals managed to secure in the 2015 election was not the result of a fundamental altering of the country's party system, nor of the parties themselves. Canada, like most systems that place significant downward pressure on the number of parties, was and remains dominated by weakly rooted catchall parties. Neither the Canadian Liberals nor the Portuguese PS suddenly transformed into anything like the FA in Uruguay, with bottom-up empowerment and mechanisms for continuous democracy. Yet all of these parties and party systems achieved the same result, albeit through different means: they turned away from orthodox neoliberal austerity that would have exacerbated (or in the Portuguese case already had exacerbated) the polarizing effects of economic trauma, and perhaps more importantly, demonstrated to citizens that voting matters. By electing parties of the center-left, citizens could voice their demands, however vague or inchoate, for a break with moribund economic ideas that had given rise to the crisis in the first place.

This does not mean the differences between Uruguay and our other cases are irrelevant. Voice in Uruguay is deeply institutionalized in both the party system and the formal mechanisms of democracy; in Canada and Portugal, responsiveness was mostly a happy historical accident, albeit one that minimally permissive institutions allowed to occur. We are thus somewhat pessimistic about the ability of these latter cases to stave off discontent over the long term. There is every possibility that the PS and the Liberals will fall victim to their own success: increased support due to responsiveness may allow the center-left to govern alone, and without the pressure of third parties on their flank, and they may well fall back into the outdated Third Way habits that have defined them in recent decades. Indeed, we see signs of this process already in Canada, where Trudeau rashly called snap elections hoping to establish a majority liberal government in 2021.[10]

Yet even if these periods of increased responsiveness prove transient, it is difficult to argue that Portugal and Canada's sociopolitical trajectories were not vastly improved by them. These countries were able to avoid the pathologies of voicelessness at a crucial moment in their political histories, and while we might wish that voice and responsiveness were institutionalized when the opportunity to do so was ripe, we should not underestimate the importance of even this temporary reprieve from democratic discontent. This was critically important because, as we discuss in Chapter 9, once discontent gains sufficient momentum, there is little anyone can do to stop it.

---

[10] Ultimately, this was a partially failed gambit by Trudeau. The Liberals were able to maintain their minority government, and the balance of seats in parliament remained shockingly stable – the Liberals lost one seat and the Conservatives kept the same number of seats, on net.

9

Populism in Power

Polarization, Charismatic Attachment, and Conspiracy Theories in Trump's America

By this point in the book, our theory's work is largely done. Our primary goal was to explain the emergence of discontent, and we have done so as well as we can. Yet one major question remains largely unexamined: what happens to all the resentment on which discontented movements and leaders thrive when they take control of government? It is a question that no book that seeks to provide a comprehensive account of discontent can ignore, and we grapple with it in this chapter by examining the administration of Donald Trump.

We cannot possibly do justice to all the twists and turns of the Trump government in a single chapter, and others have already covered this ground repeatedly; indeed, dissections of Trump's mandate have become something of a cottage industry. Instead, we focus on specific elements of Trump's time in office through which we can learn something about discontent: how it feeds off a self-sustaining cycle of polarization and charismatic attachment; the damage it can do to social cohesion and the ability of governments to respond effectively to new crises; and the role conspiracy theories play in protecting followers from the psychological distress that results when discontented leaders falter.

9.1 THE CHALLENGES OF POPULIST GOVERNANCE

Understanding Trump's presidency requires understanding why populists generally do poorly in government (Houle and Kenny 2018). Much of the problem stems from the inherently oppositional nature of populism. Unlike ideologies such as communism or fascism that also oppose established political systems but have clear (if unrealistic) visions of how society should be organized, populist movements are defined almost entirely as the negative image of their elite antagonists (Panizza 2005). As such, taking power provokes an identity crisis: by overpowering the elites they despise, the populist social narrative is undermined; the anti-elitists *become* the elite. Furthermore, their oppositional nature means populists have little immediate need to deal with the nuances and challenges of government prior to being elected. As such, they typically offer oversimplified explanations for social problems, and the solutions they propose are usually reductionist, unrealistic, or unachievable. At the same time, populists are largely ill-suited for the demands of governance, due to a combination of a lack of interest, strong affective aversion to other political actors, personality traits of populist leaders, and political inexperience.

The result of all this is that populists are often unable to successfully pursue the kinds of transformative policies that would satisfy the high expectations of their followers, which of course they helped elevate as insurgents. The most successful populists typically come to power during severe crises when political institutions have collapsed and are thus able to reshape political regimes in their preferred image. Typically, this involves concentrating power in their own hands and enervating horizontal accountability, for example by expanding the use of executive decree power or staffing courts and independent bodies with sycophants. Without the ability to act unilaterally, populists tend to flounder. Consequently, they must craft strategies that do not involve policy satisfaction to sustain their movements.

9.1.1 The Dog that Caught the Car: Trump Enters the White House

There were few people more flummoxed by Trump's surprise victory in the 2016 election than Trump himself. Some confidants of the former president have claimed that his decision to enter the race was driven by the desire to market his personal brand (Peterson-Withorn 2019) or as revenge against Barack Obama for publicly mocking him, rather than a real interest in holding the office (Wang 2017). Whatever his true motivations, Trump shared a trait common among populist politicians: a lack of interest in, or understanding of, governance.

Throughout his campaign, Trump largely avoided making the sort of concrete promises that (ideally) would allow voters to hold him accountable for fulfilling or breaking them should he win through.[1] Trump took

---

[1] This problem is not limited to Trump. Systems like that in the USA with many veto players make it very difficult for voters to accurately determine responsibility for policy

vague, frequently shifting, and occasionally contradictory positions on major issues that did not relate directly to his "America First" ethos (e.g. Social Security, healthcare). He was more consistent on his signature issues, namely, those that sprung from his general view of the world as made up only of those who exploit others and those who get exploited, such as trade and immigration. Yet even on these issues, his proposed solutions ranged from the unrealistic to the hubristic. Trump pitched himself as such a consummate negotiator that he would be able to rene-gotiate trade deals (and thus reindustrialize the United States), force Mexico to pay for his border wall, and overcome gridlock and judicial challenges to his immigration agenda through force of personality alone. Trump failed to grasp that his experience running a business populated by toadies and family members was hardly germane to running the gov-ernment, with all its veto players, coequal branches, independent agen-cies, and competing spheres of influence.

So long as Trump's campaign remained quixotic, his vacillation and self-aggrandizement were more assets than liabilities. As with most popu-lists, Trump needed to build an emotional coalition around anti-system resentment that crossed traditional social cleavages, unifying financial elites, social conservatives, and disgruntled members of the left behind. This is a perennial problem in modern US politics, where party politics have long made strange bedfellows and where satisfying one part of a coalition often alienates other factions (Ginsberg and Shefter 1999). As an insurgent, Trump could balance these factions by avoiding specific promises and focusing on attacking and stereotyping social groups that his supporters were already inclined to dislike and distrust.

9.1.2 Dysfunctional Institutions and Populism in Government

Once in power, this strategy crashed headlong into the realities of gov-ernance in the United States. Contrary to the populist narrative of elite malevolence as the root of all political evil, there are structural and insti-tutional factors that impede effective policymaking in the United States, regardless of the character of leaders. The primary culprit is the plethora of veto points and players (Tsebelis 1995) in the US system, including bicam-eralism, malapportionment and the filibuster in the Senate, judicial review,

---

successes and failures. This challenge in turn incentives leaders to make unrealistic policy promises, knowing they can always blame others when their plans fail to materialize. The Republican Party's self-call of their own bluff on repealing Obamacare is a case in point.

and federalism. Briefly put, the institutions of the United States are designed to avoid polarization by forcing compromise and consensus-building, and resisting momentary electoral trends like the election of a populist.

Problems with this system had been brewing for decades but boiled over after the Tea Party–backed takeover of the legislature by the Republican Party during the Obama presidency. This radicalized faction, unified in part by their extreme neoliberalism but perhaps more so by their hatred of Obama, drove legislative elites further apart while both reflecting and deepening social polarization. Whatever its capacities in preventing polarization, the US system tends to grind to a halt when that prevention fails. As a result, and despite his party holding both chambers of the legislature, Trump would have faced a hard road pushing his policies even if his perceptions of his own skills were accurate.

These difficulties are most apparent in the limited legislative output during Trump's first years in office. Although his party controlled both chambers of the legislature, Trump had only two major policy efforts in Congress: a failed attempt to repeal Obamacare, and a tax cut for corporations and wealthy individuals.[2] Neither did much to bolster Trump's image as a champion of the working class. Trump did attempt to secure a major infrastructure deal, which would have included the kind of major construction projects to which he could have pointed as fulfillment of his commitment to blue-collar workers. Yet the plan went nowhere in the face of opposition from Democrats, who opposed the heavy involvement of private industry in funding the plan and demands that some of the money pay for the border wall, with an assist from anti-deficit members in the Republican Party (Shelbourne 2018).

Trump was more successful in pursuing his signature cultural issues, in part because in this policy domain he could push the limits of executive power and even skirt the law to get what he wanted. He managed to craft a ban on immigration from majority Muslim countries that passed constitutional muster, at least according to a sympathetic and credulous Supreme Court, and he secured funding to build part of his promised border wall by declaring a dubious state of emergency (Baker 2019, Navarre 2020). However, his efforts to repeal the Deferred Action for Childhood Arrivals and to add a citizen question to the 2020 census were rebuffed

---

[2] In the case of Obamacare, Trump was stymied by supermajoritarian requirements for legislation to move through the US Senate. Arcane budget rules allowed the Republican Party to pass its economic package, which included zeroing out Obamacare's unpopular insurance mandate, with a bare majority.

by the Supreme Court due to the administration's failure to follow legal requirements and, in the case of the census questions, a mendacity so brazen the court refused to accept Trump's explanation for adding the question. The infamous Family Separation policy (officially known as Zero-Tolerance), was later found to have no measures to reunite families or effectively track children (OIG 2018), and under massive public outcry Trump quickly ended the policy two months later (Politico 2018).

These examples underscore the extent to which Trump failed to elide checks on his authority, something with which populists in less institutionalized democracies need not contend (Weyland and Madrid 2019). They also emphasize the general lack of managerial competence that defined Trump's presidency. A constant rumble of backbiting and internal dissension spurred a stream of embarrassing leaks, which was exacerbated by an equally continuous series of high-profile defections (Woodward 2021). It is impossible to say exactly how this affected Trump's ability to govern, but it clearly provided a great deal of unnecessary distraction in a situation where the political situation required sustained and disciplined focus.

9.2 THE PERSISTENCE OF POPULISM: CHARISMATIC ATTACHMENT AND AFFECTIVE POLARIZATION

A mainstream politician that promised so much and accomplished so little would likely find their support relatively waning quickly. Trump was not entirely immune to the continuing lack of meaningful policy victories under his watch, but he did manage to hold his coalition better than one might expect. To understand why, and to understand Trump's tactics as his administration floundered, we need to discuss the process of charismatic bonding or attachment.[3]

The direct, emotional relationship citizens form with leaders is a crucial factor in the trajectories of many populists, especially those who emerge in presidential systems that encourage personalistic leadership. Indeed, the co-occurrence of populism and personalism is so frequent that many scholars define populism in terms of these emotional and unmediated relationships (Weyland 2001, Weyland and Madrid 2019, Merolla, Ramos, and Zechmeister 2007, Merolla and Zechmeister 2011, Andrews-Lee 2019). While we do not agree for reasons outlined in

---

[3] Bonding is more commonly used in existing scholarship. We prefer the term "attachment" because "bond" implies a mutual connection, whereas attachment better captures the one-sided nature of the leader–follower relationship the concept describes.

Chapter 2, the connection here is clear enough that no study of populism or democratic discontent could be complete without addressing it.

Madsen and Snow (1991) provide the most comprehensive study of the psychological correlates of charismatic attachment. They point to the combination of two factors that facilitate this type of leader–follower relationship: a threatening and hostile social environment and a crisis of self-efficacy. In simpler terms, people are vulnerable to charismatic co-optation when they see their social situation as hopelessly negative and when they believe they have no ability to correct the situation through their political choices and behavior. Attachment occurs when a larger-than-life figure emerges who these vulnerable citizens perceive as superhumanly capable. This triggers a process of "proxy control," where individuals escape the profound anxiety produced by a lack of environmental control (Bandura 1977) by embracing the leader with blind faith (Madsen and Snow 1991, 14–19).

As the leader begins to challenge the existing system, the bond deepens only if the leader can demonstrate in dramatic ways their ability to overcome the previously insurmountable barriers erected by "the system." Reviewing the rise of Juan Perón in Argentina, Madsen and Snow (1991, 48–50) point to Perón's liberation from prison after mass protests as the moment that crystallized and cemented the bond between the leader and his movement. A similar set of events helped solidify the government of Hugo Chávez, who was restored to power after a brief coup following mass protests supporting him (Rhodes-Purdy 2017c, 151–152). These events do more than signal the invulnerability of the populist; it ties that invulnerability to the actions of followers, whose unwavering support allows the populist to arise anew from their most difficult moment. As a result, followers can experience vicarious efficacy through their identification with the leader: the psychological distinction between the leader and the follower erodes, with the latter enjoying a sense of purpose and empowerment drawn from the leader. With such strong identification, the ability of followers to critically evaluate their leader's actions withers away.

The correlation between populism and charisma is straightforward. The populist worldview strongly implies both significant social threat and a lack of efficacy, given that representatives are perceived as traitors who care little about ordinary citizens. Experimental research has shown that priming populist attitudes significantly decreases perceived external self-efficacy (Rhodes-Purdy 2021a). As we discuss in Chapter 5, Trump's social narrative was awash in perceived threats to "real Americans," most of which emanated from abroad or were otherwise presented as foreign or alien. He also emphasized the lack of effective political channels in the USA, while also claiming to serve as his followers' voice. And while nothing so dramatic as being liberated from prison was ever necessary during Trump's rise, his repeated ability to bounce back from scandals and mistakes that would have sunk ordinary politicians, culminating in his upset victory in 2016, served a similar function. By the time he took power, Trump's hold on his core followers (if not on the Republican Party coalition as a whole) was ironclad. Trump himself expressed it best when he claimed that he could shoot a person in broad daylight on a major street with no repercussions.

9.2.1 Maintaining Attachment: Elite-Cued Polarization

Charismatic attachment is not self-sustaining: it must be maintained and reinforced over time, a process that Madsen and Snow (1991, 23–32), following Weber, call "routinization." The gradual erosion of charisma occurs for several reasons, among the most important of which is the simple fact that populists undermine themselves as soon as they take office. By vanquishing their foes, they intrinsically reduce environmental threat while increasing (perceived) voice among their followers (Rhodes-Purdy 2015, 138–139). Trump faced greater challenges in maintaining attachment than more successful populists, as his ability to demonstrate his power (and, vicariously, that of his followers) was much more limited. Hugo Chávez, for example, was able to rewrite the entire Venezuelan Constitution to his liking shortly after being elected, and gradually colonized virtually all organs of the state with loyalists. By the time of his death, he faced few checks on his actions. Populists have a variety of options available to routinize charisma. Typically this involves developing organizational capacity, through building up political parties (Roberts 2006) or through the use of limited participatory programs they can control (Rhodes-Purdy 2015, 2017c, ch. 5). Barring this, populists can maintain control simply by delivering tangible benefits to supporters, although this typically requires eroding horizontal accountability so the populist can legislate without constraint.

Trump, on the other hand, had no chance of altering the Constitution even slightly, given the notorious difficulty of constitutional amendment in the USA. Unlike his Latin American counterparts, the relatively weak legislative powers of the presidency strictly limited his ability to unilaterally make policy (Weyland and Madrid 2019), although he pushed the boundaries of that power as far as he could. Nor would he be able to rely on a fawningly compliant judiciary, even as he appointed members to it as a record pace, as he learned to his sorrow when he attempted to use the courts in his attempts to overturn the 2020 elections. He showed little interest or aptitude for organizing his followers into a force that could endure and perpetuate itself, and his inability to deliver benefits through policy worsened after the Republican Party lost control of the lower chamber after the 2018 midterm elections.

Instead, Trump maintained his relationship with his followers by using the same tactics he had employed to build his political brand in the first place, namely by stoking aggression against his enemies. This is typical for populists, who aggressively target their political opponents and opposing social groups, deliberately polarize society, and increase the costs of being in opposition (Corrales 2010, 2011, Corrales and Penfold 2015). By consistently reinforcing resentment, populists can promote solidarity within the movement and maintain mass mobilization and engagement of their movements.

Polarization in US politics has been on the rise for some time, driven by a variety of factors. First, over time, parties have become more ideologically unified, with Republicans consistently adopting conservative positions and Democrats consistently adopting liberal positions (Abramowitz and Saunders 2008, Levendusky 2009, Lelkes 2016, Abramowitz and Webster 2016). This polarization is not simply ideological but also has affective components – citizens increasingly *dislike* members of the opposing political party (Iyengar and Westwood 2015, Mason 2018).

That said, much of the current polarization has not arisen organically from below but has been engendered by the deliberate action of political elites. Classic models of public opinion show that citizens tend to have relatively poorly constrained ideological positions (Converse 1964), and political elites tend to drive the political attitudes of the masses (Zaller 1992). Elites polarized earlier, and more quickly, than the mass public (McCarty, Poole, and Rosenthal 2006). Recent work shows that, even today, political elites have higher levels of affective polarization than the mass public (Enders 2021), and elites have increasingly made affective, out-group-focused public appeals to voters (Lee 2016). By pushing these negative, highly affective messages, political elites can serve to drive hatred of the opposing party, and affective connections toward citizens' preferred party or preferred leaders.

We also see evidence of this in the experimental data we presented in Chapter 4. In our video treatment study (Study 2, see Chapter 4 for details), we found that exposing participants to a video of Steven K. Bannon discussing his views on immigration and race increased cultural discontent among both self-identified liberals (Est. = 0.049; SE=.023; p-value = 0.035) and conservatives (Est. = 0.108; SE = 0.047; p-value = 0.022). Discourse analysis of Trump's campaign rhetoric was considerably more negative and directed at castigating opponents than those of other candidates (Gross and Johnson 2016, Kayam 2020). Combined with our findings from Chapter 5, showing that support for Trump was positively associated with resentment and cultural discontent among conservatives, the role of deliberate polarization is consistent with our evidence.

9.2.2 Reciprocal Polarization and Left-Wing Cultural Discontent

In short, Trump's strategy to maintain his bond with his followers was to keep them angry: at the globalists, immigrants, urbanites, and so on. He could not do much to improve his followers' lives, but he certainly could lash out at their enemies, and his ability to do harm satisfied his need to demonstrate power and capability to his supporters. While Trump's strategy helped keep him in his loyalists' good graces, it came with a cost, as Trump and the Republican Party learned during the midterms of 2018. According to an analysis of validated voters by the Pew Research Center,[4] both Democratic and Republican voters came in highly motivated, but new voters (those who had not participated in the 2016 elections) broke heavily for the Democrats, contributing to the party's forty-one-seat gain in the House, which allowed them a comfortable majority in the chamber for the first time since 2008.

In other words, Trump's deliberate inflaming of cultural conflicts impacted liberals as well as conservatives. The same policies that helped keep conservatives motivated and loyal by playing to growing ethnonationalism incensed progressives, who responded with ever-increasing outrage to Family Separation, the Muslim immigration ban, and Trump's continuing attacks on transgender persons and minorities. We see these effects in our data: cultural discontent increased among liberals in both Study 2 (referenced earlier in this chapter) and in Study 1, which used a writing exercise rather than videos. Written treatments can be doubly useful, both priming the desired attitude while also providing a window

---

[4] www.pewresearch.org/methods/2020/09/08/democrats-made-gains-from-multiple-sources-in-2018-midterm-victories/.

(through the open-ended responses) to participants' thinking. Among self-identified liberals in the cultural discontent condition, thirty-nine out of sixty-eight specifically mention Trump or the cultural issues he championed (such as immigration) as the source of their alienation.

The reactions of conservatives and liberals may be diametrically opposed but the mechanisms are the same: resentment accentuates in-group/out-group distinctions, increasing hostility toward the latter and solidarity with the former. Furthermore, this group polarization encourages conformity within the in-group, driving moderate liberals further to the left, especially on cultural issues, as the right radicalizes (see Mason 2018). These dynamics can be seen in the shifting policy positions of mainstream Democratic leaders. Hillary Clinton spent the 1990s as a moderate-to-conservative Democrat, a position she maintained on economic issues while embracing policies like gay marriage, criminal justice reform, and abortion rights during the 2016 campaign.

Given Trump's continuing hold on government and his increasing power over his party, this growing sense of cultural discontent also increased populist sentiments on the left. Although the divide between progressives and moderates within the Democratic party had troubled the party for years and grew throughout the Obama era, candidates taking system-challenging positions grew rapidly in prominence. Relative political newcomers (Elizabeth Warren) and those who had languished in obscurity (Bernie Sanders) became major players in the party. The 2018 midterms also elevated a new group of vocal Democratic Representatives like Alexandria Ocasio-Cortez and the rest of the so-called Squad who supported unabashedly leftist policy change, often to the frustration of establishment Democratic leaders.

9.2.3 Statistical Analysis of Left-Wing Polarization

To analyze the influence of left-wing polarization, we created measures of support for Bernie Sanders and Alexandra Ocasio-Cortez by taking their feeling thermometers from the PSAS and subtracting them from the thermometer for Biden, as we did with Trump and Romney in Chapter 5. We then rescaled the support measures so they range from zero to one and regressed them on the dimensions of populism, cultural discontent, and a set of control variables (ideology, economic distress, income, education, Latine dummy, gender, age, region, and race) using Tobit regression. We estimated two models for each figure, one including both populism and cultural discontent, and one omitting the populism measures to account

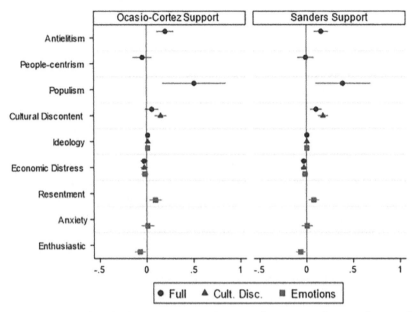

FIGURE 9.1 Cultural discontent, populism, and support for Sanders and Ocasio-Cortez

for possible mediation and collinearity. Finally, we regressed support for each figure on anger, anxiety, and enthusiasm. The results are presented in Figure 9.1.

Both Sanders' and Ocasio-Cortez's support was significantly associated with populism as a syndrome and anti-elitism, the more aggressive and hostile dimension of populism. Sanders' support was significantly influenced by cultural discontent even when populism was included, while support for Ocasio-Cortez was only affected when populism was not included, indicating that the entire effect of discontent was mediated through populism, as our theory predicts. Finally, resentment drove support for both figures. Observational data taken at a single point in time cannot definitely establish the influence of a dynamic process like polarization, but these data are largely consistent with our argument that polarization along cultural lines has driven liberals to develop their own populist impulses. And the experimental data presented earlier, including the video experiment in Study 2 and the content of responses to the writing exercise in Study 1, strongly suggest that cultural discontent on the right, and resentment arising from it, is the driving force behind this process.

9.2.4 Mutually Assured Destruction: Governance and Reciprocal Polarization

As alluded to earlier, the US political system is not terribly well suited to managing two political factions that see one another as bitter enemies. As Trump and his opponents traded barbs, a vicious cycle ensued where hostilities between Trump and the Democrats constantly intensified, and Trump's ability to accomplish any real policy victories died with the loss of his party's majority in the House. The changing of the guard in Congress only increased already heightened scrutiny of Trump's ability to perform the duties of his office, the shambolic nature of his administration, and his penchant for abusing the powers of his office for his own material or political gain. As time wore on, these failings became ever more difficult for even his most ardent followers to ignore.

9.3 A CONSPIRACY IS A WARM BLANKET: COPING WITH POPULIST FAILURE

Realizing that a populist leader is a giant with clay feet is, to the charismatically attached follower, akin to a loss of religious faith. Not only would the follower feel gullible and foolish, but they would lose the sense of vicarious efficacy and empowerment that brought them close to the leader in the first place. No research of which we are aware has examined specifically the psychological toll exacted by such disillusionment, but we can safely assume based on the passionate nature of charismatic attachment that it would be a heavy one.

Humans will typically avoid this kind of distress if possible. Mechanisms like cognitive dissonance (where the connection between two ideas would be too painful to bear and thus an individual will not connect them) and repression are two of the best known strategies, although there are of course many more. We seek to add a rather odd and counterintuitive item to that list: conspiracism. Conspiracy theories[5] seem at first glance to be spectacularly ill-suited for providing psychological comfort: who, after all, would find wild stories about omnipotent and malevolent forces secretly controlling the world to be a balm to a troubled mind? By tracing the rise of conspiracism over the course of

---

[5] Following the literature, we conceptualize conspiracy theories to be those allegations that a group of individuals is working in secret for their own gain; the difference between a conspiracy and a conspiracy theory is that the latter may or may not be true (Douglas et al. 2019, Sunstein and Vermeule 2009).

Trump's tenure, we show that conspiracy theories can serve as a coping mechanism by explaining away the populist's shortcomings and inadequacies, thus preserving the all-important emotional connection between the leader and their followers.

9.3.1 Of Pizzas and Pedophiles: The Emergence of QAnon

Trump, like most populists, readily indulged in conspiracy theorizing; indeed, his entry into politics came via the "birther" conspiracy theory that Barack Obama was not born in the United States. His rhetoric about cabals of globalists secretly controlling the US government was always uncomfortably close to old anti-Semitic canards. The most florid and bizarre conspiracies associated with Trump, however, emerged later in his administration, after his connections to Russia began to be scrutinized and as his inability to keep his promises through dramatic legislative victors became undeniable.

Three such conspiracy theories are particularly relevant to us: Pizzagate, QAnon, and Stop the Steal (STS). Pizzagate was not initially focused on Trump, but instead the claim made by a known white supremacist that prominent Democrats had been found running a child sex-trafficking ring; the story was gradually embellished to the point that a man entered a pizzeria in Washington, DC with a rifle in an attempt to liberate the entirely fictitious trafficking victims held therein (Robb 2017). For all its pathos, this theory was notable mostly for its banality. The story was little more than a modern take on the Blood Libel, an ancient xenophobic narrative, most frequently directed at Jews, that has emerged repeatedly throughout history, most recently in the Satanic Ritual Abuse panic of the 1980s. As such it conformed closely to the so-called "paranoid style" of politics described by Hofstadter (2012): a toxic combination of hyperactive threat detection, deeply held prejudices, and, as Pytlik, Soll, and Mehl (2020) argue, a predisposition to jump to conclusions on razor thin "evidence."

Pizzagate might have remained a relatively minor and tangential aspect of Trumpism had it not contributed to the QAnon conspiracy theory that gained wider infamy when its adherents participated in the January 6th *putsch*.[6] The genesis of QAnon can be found in Pizzagate, and this evolution makes it far more interesting for our purposes. For a

---

[6] The QAnon conspiracy has many branches and is frequently filled with in-fighting about which interpretation is correct. That said, not everyone that was involved in the protests and infiltration of the Capitol would consider themselves a part of QAnon; of those that do, there will be a rather diverse range of what strand of Q theory they subscribe to.

theory that eventually made claims about everything from incipient mass executions against US elites to the CIA's role in North Korea, QAnon had relatively humble origins. The story began when an anonymous[7] figure calling themselves "Q," purporting to be a high-ranking national security official, began leaving notes on internet message boards claiming that Robert Mueller's investigation of Trump's Russia ties was a sham. In "fact," Trump and Mueller were working *together* against the so-called Deep State: criminal political leaders who were essentially identical to the globalist cabals from Trump's campaign rhetoric. The connection between this and Pizzagate happened early on, and the politicians who were formerly simply corrupt and treasonous became cannibalistic, Satan-worshiping pedophiles. Q promised mass arrests, convictions, and executions on a biblical scale. Speaking of biblical, Trump rapidly became the messianic figure in Q's apocalyptic narrative, the one who would save the United States from the clutches of evil.

9.3.2 QAnon and the Obscuration of Failure

QAnon holds more interest for us because it, and many other conspiracy theories like it, had origins and purposes that were very different from the paranoia-induced paroxysms described by Hofstadter. QAnon instead served a protective purpose: it provided a narrative that could explain, first, why an almost universally respected Republican figure like Mueller might be targeting Trump, and then later metastasized to explain away virtually all of Trump's failures and foibles. Any event, no matter how apparently damaging to the populist, could be reinterpreted as another feint to fool the Deep State cabal. As Stephan Lewandowsky puts it, "[c]onspiracy theories often serve an ironic function of providing a sense of order in chaos. People would rather believe that there are evil masterminds out there ... than accept the occurrence of random events" (Coaston 2020).

We concur with this logic, namely that conspiracy theories can have a psychological protective function, one which is particularly important to populism and populists. Due to their typical inability to govern successfully (unless they can reshape the institutional ecology in which they operate to their advantage), populist leaders often desperately need some way to excuse their failure, while populist followers need a way to

---

[7] Although the identity of Q remains unconfirmed, a recent documentary (*Q: Into the Storm*) provides compelling evidence that Q is Ron Watkins, the operator of one of the message boards where Q frequently posted.

shore up their faith in the face of obvious contrary evidence. This is also in line with current literature on conspiracy theories which holds that conspiracies are "a form of threat perception, and fears are fundamentally driven by shifts in relative power" (Uscinski and Parent 2014, 131). In other words, those that are out of power are more likely to endorse or express belief in conspiracy theories (Miller, Saunders, and Farhart 2016, Uscinski, Klofstad, and Atkinson 2016). Our approach amends the understanding of "out of power" to include situations where populists remain in office but fail to produce the kind of dramatic unraveling of the status quo they promise during their insurgent phases.

9.3.3 Conspiracies, Emotions, and Cultural Discontent: A Statistical Analysis

Trying to analyze the relationships between such tightly interwoven phenomena as populism and conspiracism is difficult. Isolating the protective mechanism is especially challenging, as we have no real way to parse the reasoning of conspiracists in large-sample surveys or experiments, and thus cannot test this hypothesis directly. We can, however, test the implications of the hypothesis. For one, our theory suggests that conspiracism is related to both anxiety and resentment, but in very specific ways. Conspiracism should be increased by anxiety: weakening faith in a leader one previously trusted without question certainly qualifies as an unfamiliar environment, and the information search and openness to new ideas triggered by anxiety clearly lend themselves to conspiratorial thinking. Yet the emotional *consequences* of conspiracism are less clear. The paranoia model elaborated by Hofstadter would suggest a further descent into anxiety, or even something more primal like terror: the idea that omnipotent threats lurk around every corner is frightening on its face.

We have no doubt that paranoia plays a role in many conspiracy theories, but during the twilight of a populist government, that role is subordinate to the protective role. Conspiracy theories like QAnon have clear paranoid content but their function is totally divorced from the inhibition of motivation produced by anxiety: the point is to *escape* anxiety, as well as the contradiction of charismatic faith and undeniable failure, by engendering resentment. Conspiracy theories, as the earlier Lewandowsky quote points out, provide specific targets who can be blamed for the troubles and controversies that populist followers confront. As such, our approach would predict that resentment, rather than anxiety, results from conspiracism.

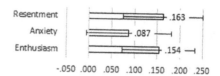

FIGURE 9.2 Regression analysis of conspiracism on emotions.

In an experimental analysis presented in a separate paper (Navarre, Rhodes-Purdy, and Utych 2021),[8] we used video treatments depicting conspiracies that turned out to be true (pro-conspiracism) or are ludicrously false (anti-conspiracism), as well as a control condition to either prime or inhibit conspiratorial ideation in 844 US resident adults recruited via Mturk. We then regressed measures of anxiety and resentment on conspiracism to determine emotional consequences. We used this study and Study 2 in this book to analyze the emotional antecedents and consequences of conspiracism. We found that conspiratorial ideation was caused primarily by anxiety but produced considerably more resentment. These findings, we argued, supported the role of conspiracy theories as coping mechanisms rather than as manifestation of paranoia.

Here, we reinforce these findings using observational data from the PSAS-US. We regressed our measures of anxiety, resentment, and enthusiasm, along with the usual control variables, on conspiratorial ideation. The results are presented in Figure 9.2.

Keeping in mind that we can only observe conspiracism after it has already developed with these data, the results are consistent with our interpretation of conspiracy theories as coping mechanisms. Anxiety was associated with conspiracism, but the effect was only marginally significant (p = 0.067). Resentment and enthusiasm had nearly twice the effect and were highly significant (p < 0.000). The effect of enthusiasm is a bit counterintuitive but not, considering our approach, as surprising as it seems. It fits with the role of conspiracy theories in overcoming anxiety and encouraging motivation.

We also see evidence that these emotional responses are not entirely spontaneous, but rather shaped by political ideas and leaders. We conducted another regression analysis, this time adding populist attitudes[9] and our measure of Trump support from Chapter 5. We found

---

[8] For a similar analysis see Balta, Rovira Kaltwasser, and Yagci (2022).

[9] For experimental evidence that the emotional and attitudinal relationships we analyze here are causal, see Navarre, Rhodes-Purdy, and Utych (2021).

significant associations between conspiracism and anti-elitism (Est. = 0.461; SE = .058; p = .000), populism (Est. = 0.470; SE = 0.235; p = 0.046), and support for Trump (Est. = 0.200; SE = 0.035; p = 0.000).

9.3.4 The Real Storm Comes: Conspiracy Theories at the Dawn of the Covid-19 Crisis

To bluntly summarize the preceding discussion, conspiracies are the opiate of the populist masses, distracting and soothing the mind in an intolerable situation, which is fitting enough given the quasi-religious nature of many conspiracy theories. Yet, like opium, conspiracy theories can easily induce a delirium from which it can be difficult to escape, especially when new threats emerge in an already hostile environment. Followers of QAnon had long predicted a coming "storm," namely, a series of mass arrests and executions of Trump's enemies for various crimes. In 2020, a storm arrived, but not the one QAnon followers expected. Rather than a political revolution (or coup, depending on one's perspective), the storm came in the form of a once-in-a-generation pandemic that, in a few short months, destroyed all the economic progress made during Trump's presidency and set the stage for a new phase of democratic discontent.

9.4 AUTUMN OF THE POPULIST: CORONAVIRUS, STS, AND JANUARY 6TH

There are reasons to question the relevance of conspiracism to politics. Some argue that "belief" in such narratives are merely ways of signaling membership in a group (Berinsky 2018), or meaningless eccentricities that do not motivate political behavior in ways that cannot be explained by more grounded variables like populist attitudes or cultural discontent. The most compelling evidence to counter these dismissive interpretations can be found in two mass assaults on edifices of democracy at both state and national levels.

9.4.1 Conspiracism and Resistance to Covid-19 Restrictions

In May of 2020, armed protesters entered the Michigan statehouse to express their fury at government responses to the Covid-19 crisis, including economic shutdowns and mask mandates. The national response to Covid-19 was uncertain until the spring of 2020, when the Trump administration, under advice by public health officials, finally declared a state of emergency and recommended a major economic shutdown to stop the spread of the highly contagious coronavirus. Most states acceded to the recommendation, but the curve proved maddeningly difficult to flatten, and the shutdown dragged on longer than most people expected. Such state intervention in the economy was bound to arouse the fury of both radical neoliberals, who tend to oppose even minor governmental economic activity, as well as those whose livelihoods were negatively impacted by the sudden cessation of so much economic activity.

Trump gradually turned against his own public health advisors and officials, demanding that economies reopen themselves far earlier than most infectious disease specialists thought safe. This turn was all it took for polarization to begin imbruing the public health response: Trump began to promote treatments for Covid-19 that ranged from unproven (hydroxychloroquine) to the ludicrous (injections of bleach). He publicly mocked masked wearing and refused (for the most part) to actively promote vaccination.

Of course, it is possible to sympathize with those who are angry and anxious over the economic damage wrought by the economic shutdown while still accepting that such policies were necessary to preserve the lives and health of millions of people; however, the resistance to Covid-19 restrictions like masks strikes many as bizarre. Why such rage against such modest interventions, especially since they could facilitate a more rapid and complete economic reopening?

This resistance becomes much more intelligible when recognized for what it is: another manifestation of conspiracism. With the populist set against public health measures, the conspiratorial mindset of his followers began to bleed into the conversation around Covid-19. The protesters who stormed the Michigan statehouse were a mixture of citizens enraged by the economic slowdown and those who saw masks, vaccines, and shutdowns as nothing more than additional methods for the powers that be to control the people. Many argued that Covid-19 itself was a hoax. QAnon gradually incorporated Covid-19 into its metanarrative, with some arguing that masks were part of the plot to facilitate child sexual trafficking by obscuring their physical features (Spring and Wendling 2020).

The role of Trumpism, conspiracism, and cultural polarization is apparent in our survey data. The PSAS-US included several questions regarding attitudes toward Covid-19 restrictions: whether the risks of the Covid-19 vaccine are greater than those of the disease; whether mask mandates violate people's rights; whether economic shutdowns did more harm than good; if the person planned to get vaccinated against Covid-19

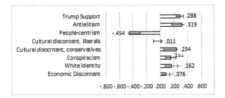

FIGURE 9.3 Regression analysis of Covid-19 restriction resistance.

as soon as possible (the survey was published after vaccines had been approved but before they were widely available); and whether the respondent always wears a mask in public. We used CFA techniques to combine these into a single index of Covid-19 restriction resistance, where higher scores indicate more resistance and less obedience. We regressed this index on support for Trump, populism, cultural discontent, ideology, conspiracism, economic distress, the usual control variables, and a dummy variable indicating if the respondent knows someone who was significantly sickened or killed by Covid-19. We estimated another model in which we include Jardina's (2019) measure of white identity politics (this model necessarily includes only white respondents). The results are presented in Figure 9.3.

To begin, we see again the importance of economics in Trumpist discontent: economic distress significantly predicted Covid-19 restriction resistance in both models. This is hardly surprising, as millions lost their jobs and incomes, or had businesses decimated or shuttered entirely due to the shutdown. However, the clearest pattern gleaned from these results is that Trumpism, including its anti-elitism, conservative cultural discontent, and conspiratorial ideation, was the key force driving resistance to measures necessary to curb the spread of coronavirus. All of these factors had significant associations with resistance, although the effect of cultural discontent was much weaker and insignificant among liberals (Est = 0.011; SE = 0.058; p = 0.850) than among conservatives, where the association was much stronger (Est = 0.234; SE = 0.093; p = 0.013). We also see that white identity politics are also associated with resistance, even when controlling for factors such as Trump support.

This last relationship requires a bit of logical deduction to explain but doing so sheds considerable light on why so many people, especially supporters of the former president, refused to take basic precautions in the midst of a pandemic. In a deeper analysis of these issues, we found that anti-elitism conditioned the influence of white identity: among those with intense anti-elite attitudes, the effect of white identity salience was accentuated (Utych, Navarre, and Rhodes-Purdy 2022). We conclude in this paper that white identity politics are inherently based on grievance and a sense of political exclusion, rather than positive solidarity seen among other racial groups. Having never experienced the marginalization that encourages such solidarity, white identification only emerges when individuals perceive themselves as victims.

Taken with the other results, we see strong evidence for the notion that Covid-19 restriction resistance was simply a new manifestation of the polarization and anti-system ideation that Trump had worked to inculcate in his followers. Masks and vaccines became part of the conspiracy. Only this manifestation had devastating consequences: we will never know how many thousands have died or will die because of the dynamics of polarization the populist exploited for his own gain.

9.4.2 Start the Steal: Fraud Conspiracies and the Insurrection of January 6th

Prior to Covid-19, Trump pushed the limits of US political institutions as far and as hard as he could, but for the most part they stood fast, as Weyland and Madrid (2019) predicted. But the strain on these norms and conventions grew as Trump deliberately encouraged polarization and flirted with both conspiracy theories and white nationalism. Even if competing factions in democracy share no interests and see each other as antagonists, they must still accept each other as members of the same nation and as thus entitled to respect for their political rights to function. This is difficult to sustain in a populist society where one sides sees the other as a Manichaean threat.

As the 2020 elections reached their conclusion, it became clear that Trump supporters' inability to accept that Trump could fail was sufficiently entrenched that it would inevitably mar the transfer of power should Trump lose. The populist himself contributed to this perception; Trump repeatedly claimed he could only lose a fraudulent election and that fraud would be made easier via the expanded voting-by-mail rules necessitated by the pandemic. As such, it was hardly surprising that Trump would refuse to accept the results of the election despite a decisive (if narrow) loss.

Nor was it shocking that Trump's supporters embraced his fraud narratives, primed as they were to believe in conspiracies, which is what the STS movement amounted to. The details of the conspiracy were typically bizarre, involving (among other things) foreign powers submitting

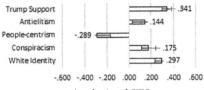

FIGURE 9.4 Analysis of STS support.

mail ballots tainted with bamboo, the deceased former populist leader of Venezuela, and legions of dead voters. However, what seems bizarre makes more sense when interpreted through the lens of a failing leader with charismatically attached followers resorting to conspiracism to cope. Any idea, no matter how implausible, is preferable to admitting the truth: that one's faith was misplaced, and that failures of governance were due to the incompetence of one's chosen leader.

To better demonstrate this, we again turn to the PSAS-US. We asked respondents a series of questions about the STS movement (we described this movement as believing that Trump lost the election to fraud and was associated with the January 6th disturbance at the Capitol).[10] We then regressed this measure of support for STS on the various aspects of democratic discontent we have discussed thus far: populism, conspiracism, cultural discontent, and support for Trump himself, as well as economic discontent (the effect of which was not significant) and the usual control variables. We again conducted a second model with white identity included, as we have shown evidence throughout this book and this chapter that this form of political identity is intimately connected to the feelings of exclusion and resentment that underlie Trumpism. The results are presented in Figure 9.4.

These data are consistent with our interpretation of STS as a manifestation of Trump-induced conspiratorial ideation. Trump support was the single strongest predictor of STS support. Anti-elitism, white identity, and conspiracism were also significantly associated with STS. The effect of people-centrism is interesting as it follows a pattern seen throughout this book, namely that this dimension of populism tends to be less important or even contradictory in its relationship with right-wing populism

[10] Questions include support for the goals and methods of STS, whether the actions of STS were mostly violent, whether the actions of STS were necessary, and whether members of STS were mostly good, decent people. Results of these analyses were similar when we used a single question measuring agreement with the contention that the 2020 elections were plagued by fraud of sufficient gravity to change the results.

and associated attitudes and behaviors. In this case the connection makes a great deal of sense: supporting a movement that assaulted the seat of democracy in an effort to thwart the peaceful transition of power to the victor of that election bespeaks a strong aversion to democratic principles. The effect of white identity is the most powerful predictor of support in the model that includes it, and is larger even than Trump support. This shows the extent to which Trumpism became enmeshed with white identity politics by the end of his administration, and how much those politics are defined by democratic discontent. Finally, we also found that cultural discontent influenced sympathy for STS, although in a somewhat roundabout manner. The direct effect of cultural discontent was significant and negative for liberals (Est. = −0.108; SE = 0.046; p = 0.019) but insignificant for conservatives (Est. = −0.09; SE = 0.075; p = 0.229). Here again, we see the polarizing influence of right-wing radicalism on the left, with discontented leftists more emphatically opposed to the actions of the right and more likely to view them in hostile and suspicious terms. Cultural discontent did indirectly encourage support for STS among conservatives by activating ideology: among the culturally contended, conservatism did not significantly influence STS sympathy (Est. = −0.009; SE = 0.010; p = 0.409), but the effect of conservatism among the discontented was strong and positive (Est. = 0.051; SE = 0.010; p = 0.000).

9.4.3 Why We Worry about Conspiracy Theories

Watching the January 6th insurrection unfold live on television, we imagine it was difficult for anyone who believes in democracy not to feel horror and outrage in equal measure. Yet in a scholarly work we must rise above these instinctual reactions,[11] and one way to do so is to ask a simple question: what if the Trumpists were right?[12] How would any of us react if we sincerely believed that a movement to which we were totally committed had won the right to remain in power through elections, only to have victory snatched away by elites that had been exploiting and ignoring us for years?

   It would be easy to dismiss this by arguing that the STS movement and unaffiliated believers in electoral fraud conspiracies do not "truly" believe the election was stolen but are merely engaging in motivated

---

[11] Which is not to say we should attempt to banish our emotional responses, because as we have argued throughout this book, emotions are not so easily banished, and are often quite useful in making sense of the world around us.

[12] Just to be clear: they were not.

reasoning. They desperately wanted Trump to remain in power, refused to accept that the majority disagreed, and violently attempted to overturn a fair election accordingly, with voter fraud a flimsy pretext and one with the added bonus of justifying restrictive voter laws that might change the outcome the next time.

We have no doubt that such motivated reasoning plays a role here, but the role that conspiracism plays in conjunction with charismatic attachment gives us pause. Motivated the reasoning might be, but not in the calculating and nefarious manner described above: STS adherents and other Trumpists were desperate for more than maintenance of their leader in power, but for any set of beliefs that might help them avoid the truth: that their leader was a narcissistic charlatan who cared little for anyone but himself and lacked the skills and the motivation to do much of anything that was not to his immediate benefit.

The evidence of this lies in the simple truth that many believers in STS are also skeptics of Covid-19 (in the PSAS-US the correlation between the two is 0.580) and the methods used to combat it, including vaccines that Trump advocated for and for which he deserves a certain amount of credit. And yet these individuals have refused en masse to get a safe and effective vaccine that could save their lives and the lives of their friends and family. As the Delta variant swept the country, reports emerged of such people demanding quack remedies or self-medicating with drugs purchased at farm and feed stores in lieu of the vaccine. A whole host of conspiracy theories emerged around the vaccine: that they alter DNA, cause miscarriages, or contain tracking devices courtesy of George Soros or Bill Gates. What precisely is the motivation behind *these* self-injurious delusions?

Conspiracy theories are, contrary to typical motivated reasoning narratives, independently dangerous. When people retreat from reality, they develop a mindset that is so distrustful of political authorities and institutions that anything associated with them becomes practically radioactive, to be avoided or attacked but never accepted. This can lead people who might otherwise value or even idolize the US system of government to attempt to destroy that very system, as occurred on January 6th, or it can lead them to avoid medical care that might save them from serious illness or death.

9.5 CONCLUSIONS: WHERE DO WE GO FROM HERE?

Scholars typically avoid taking strong positions on the topics they study. This is admirable but nearly impossible when said scholars strongly believe in the value and importance of democracy, as we do, while studying a topic which poses serious threats to democratic regimes, as ours does. Therefore, we feel free to admit that we, along with much of the rest of the country, breathed a sigh of relief when Trump finally decamped for Florida, with the peaceful transition of power successfully concluded, albeit with the word "peaceful" requiring a fairly large asterisk.

The relief did not last. The months since Biden's inauguration showed the continuing hold that Trumpism has on the Republican Party. That hold is in many ways stronger than the hold of Trump himself, who was recently booed at a rally for the having the temerity to speak a few mildly positive words about vaccination. The ethnonationalist populism Trump pushed and the conspiratorial mindset that went along with it are still here, and are now being championed by a new (if less charismatic) group of followers like Marjorie Taylor-Greene, Mo Brooks, Matt Gaetz, and Madison Cawthorn.

Although we find ourselves disheartened by the endurance of Trumpism, we are hardly surprised. As we have alluded to throughout this chapter, the dynamics of populism in power are separate from those of its emergence. Trump rode a wave of economic resentment and the cultural discontent it engendered to the White House. Yet, while he occupied that space the economy continually improved, while democratic discontent deepened and spread across the aisle to progressives. To put it succinctly, one cannot unring a bell. Cultural discontent, once triggered by economic trauma, follows its own malign logic: by accentuating identity boundaries and targeting out-groups, it multiplies the threat faced by said out-groups. This sets in motion a reciprocal process where the targeted groups respond in kind, with a vicious cycle of polarization ensuing. Add in a host of delusional beliefs that paint one's social adversaries as irredeemably evil, and the cycle only intensifies further. As we argue in Chapter 10, democratic discontent may be averted, but turning it back will be a far greater challenge.

10

Conclusions

Is Neoliberal Democracy Sustainable?

Throughout this book we have alluded to the inherent tension between neoliberal capitalism, with its inequities and the insecurity wrought by its creative destruction, and substantive democracy. In this concluding chapter, we address this topic more explicitly, tracing the implications of our findings for the future of both neoliberalism and democracy. To be blunt, we are not very optimistic, although we are not entirely without hope. We doubt that the populist movements of today will topple democracy tomorrow. Instead, we see the current trajectory of the democratic world as akin to a drunkard's walk, lurching back and forth between stability and periods of discontent, but moving ever closer to the eventual fall. Even as periods of discontent wax and wane, the damage done to democratic norms and institutions will carry from one episode to the next. The likeliest result are diminished and debased democracies which exhibit increasing governance problems, social polarization, and various forms of illiberalism and anti-pluralism.

We conclude the book by discussing political changes that would help avoid this fate. Most of our suggestions amount to fortifying democracy so that it can effectively dominate markets and force capitalism to function in a socially responsible manner. We should note that much of this chapter looks forward in time, beyond the present moment and thus outside the scope of any available data. As such, our discussion here is much more theoretical and speculative than in earlier chapters. Since we, like everyone else, see through a glass darkly, we both welcome and encourage a heightened degree of skepticism. We are less interested in firmly proving arguments than in raising new questions, highlighting possible implications of our findings for normative political theory and philosophy, and suggesting future avenues for both empirical research and political thought.

This book has covered a substantial amount of theoretical and empirical ground, and before speculating based on those findings, a summary is in order. In Chapters 1–3, we argued that phenomena such as populism, conspiracism, cultural polarization, outbreaks of contentious politics, and regime antipathy were all to some extent either direct manifestations of or influenced by the democratic discontent that emerged during the Great Recession(s). Reviewing the literature on these distinct manifestations revealed a common analytical divide between economics and culture. Each side can point to positive findings: macro-level institutions tended to find evidence of economic causation, with a less consistent but mostly null effect of culture, while individual-level analyses tended to find the opposite.

In Chapter 3, we rejected this dichotomy as illusory. This was not a simple matter of throwing the division between culture and economics aside, as each approach makes irreconcilably different assumptions about human motivation. On one side, we find rational and calculating utility-maximizers with a narrow focus on material well-being; on the other, we see people focused on norms, morals, and identities. Emotions resolved this impasse. Economic trauma, which spreads far and wide during economic crises, produces enduring arousal of negative emotions, namely anxiety and resentment. These emotions in turn trigger cognitive and motivational changes that predispose people to embrace discontented narratives. We also provide evidence that these emotions intensify identity conflicts, leading individuals to be more suspicious of and hostile toward perceived out-groups.

In the latter half of the book, we applied this theory to within-case and comparative analyses of countries that experienced significant discontented episodes. Rather than revisit the specifics of each case, we wish to highlight the most important findings gleaned when taking all the case studies together. First, the resentments borne of economic crises do not create group conflicts or contentious issues out of whole cloth, but instead exert sustained pressure on the social fabric. When discontent erupts, it does so at the weakest seams, coalescing around the most salient cleavage lines. This can be racial and ethnic divides (the USA), anxiety over the loss of national sovereignty (the UK, as well as Spain relating to both the role of the EU and the Catalan independence issue), and even issues like corruption (Brazil) or inequality (Chile) that are not cultural in the strictest sense of the term.

All these dynamics are shaped and molded by politics, particularly the health and robustness of democracy prior to the crisis. Economic discontent emerges from the interplay of objective and subjective factors. The objective reality of economic tumult that comes with a period of crisis certainly takes a toll on the emotional well-being of individuals, and thus on the peace and stability of the political system. Yet not all economic harm is created equal; perceptions of damage are subjective, and the most crucial factor that shapes those perceptions is the presence or absence of democratic voice. Countries with unresponsive democracies, due either to oligopolistic or inchoate party systems, lost citizen support much more readily than those that could muster even a weak form of citizen voice at critical moments (e.g. Canada, Portugal). And relatively modest downturns, such as the Chilean slowdown of 2018, could have repercussions akin to those of more severe recessions when citizens had little hope that the state would hear or respond to their demands.

In a sense, this book promotes cooperation and understanding across paradigms. We laid out over the preceding chapters how economics, culture, and politics are the very antithesis of nonoverlapping *magistra*. Particularly when the issue at question is the thoughts, feelings, and choices of ordinary people, these domains of social life are unified, because our units of analysis (i.e. people) exist simultaneously in all of them, and conditions in one area affect those in others. This presents a challenge to scholars, given our preference for neat and (relatively) parsimonious explanations for complex social processes. We hope we have shown a way to manage those difficulties, through the application of political and psychological theory and the use of mixed methods research where the weaknesses of one method are balanced by the strengths of another.

10.2 CAN NEOLIBERAL DEMOCRACY SURVIVE?

No work of research can answer every question it raises, and this one is no exception. Although our theory appears useful in contexts as diverse as Latin America, the North Atlantic, and southern Europe, we hope that scholars of other regions will apply it to see if complications such as post-communism (eastern Europe), recent decolonization (Africa), or declining social democracy (Scandinavia) change how it operates. We would also encourage students of other topics who grapple with the conflict between economic and cultural theories to borrow our APE approach to see if it might resolve those conflicts.

However, the most critical open question in the study of democratic discontent is whether it represents a genuine threat to democracy in the long run. One can easily observe underdeveloped countries where there can be no doubt; post-Chávez Venezuela comes immediately to mind. But that does not imply that populism and related political tendencies will become the kind of existential challenge to democracy that fascism was during the mid-twentieth century, or that communism was during the Cold War. On this point we tend to agree that history is over: we do not see a vague world-view like populism becoming a meaningful foil to liberal democracy, and nationalism has a way of destroying itself in the long run. What is likely, however, is that having vanquished their common foes, the two components of (neo)liberal democracy will increasingly turn on one another. Regardless of whether one favors the modifier or the noun, there is no happy ending here: unlike the grand ideological struggles of the twentieth century, this will be a struggle not of polar opposites but of two mutually contradictory worldviews that nevertheless depend on one another to survive and thrive.

10.2.1 Capitalism and Democracy

Political theorists and scholars of democracy have extensively analyzed the various synergies and contradictions between capitalism and democracy. Both the US founders and more modern liberals (Friedman 2020) have argued that free markets and private property were necessary preconditions for other freedoms, including the freedom of participation embodied by political democracy. There is some support for similar arguments in empirical studies: the correlation between advanced capitalism and democratic consolidation is among the strongest and best-supported in political science (Burkhart and Lewis-Beck 1994, Przeworski and Limongi 1997). Scholars have found that the dynamics of class competition (Rueschemeyer, Stephens, and Stephens 1992) and property rights regimes (Acemoglu and Robinson 2006, Baland and Robinson 2008) engendered or required by capitalism provide uniquely hospitable ground for democracy.

Students of capitalism are less enthusiastic about this symbiosis. Iversen and Soskice (2019), in a book defending the compatibility of capitalism and democracy that we discuss in detail shortly, provide a useful overview of this scholarship. Those who favor capitalism (Hayek 2007, Schumpeter 2008) fear that the political equality of democracy will lead short-sighted citizens to abandon capitalism in favor of state interference in the economy, to the point where economic liberalism will eventually give way to something like socialism. They are joined by early liberal theorists (Locke 2003, Montesquieu 2001) and practitioners such as the US founders, who attempted to design and implement political institutions that would limit the public role to the periodic selection of leaders from a "natural aristocracy" that would have the wisdom to preserve capitalism against the prevailing winds of public opinion.

Iversen and Soskice describe this literature primarily to rebut it; in their book *Democracy and Prosperity*, the authors provide the most thorough and convincing argument in recent years about the necessity of democracy to capitalism, and vice versa. We cannot possibly do justice to the book's argument here, but simply put they find that advanced capitalist democracy is historically uniquely resilient, and that democracy enhances capitalism by providing the infrastructure (including physical infrastructure and knowledge infrastructure like public universities) it needs to survive and advance and by incentivizing most groups (if not the left behind) to act as responsible citizens, supporting reasonable and competent political factions. They largely dismiss the recent eruption of populism as transient and driven by the marginalization of some groups that are unable to adapt to the postindustrial new capitalism. The plight of the left behind is political, rather than economic, and the authors are confident that it will eventually be resolved through democratic means.

Iversen and Soskice make a compelling argument; nevertheless, it suffers from several serious flaws. Perhaps the most critical flaw is that the typical voter they envision is unrecognizable to us. They see an electorate coolly calculating incentives, costs, and risks, and behaving accordingly. Although we have emphasized the importance of economic phenomena for explaining political behavior throughout this book, the vision of the rational voter promoted by Iversen and Soskice neglects the overwhelming and immediate importance of values and identities to which we also point. If values, norms, and identities manner, and we have spent this entire book arguing that they do, then the harmony between capitalism and democracy becomes much more questionable, because the two seek to impart irreconcilably different sets of beliefs and norms in society.

10.2.2 Authoritarian Governance in the Economy

The preceding discussion may have surprised some readers: after all, are not capitalism and democracy mutually founded on respect for individual rights, limited government, and the equality of persons? Perhaps in theory, but not in practice, as Elizabeth Anderson (2017) explains in her book *Private Government*. Anderson contextualizes liberal capitalism throughout history, thus revealing its shifting position in the ideological struggle between left and right. As originally formulated by thinkers like Ricardo and Smith, economic liberalism was almost radically egalitarian; the foundational works of capitalism envisioned a society of independent proprietors exchanging goods and services, free of the domination of feudal estates and guilds that hampered social and economic mobility. Smith particularly believed that a market so arranged would promote economic equality by eliminating privilege (Boucoyannis 2013).

This of course does not remotely resemble the capitalism we know today. Several factors contributed to this failed prediction, but Anderson emphasizes the fact that early liberal theorists failed to appreciate the power of collective action. Firms may be dreadful for the employees they dominate and exploit, but they also have an overwhelming advantage: they can apply selective incentives to ensure subordination of the individuals to the group (Olson 1971), and are thus far more efficient and productive than disorganized individuals. As a result, capitalism came to be dominated by ever larger firms, eventually metastasizing into the multinational corporations of today. This was no minor error of foresight (although early capitalists could hardly be faulted for failing to perfectly divine the future); it fundamentally changed the status of liberal capitalism from an equalizing (and thus politically left-wing) force. Instead, economic life in advanced capitalism is defined by hierarchy and inequality. Governance within firms is fundamentally authoritarian and illiberal; employees have few rights, and little say in how the organizations in which they are embedded function.[1] Other stakeholders (e.g. consumers) can occasionally influence firms through the use of voice or by "exiting" their relationship with the firm (Hirschman 1970). Yet mostly they are powerless, because the firm is a true collective actor, capable of imposing punishments and incentives to achieve university of purpose, while employees and consumers are (for the most part) left to press claims and demands alone. For a time during the twentieth century these facts were obscured by strong unions and the managerial capitalist ethos that emerged after World War II. But by the dawning of the age of the Great Recession, the bureaucratic authoritarianism of business firms was undeniable.

---

[1] Authority in firms where the workforce is unionized, as in most of Europe, is somewhat less arbitrary, but typically no less undemocratic and authoritarian.

We do not wish to unfairly paint all firms with the same brush: many treat their workers and customers well and plenty of bosses are not petty tyrants. Competition does provide some incentive for firms to behave themselves. Yet the fact remains that most citizens in democracies spend at least half their waking hours in illiberal authoritarian environments. This is particularly true of the left behind; educated urbanites are more likely to work in the public sector where they often have stronger job protections and support from capable unions, while those in the private sector often have sufficient skills to enjoy some insulation from the worst caprices of corporate authority. Workers with limited skills, on the other hand, who wish to escape the drudgery of the firm have few alternatives beyond self-employment, with all the attendant risks of inefficiency. The antidemocratic effects of economic authoritarianism are compounded by the decline in recent years of civic organizations and horizontally organized public spaces (Putnam 2000, Barber 1996). Without these voluntary organizations, employment in authoritarian economic firms represents virtually all the time many individuals spend in organized social environments.

10.2.3 Fearful Symmetry: The Link between Economic Authoritarianism and Ethnonationalism

The authoritarianism of the firm is only one way in which the neoliberal ethos has diffused through society. The ascendency of neoliberalism over democracy has tilted the distribution of values away from the latter and toward the former. To see this in action, one need only look at the spectacle of anti-mask mandate protests and vaccine refusal during the Covid-19 pandemic. Although the causes of Covid-19 restriction resistance were analyzed in Chapter 9, we did not discuss a more nebulous but still powerful influence on them: the infantile notions of "freedom" and "liberty" that have been propagated by neoliberal extremists. One of the more peculiar features of the late Trump era has been the issuance of books or speeches by former Republican Party and conservative elites (e.g. John Boehner, Mark Sanford, Paul Ryan) castigating the party for embracing Trump and deviating from true "principled conservatism," which inevitably includes things like limited government and personal freedom. The details differ but the core story presented in all these they-a-culpas is the same: a party dedicated to small government and free enterprise has been mysteriously crashed by a rowdy mob of white nationalist hooligans.

It just goes to show that charismatically attached followers of populists are not the only ones who struggle with critical self-reflection. Leaving aside the mercenary use of white nationalist tropes to justify the erosion of welfare capitalism (recall Regan's racialized welfare queens), the neoliberal advance paved the way for the ethnonationalist populism we see today. There is a direct line of descent from the "greed is good" ethos of Regan-era conservatism to the contemporary vaccine refusenik, who insists that their freedom to spread a preventable illness takes precedence over the freedom of everyone around them to live and breathe. Donald Trump and others like him elsewhere in the world are not deviations from the neoliberal ethos. They share a hypocritical conception of "freedom," where certain actors (firms for neoliberals, the dominant cultural group for ethnonationalists) retain the unacknowledged privilege of unity, group identity, and collective action, and should be free to act without restraint. What we see here is the toxic synthesis of neoliberal atomization and parochial group chauvinism predicted by Barber (1996). The unstated assumption justifying this ridiculous claim is that the refusenik is, unlike the elitist snobs pushing mass vaccination, a true member of "the people," and thus entitled to collective action, a right they would deny to anyone who is not a member of their group. The "real people of this country" do what they will, and everyone else suffers what they must.

In this contortion of logic, the FR has taken its cues from the market economy: like "the people," modern capitalism gives the exclusive right to collective action to the firm, while attempting to wear away the rights of citizens (through the gradual hollowing of the democratic state and the relegation of an ever-increasing set of issues to technocracy, rather than politics) as well as unions and consumers. Anti-Covid-19 restriction protests also betray a rueful sort of irony, as the proponents of this conception of freedom in the realm of public health are often victims of a similar conception in the economic sphere. In other words, many of these left behind Covid-19 deniers *suffer* from unequal access to collective action as workers and consumers, even as they seek to benefit from it in the culture wars. While we lack data and can only speculate, we cannot help but wonder if disease mitigation strategies are what these people are truly angry about. At the risk of extrapolating too far, we wonder whether these protests represent "weapons of the weak," as James Scott (2008) once called them. In other words, perhaps these protesters are venting fury at the capricious and unaccountable authority they face every day at work (or school, as we discuss later), but which they may not challenge.

The collective rage among some circles over Covid-19 restrictions provide these individuals with a safe and acceptable way to express their anger.

10.3 HOW DO WE FIX IT?

Neoliberal capitalism and democracy, deprived of common foes to unify them, have begun the inevitable process of devouring one another, with the former thus far playing the role of the glutton. Since we concede that democracy and markets are each necessary preconditions of the other, resolving this dilemma is not a simple matter of choosing one or the other and hoping it prevails. Allowing capitalism to undermine democracy will likely produce repeated bouts of discontent, especially populism, which in turn will weaken democratic institutions through polarization. And there is little evidence that modern democracy can function without markets.

Based on theoretical work on the relationship between capitalism and democracy, as well as our own findings in this book, we conclude that resolving the dilemma between markets and democracy requires reconciliation through the domination of one over the other. Either democracy or neoliberalism must eventually establish the fundamental logic of society, with the other relegated to a supporting role and confined within strict limits. This idea is hardly new: classical liberals argued that representative institutions must be carefully circumscribed through horizontal accountability to ensure that democracy would not supplant the liberal individualism of capitalism. Later theorists of capitalism (Schumpeter 2008) and liberalism (Riker 1988) renewed and updated this suggestion for the era of advanced capitalism. Although not directly pertaining to the conflict between neoliberalism and democracy, several studies of the recent surge of discontent have embraced the logic of constricting democracy to protect liberalism (Levitsky and Ziblatt 2018, Mounk 2018). Even progressive thinkers, who are typically more supportive of popular democracy than liberal academics, have begun to explore elevating certain institutions above democracy to protect the rights and interests of marginalized groups (Kendi 2019). Advocates of guardianship can find some support for their positions in our findings, especially our argument in Chapter 9 that populism can trigger a self-perpetuating cycle of polarization once in power. Preventing the start of such a cycle, some might argue, is of such overriding importance that it must take precedence over all other matters, including the provision of democratic voice.

Astute readers have probably guessed that we do not concur with these arguments. We have both philosophical and empirical objections. For the former, we note that the schemes these thinkers suggest amount to elaborations on the concept of political guardianship. Guardianship has its roots in Plato's philosopher kings, embodied in a modern context as economic technocrats, party elites (Levitsky and Ziblatt 2018), or special state organs such as a Department of Antiracism (Kendi 2019). Simply put, guardianship allows some class of persons (typically a highly educated group with specialized knowledge)[2] to exert ultimate control over society; day-to-day issues of governance are left to democratic officials, but they can always be overruled by the guardians. To counter the proponents of guardianship we rely on Robert Dahl's critique in *Democracy and Its Critics* (1989, ch. 4). Dahl argues that whoever the guardians may be, without accountability and divorced from the common run of social life, they will inevitably become a social interest group unto themselves, and pursue their own ends, rather than those of the citizenry. In short, benign guardianship cannot last indefinitely.

Indeed, the isolation of political elites and the lack of democratic competition that enables it were part of the reason why discontent surged in the first place. The best evidence of this is found in Chile, where democratic elitism and technocracy gradually led to the *estallido social* despite an admirable record of policy success, but all our discontented cases suffered from significant democratic deficits related to voice and responsiveness. This brings us to our empirical objection to guardianship, namely the fact that it precludes the possibility of strong voice. Throughout this book, we have highlighted numerous ways that the absence of democratic voice exacerbated the effects of economic crises: more negative evaluations of economic outcomes, more extreme emotional reactions to those outcomes, and more hostility to democratic institutions and parties as a result. Even when guardians are extremely competent (as in Chile), they will always slip sooner or later, and even modest failures can produce significant surges of discontent. Weakening democracy in favor of guardians would therefore inevitably lead to exactly the political outcomes it seeks to prevent.

If the effects of voice on discontent are a caution against guardianship and elitism, they also point to a more promising solution. In Chapter 9, we showed that voice, whether strong or weak, was sufficient to stave off discontent in Canada, Portugal, and Uruguay. In the struggle between democracy and neoliberal capitalism, the most promising solution is to maximize democracy and throw out the "neoliberal." We are not

---

[2] This group typically includes the advocate of the specific brand of guardianship in question, which we are sure is merely coincidental.

anti-market radicals, this book is neither red nor little, and we do not mean to imply that the socialization of the means of production would be necessary to save democracy. Quite the contrary; abandoning neoliberalism in favor of strong democracy would also strengthen markets and preserve the stability of market economies in the long run. In this we concur with recent work arguing that robust social democracy is the best guard against democratic discontent (Berman 2019), although renovated democracy in the postindustrial era will likely differ from social democracy in significant ways, given underlying structural changes. Markets would also benefit from this solution in the long run. If Iversen and Soskice (2019) are correct that markets and democracy are mutually necessary, strengthening democracy will help preserve the stability and integrity of the market economy. On the other hand, if the insecurity and instability of extreme neoliberalism is allowed to prevail, our findings show that a steady erosion of democracy is the most likely scenario, which will in turn threaten capitalism.

10.3.1 Resocialization of Risk

Turning to specifics, there are two major sets of reforms that we feel are necessary to ensure the future of democratic market economies. The first is the resocialization of economic risk. We have already spilled buckets of ink on the connection between economic insecurity and cultural and democratic discontent, and we will not revisit the issue any further, as anyone who is not convinced by now likely never will be. We do, however, have a few ideas on the matter that we have not explored thus far. First, the last thing anyone needs at the moment is a turn to revanchist statism. The British Labour Party learned this lesson much to its sorrow after yet another series of defeats after electing old-style socialist Jeremy Corbyn as its leader.[3] A return to the heyday of nationalization and statist democratic socialism may have appealed to a small but intense group of disaffected leftists, but outside this group it failed to spark any interest, reinforced the reputation of the Labour Party as economically irresponsible, and thus damaged the party's long-term electoral prospects. Nationalization may make sense in some circumstances (particularly natural monopolies like transit or energy infrastructure) but is not a winning political strategy, nor a promising solution to the crisis of neoliberal economics generally.

---

[3] Corbyn's lackadaisical approach to anti-Semitism in his ranks also contributed.

Furthermore, leftists and progressives are perhaps a bit wide of the mark in focusing on poverty reduction and economic inequality. Both are undeniable social problems, but addressing the former can unintentionally accentuate the divide between the poor and the rest of society, because it often implies means-tested solutions that set up resentments between the middle sectors, who must pay more for programs they hope never to need, and their less fortunate co-nationals. Inequality, meanwhile, has proven stubbornly difficult to politicize, mostly because citizens seem to focus more on material well-being and trajectory than on comparisons with others.

Insecurity, on the other hand, touches everyone, including the educated middle sectors who so offend the left behind. Even a college education is no longer the ticket to economic prosperity and security it once was. Competition from skilled service workers in developing countries, the increasing automation of tasks even in the information economy, and the rise of the "gig economy" and temporary skilled employment for writers, programmers, and the like, have all led members of the intellectual aristocracy closer to the economic position in which the left behind have long found themselves. As such, we believe that universalistic programs are likely to be more successful, both at alleviating insecurity across a broad subsection of society and at sustaining themselves politically. This runs directly counter to current conventional wisdom; neoliberal social policy holds that only the very poorest – those who are unable to provide for themselves – should be the targets of aid. There are some practical advantages to this approach; chief among them is that it maximizes the impact of social spending by directing aid to those who most need it[4] and for whom even modest monetary gains can make an enormous difference.

However, the neoliberal era has demonstrated that means-tested programs are inherently unsustainable and are thus unlikely to ward off democratic discontent. They are simply too vulnerable to encroaching resentment, especially during difficult times: as the financial health of more prosperous citizens erodes, they become less willing to contribute to welfare programs from which they receive no benefit. They also provide a dangerous beachhead for ethnonationalism in societies like the USA where race, ethnicity, and class overlap to a significant degree. Political movements wishing to cut such programs will be tempted to

---

[4] Though the burden placed on those who often have the least means to navigate the complicated eligibility requirements of means-tested programs makes this statement more theory than practice.

stoke racial resentments to build antagonism against them. Universalistic programs give the middle class a stake in maintaining the system: one need only look at the fiercely protective reaction Canadians and Britons have toward their health systems to see this.

Even programs that are not totally universal, that is, those which exclude some small proportion of the ultrarich, can help to minimize the racial, ethnic, and class-related divisions that means-tested programs so often stoke. Consider the rhetoric during the 2020 US election regarding free college tuition – the targets as "undeserving" of this policy were not marginalized groups in society but the obscenely wealthy. If policy debates focus on, say, how unfair it is that billionaires like Jeff Bezos' and Elon Musk's children can receive a college degree for free, and where excluding lines should be drawn, this removes quite a bit of the racialized rhetoric that has traditionally surrounded social welfare programs in the United States (Gilens 2009).

Even in our polarized era, benighted as it may be by discontent, we see some signs of progress here. Even a resolute centrist like Joe Biden has clearly realized that the state needs to do more to protect its citizens' economic well-being. His recent economic proposals (as of this writing working their way through the Kafkaesque labyrinth that is the legislative process) would expand family leave, childcare, and fiscal support for families, to name only a few. We encourage the left to lean into these sorts of reforms, namely those that require little if any navigation of complex administrative politics to access and provide support to the struggling middle sectors as well as the working class and poor. Such programs could be used to build cross-class solidarity, which over time could open the door to more innovative and dramatic reforms, such as a reduction in the length of the workweek or universal basic income programs.

Even on the center-right, we see some (extremely tentative) signs of movement in this direction. Mitt Romney, a moderate Republican senator, recently proposed a child tax credit with monthly cash disbursement similar to what was included in the most recent stimulus bill, with a termination of the Temporary Assistance to Needy Families program as part of the package. In this, we see a way forward for conservative parties to become a productive part of a post-neoliberal era: a replacement of means-tested support that often subjects its participants to humiliating conditions and impenetrable bureaucracy with a market-friendly, universalistic alternative. Devotees of the free market should take note: this sort of program, applied to other areas of social support, could easily be a way to restore the electoral viability of conservatism without resorting to alliances with ethnonationalists, while both improving social harmony and order and preserving the predominance of markets.

We should not be naive here; there are, of course, enormous challenges and equally massive opportunities for blunder and failure as the democratic world moves on from neoliberal orthodoxy. We see two primary impediments, the latter of which will segue into our second major area of reform. But first, we must acknowledge the difficulties that globalization implies for the socialization of risk. Having already discussed this issue at length in various places throughout the book, we will simply restate that global economic competition has shifted the balance of power away from states and toward transnational economic actors. Although we largely concur with Iverson and Soskice's assertion that the "race to the bottom" issue is overblown and capital not nearly as mobile as many assume, we also believe this problem could easily intensify should states start moving unevenly toward greater social support for citizens. In short, more aggressive movers may well suffer damage that advantages the timid, thus putting ambitious reform efforts in jeopardy.

Here too, we see reason for hope. Scholars such as Thomas Piketty (2018) have begun to grapple seriously with this problem and have begun crafting (admittedly hypothetical) solutions such as a global wealth tax. Political leaders have also taken note, as can be seen in the early moves made by advanced democracies to begin setting a floor on corporate taxes. The key to globally aware reform will be to provide security to the middle and working classes in developed countries *without* beggaring their neighbors in the underdeveloped world, as the recent hostility to trade embraced by populist nationalism does. There are historical precedents for how this might be managed. During the 1990s, the United States signed a pilot trade deal with Cambodia that gave the country preferential trade status in exchange for maintaining pro-social policies like workers' rights and the advancement of women (Sibbel 2007). The program eventually lapsed due to lack of a constituency in the USA but was very successful while in operation and could provide a model for a post-neoliberal trade regime.

The notion of international coordination on economic policy raises the question: would supranational governance of some sort be necessary to secure reforms of sufficient gravity to close out the age of discontent? To this we respond with an emphatic "no." We have no objection to the idea of supranational governance in theory, but one need only look to the conflicts over Brexit and austerity in southern Europe to see the potential for disaster. We have seen, time and again, how difficult real, substantive change is on a national or even subnational level. We do not have much faith that a supranational organization, allowing for considerably more heterogeneity in political worldviews, would serve to cure any of these problems. Entertaining the notion of new supranational organization is putting the cart before the horse; it would be far more prudent to fix the institutions we currently have, rather than imagining new ones on a much grander scale.

10.3.2 Toward a New Democratic Era

This leads us to our final, and we believe most crucial, proposed reform: democratization. The reforms we have mentioned thus far will be extraordinarily difficult to implement without a resuscitation of democratic representation and voice. The erosion of risk socialization was enabled in the first place by anemic democracies that allowed the political elite to converge around neoliberalism while suffering few electoral repercussions. The clearest evidence of this is that the states with the most robust democracies, such as Scandinavian social democracies and (within our sample) Uruguay, were also those who were least enthusiastic in slashing their safety nets. The era of recession and discontent in which we find ourselves has aroused much of the political elite from its earlier stupor; but crafting a post-neoliberal world will require concentrated and sustained political pressure. This in turn will require an engaged citizenry, embedded in strong organizations, operating in institutional contexts that force elites to respond to such pressure.

10.3.3 Continuous Democracy

No matter what reforms states implement, eventually there will be problems, people will suffer, and economies will go through periods of struggle. All human history points to the inevitability of economic crisis. To prevent such strife from engulfing culture and politics, democratic states must rebuild their legitimacy, and the most effective way to do so is to enhance citizen voice. We cannot be as specific on democratic reforms as we were on economic ones, because every democracy is different, and reforms will need to be pursued within and tailored to each country's historical and institutional context. We can, however, outline some general principles which might guide activists and democrats as they push systems toward greater voice.

To provide sufficient citizen voice, democracies must become continuous and comprehensive. By "continuous," we mean that voice must be freed as much as possible from discrete moments in time (i.e. elections); the exercise of citizen voice should be an ongoing, constant process. This notion weighs against one of the trendier mechanisms to enable voice, namely direct and participatory democracy. Both have potential, but they also suffer from significant shortcomings (Altman 2010, Wampler 2015, Rhodes-Purdy 2017b), including suffering from the same discrete nature of representative elections: between instances, citizens remain voiceless. As has been argued elsewhere (Rhodes-Purdy and Rosenblatt 2021, Pérez Bentancur, Piñeiro Rodríguez, and Rosenblatt 2018, 2020), political parties are a far more promising vehicle for voice because they can facilitate its use on an ongoing basis. This is in line with recent work by students of populism like Jan-Werner Müller (2021), who argues that revitalizing intermediate institutions like political parties and free media is essential to resuscitating democracy.

Revitalizing parties requires a discussion of the types of parties that might best serve the provision of democratic voice. Although the specific details of the Uruguayan FA would be difficult to completely capture outside that country's unique historical development, several characteristics of the party would be useful guides for parties seeking to deepen their social roots. These include the institutional guarantee (through party rules and procedures) of grassroots control, the use of participatory meetings to set policy and strategy, and the structure of the party as a permanent coalition of social organizations. The broad front model has promise for increasingly heterogeneous societies: by securing loyalty through efficacy and voice, while resolving disputes and conflicts through internal and external democratic mechanisms, it provides an alluring way to manage the factionalism and diversity inherent to the political left in advanced societies.

Of course, institutional reform will also be necessary to accommodate and encourage this sort of party reformation. Most of the discontented states we analyze here would have benefited from a larger number of parties, particularly on the left. As we described in Chapter 9, a divided left and the competition it engendered helped force moribund parties to innovate and take risks, which eventually paid off in the form of greater citizen support in Portugal and Canada. There are certainly pitfalls here: one can easily find cases where discontent has roots in governability crises caused by an excessive number of parties; Italy and Israel spring immediately to mind. Again, Uruguay and its DSV system suggest a promising way forward: it encourages enduring (but not unbreakable) coalitions of pseudo-partisan factions, which maintain their own identities and platforms while facilitating governance. We do not mean to imply that all countries should adopt this system; rather, we should take note of the way it balances governability and representation/participation and try to craft institutional reforms along similar lines that would work in context. For example, plurality systems could adopt ranked voting systems which allow only one candidate per list, but where parties may have multiple lists with set platforms and agendas. The process of reallocating ranked votes could then proceed at the party level, then within the majority party to select a candidate from the majority list.

Reform of electoral politics can only take us so far. Political actors (especially on the left) will also need to cool their flirtations (or in some cases ongoing affairs) with antidemocratic institutional guardianship. It is difficult to criticize the use of courts and judicial review to secure rights for marginalized groups. Yet using nondemocratic means to achieve these goals has a cost. It robs the decisions of democratic legitimacy and renders them vulnerable to challenge and backlash; one need only look to the politics of abortion rights in the United States. We think it plausible that reproductive freedom might be more expansive and secure had it been pursued through democratic institutions than it is today, with a court dominated by archconservatives apparently eager to destroy what remains of the constitutional right to choose. Furthermore, reliance on the courts (or other guardians like Kendi's Department of Antiracism) tends to have a stupefying effect on the left, enervating its drive to forge new coalitions with culturally conservative but economically marginalized groups.

The example that springs to mind here is the alliance between Harvey Milk, the first openly gay elected official in the United States, and the beer truckers' union. Both sides of the alliance had to overcome mutual suspicion and even hostility, but ultimately the boycott (organized by Milk) of Coors, the last company to strike a deal with the union, proved decisive in forcing the company to meet the drivers' demands (Shilts 1982, 82–84). The unlikely alliance continued throughout Milk's tenure as San Francisco city supervisor until his assassination. This kind of coalition building was essential during the dawn of the LGBTQ rights movement, when the courts were unlikely to intervene on the movement's behalf. Should culturally progressive leftists moderate the pursuit of postmaterialist issues through courts, it would provide incentives to reach out to groups with whom they rarely interact, and potentially build larger coalitions that would both enable progressive reform and perhaps ease some of the cultural anxieties and resentments that have become so troublesome.

10.3.4 Comprehensive Democracy

None of these reforms are likely to be sustainable when so many democratic citizens spend the bulk of their public lives, from cradle to grave, in profoundly authoritarian environments. Democracy must therefore become not just continuous but comprehensive, which requires extending democracy to all social groups and into new spheres of social life. The former element is currently under significant threat thanks to the rise of the FR, often assisted by neoliberal conservatives. The ethnonationalist beliefs of the FR hold that only those who conform to the norms and morals of the cultural majority are part of the "true people" and thus worthy of participation in self-governance. As such, no matter how often such actors demand that power be returned to the people, they have few compunctions about violating the political rights of those groups they feel do not properly belong to that category.

These ideas have recently manifested in attacks on the democratic process, especially the integrity and security of elections, and these attacks were deeply racialized. Allegations were invariably directed to majority Black urban centers, with a clear implication that these jurisdictions (and by extension the constituents they serve) are corrupt and untrustworthy. And while these arguments may not have been embraced by the mainstream, neoliberal right, the proposed solutions to the issues were. Republican Party leaders rallied around new rounds of voter suppression laws that were often thinly veiled attempts to make voting more difficult for people of color. Lest anyone think these trends are a uniquely US phenomenon, the use of bogus allegations of voter fraud have metastasized around the world; Jair Bolsonaro has recently used similar claims to try to alter electoral procedures in Brazil and to intimidate judges investigating him and his family for corruption. Nor are these tactics, or the neoliberal/FR alliance that pushes them, entirely novel. As we have already discussed, neoliberals have long used ethnonationalist appeals strategically to attack the welfare state.

The first step in making democracy more comprehensive, therefore, is to remove as far as possible barriers that marginalized groups face when engaging with politics. States need to enact or revive legislation to prevent racially motivated attacks on suffrage. This is surely easier said than done, given that these reforms tend to be highly politicized. However, methods to increase access to the ballot box, through increased options for voting (both by expanding the amount of time available for in-person voting, and making voting in absentia, either via mail or, perhaps in the future, online, easier) must be pursued. Reforms such as eliminating felon disenfranchisement, lowering the voting age, and eliminating various structural barriers to voting would serve to strengthen democracy worldwide. Reforming campaign finance so that parties of the economic elite are not structurally advantaged would also improve representation among the marginalized. Finally, some of the reforms we discuss earlier in this section related to continuous democracy, specifically those that would encourage parties to actively engage with all social groups in their search to maximize votes. Given the importance of this issue, it might be advisable to adopt even more drastic reforms, such as compulsory voting.

Reforms could also occur within electoral systems. First past the post systems serve to limit the number of competitive parties, leading to disillusionment among citizens who feel they are not represented by a major party. Proportional systems seek to solve this, but systems with excessively welcoming thresholds are often resigned to perpetual minority governments, which may serve to destabilize the political system and allow, to put it charitably, less than serious parties to gain representation in government. This could lead to a rise in ethnonationalist parties in government, which we have seen throughout much of Europe.[5] That is to say, we do not have a concrete solution here, as states must grapple with which electoral system allows for fair representation of minority interests, while also maintaining a stable democratic regime.

Even if we perfect democracy in the political arena, this would do little to resolve the issue of entrenched authoritarianism in other areas of social life, especially the economy. If democratic values are to have a chance to define those of society, democratic modes of decision-making need to be extended into firms. This is not so radical as it sounds: if history is over, and democracy is the only morally acceptable principle of governance, why should we tolerate anything else in realms outside the political? Readers who still feel this is fancifully aspirational should note that precedents for it already exist, and reforms building on those precedents could proceed in a gradualist fashion. Legal reforms could abolish shareholder capitalism and provide corporate representation of consumer associations and employees; cooperatively owned enterprises already accomplish something like this. Robert Dahl (1985) made a similar argument for the extension of democracy into the economic sphere.

---

[5] Which, we suppose, is still a better alternative than one of two major parties becoming a de facto ethno-nationalist party, as we may have observed in the United States.

The process should begin even earlier in citizens' lives. All the authors of this book are both educators and parents of small children, and we therefore understand the implausibility of democratic governance within schools. And yet by virtue of these same characteristics we are acutely aware of how neoliberalism's combination of an atomized notion of freedom and authoritarianism has taken root in public education. Education today bears little resemblance to the idealism of US reformers like Horace Mann, who saw public education as a method of avoiding the "woe to the republic that rests upon no better foundations than ignorance, selfishness, and passion" (Winthrop 2020, 2). Instead, schools operate like factories, with students either products (in K-12) or consumers (in higher education), with all the trappings of industrialization-like quantitative metrics, and the incentives and punishments that go with them. As Rebecca Winthrop (2020) argues in a Brookings Institute report, schools are increasingly concerned with producing workers, not citizens. She argues that schools must return to an emphasis on civic education, teaching the skills necessary to allow students to participate in self-governance.

We do not agree that the solution here is as simple as teaching a different set of skills. The pedagogical model embraced in much of world has the neoliberal ethos at its very core. We are not very hopeful that authoritarian and antisocial methods can teach democratic skills. Instead, methods should be changed to better encourage autonomy and personal and moral development. There is no need to reinvent the wheel here, as several such pedagogical systems exist, some of which have or are currently developing extensive evidentiary support: from the Scandinavian concept of *bildung*, which emphasizes "the way that the individual matures and takes upon him or herself ever bigger personal responsibility toward family, friends, fellow citizens, society, humanity, our globe, and the global heritage of our species, while enjoying ever bigger personal, moral and existential freedoms" (Andersen and Björkman 2017, 14), to Montessori methods.[6] Empirical evidence suggests that any feared trade-off between the practical skills so prized by neoliberalism and the developmental potential of these methods is illusory. Scandinavian students routinely achieve some of the best standardized test scores in the world, and recent

---

[6] Montessori has a very bourgeois reputation in the United States, which given its prevalence in private schools is not undeserved. It was originally pioneered, however, for use with the most deprived and challenging students in Maria Montessori's native Rome, and was designed in part as a form of anti-fascist education that would give students the confidence, autonomy, and liberal values necessary to resist authoritarianism (Duckworth 2008).

high-quality studies of Montessori methods have shown they can virtually eliminate the racial achievement gap (Lillard et al. 2017).

Firms and schools are simply the most prominent examples of authoritarian enclaves in democratic societies: prodemocracy movements should encourage democratic norms in all realms of society to the extent that they are practically possible. Students should be taught democratic skills but also democratic values: the importance of compromise, the power of collective action, the need to accept legitimate outcomes with which they may not agree, the impermissibility of coercing others to accept one's own beliefs, and so on. Yet, these values cannot be taught entirely from books; they must be acquired through demonstration and experience. Schools should strive to model these values in every aspect of their operations, not just their curricula.

10.4 CONCLUDING THOUGHTS: THE HIDDEN RISKS OF DOING NOTHING

Our postmodern era is defined by paradox: humanity has never had more control over its own destiny, while humans have arguably never had less. Technological and scientific innovations have improved healthcare, advanced longevity, and created material plenty for an ever-expanding proportion of the global population. Emerging technologies like renewable energy, industrial automation, and artificial intelligence may well put an end to both scarcity and toil within our lifetimes. In some ways, life in the state of nature grows nicer, more refined, and longer by the day.

However, to facilitate the cooperation and coordination necessary to achieve the advances described above, societal organization has expanded in scale and rapidly increased in complexity. Specialized knowledge is increasingly crucial for all types of social decision-making, preventing ordinary people from understanding and participating in those processes. Our lives are structured by a nearly infinite number of decisions made by powerholders who are more remote from those they govern than ever before in history.

The logic of neoliberalism has only exacerbated this contradiction. The idea of freedom as the near total absence of social interference in the life of the individual, with exceptions carved out for the economically powerful (or among the FR, for the ethnoracial majority), have augmented the helplessness and enervation that defines postmodern life. To counteract it, we need a shift in how we think about what constitutes a "free society." In the words of Justice Harlan of the US Supreme

Court, commenting on a challenge to compulsory vaccination, freedom cannot be "an absolute right in each person to be, in all times and in all circumstances, wholly free from restraint" (Mariner, Annas, and Glantz 2005). Such freedom is intrinsically antisocial. For one, it is not possible for all citizens to enjoy such a conception of freedom simultaneously: as we see with the anti-vax movement, the freedom of some must inevitably be given precedence over others. Freedom becomes perverse: it coddles social hierarchies and systems of power and control rather than liberating individuals from them. More practically, it precludes the possibility of meaningful collective action that could counterbalance the self-destructive tendencies of capitalism. States should not unnecessarily interfere nor entangle themselves with markets. But markets cannot exist without stable societies and the public goods they provide. As such, societies of citizens acting through democratic mechanisms should be free to set whatever regulations and capture whatever portion of wealth they deem appropriate to ensure that all members have a decent and secure standard of living. Doing so is not a violation of economic freedom but a necessary precondition for sustaining it.

Some readers may well find this chapter unrealistically speculative, or excessively dramatic in the face of what they see as a transient episode that will soon regress back to the old neoliberal equilibrium. While it may be comforting to assume that this era of discontent too shall pass, we strenuously disagree for one simple reason: our findings strongly imply that, while the targets of discontent may be wildly wide of the mark in the case of the FR, the current state of society in the democratic world makes discontent inevitable, and in some cases politically necessary. One need only to look at the BLM movement to show the power discontent can have to organize groups in search of real progress. There is no doubt, faced with generational histories of slavery and discrimination, that Black Americans *should* be discontented with the fact that extrajudicial murders against members of their community so routinely go unpunished. It is entirely natural to be outraged when one sees working people lose their homes through no fault of their own, especially in an era where the obscenely wealthy only see their stock portfolios grow. When women are faced with routine sexual harassment in nearly any area of life, when refugees flee political oppression only to be met with scorn and disdain in their unfamiliar new home, when immigrants are scapegoated for the color of their skin or their national origin, when same-sex couples are denied access to a wedding venue, or when someone's race, religion, gender, or sexual orientation are targeted and attacked by political representatives, discontent is a natural result. We imagine that few readers will struggle to find their own additions to this list.

Discontent itself, in other words, is not the primary problem. Instead, the problem becomes *where* this discontent is channeled. Discontent is troubling because it so frequently rears its head in ugly (e.g. xenophobic, ethnocentric, and racist) ways, or because it is co-opted by demagogues who care little for their followers and less for democracy – instead of focusing on the root causes of political strife. The greatest tragedy of this era of discontent is the tendency of neoliberalism's victims to turn against each other, and against the politics that might provide a solution to their struggles.

The age of discontent has certainly had its dark moments. But it has also aroused societies from complacency and encouraged a new degree of political engagement among those who otherwise would have languished in apathy, and thus it might just be the perfect time to begin crafting a new kind of politics. As we showed in our discussion of responsiveness, when all faith in the system is lost, fortune favors the bold. In our current era, reformist political movements and activists can escape paralyzing risk aversion and gamble on ambitious platforms with the knowledge that they are more likely to be rewarded than at any time in recent memory. On the other hand, we could see continued paralysis and erosion of support for democratic regimes and principals, with vicious cycles of discontent and polarization slowly but steadily poisoning societies. In short, the risks of any actions must be balanced against the existential threat of inaction. The future of both markets and democracy hangs in the balance.

References

Abramowitz, Alan I. 2011. "Partisan polarization and the rise of the tea party." *Presented at the Annual Meeting of the American Political Science Association*, Seattle, WA.

Abramowitz, Alan I. 2018. *The great alignment: Race, party transformation, and the rise of Donald Trump*. New Haven: Yale University Press.

Abramowitz, Alan, and Jennifer McCoy. 2018. "United States: Racial resentment, negative partisanship, and polarization in Trump's America." *The ANNALS of the American Academy of Political and Social Science* 681 (1): 137–156.

Abramowitz, Alan I., and Kyle L. Saunders. 2008. "Is polarization a myth?" *The Journal of Politics* 70 (2): 542–555.

Abramowitz, Alan I., and Steven Webster. 2016. "The rise of negative partisanship and the nationalization of U.S. elections in the 21st century." *Electoral Studies* 41: 12–22.

Acemoglu, Daron, and James Robinson. 2006. *The economic origins of dictatorship and democracy*. Cambridge: Cambridge University Press.

Achen, Christopher, and Larry Bartels. 2017. "Blind retrospection: Electoral responses to droughts, floods, and shark attacks." In *Democracy for Realists*, edited by Christopher Achen and Larry Bartels, 116–145. Princeton, NJ: Princeton University Press.

Adams, James, and Zeynep Somer-Topcu. 2009. "Policy adjustment by parties in response to rival parties' policy shifts: Spatial theory and the synamics of party competition in twenty-five post-war democracies." *British Journal of Political Science* 39 (4): 825–846.

Adorno, Theodor, Else Frenkel-Brenswik, Daniel J. Levinson, and R. Nevitt Sanford. 2019. *The authoritarian personality*. New York: Verso Books.

Aguilar, Rosario, and Ryan E. Carlin. 2017. "Ideational populism in Chile? A case study." *Swiss Political Science Review* 23 (4): 404–422.

Akkerman, Agnes, Cas Mudde, and Andrej Zaslove. 2014. "How populist are the people? Measuring populist attitudes in voters." *Comparative Political Studies* 47 (9): 1324–1353.

Albertson, Bethany, and Shana Kushner Gadarian. 2015. *Anxious politics: Democratic citizenship in a threatening world*. Cambridge: Cambridge University Press.

Allport, Gordon Willard, Kenneth Clark, and Thomas Pettigrew. 1954. *The Nature of Prejudice*. New York: Basic Books.

Altemeyer, Robert A. 1981. *Right-wing authoritarianism*. Winnepeg: University of Manitoba Press.

Altemeyer, Robert A. 1996. *The authoritarian specter*. Cambridge, MA: Harvard University Press.

Altman, David. 2010. *Direct democracy worldwide*. Cambridge: Cambridge University Press.

Altman, David. 2011. *Direct democracy worldwide*, Kindle edition. Cambridge: Cambridge University Press.

Álvarez, Roberto, Álvaro García-Marín, and Sebastián Ilabaca. 2021. "Commodity price shocks and poverty reduction in Chile." *Resources Policy* 70: 101177.

Ames, Barry. 2002. *The deadlock of democracy in Brazil*. Ann Arbor: University of Michigan Press.

Andersen, Lene Rachel, and Tomas Björkman. 2017. *The Nordic secret*. Stockholm: Fri tanke.

Anderson, Benedict. 2006. *Imagined communities: Reflections on the origin and spread of nationalism*. London: Verso Books.

Anderson, Christopher J. 2007. "The end of economic voting? Contingency dilemmas and the limits of democratic accountability." *Annual Review of Political Science* 10: 271–296.

Anderson, Elizabeth. 2017. *Private government*. Princeton, NJ: Princeton University Press.

Anderson, John R. 1983. "A spreading activation theory of memory." *Journal of Verbal Learning and Verbal Behavior* 22 (3): 261–295.

Andrews-Lee, Caitlin. 2019. "The revival of charisma: Experimental evidence from Argentina and Venezuela." *Comparative Political Studies* 52 (5): 687–719.

Angyal, Andras. 1941. *Foundations for a science of personality*. New York: The Commonwealth Fund.

Arendt, Hannah. 1973. *The origins of totalitarianism*, Vol. 244. Boston: Houghton Mifflin Harcourt.

Autor, David Dorn, Gordon Hanson, and Kaveh Majlesi. 2020. "Importing political polarization? The electoral consequences of rising trade exposure." *American Economic Review* 110 (10): 3139–3183.

Baiocchi, Gianpaolo. 2001. "Participation, activism, and politics: The Porto Alegre experiment and Deliberative democratic theory." *Politics & Society* 29 (1): 43–72.

Baker, Andy. 2009. *The market and the masses in Latin America: Policy reform and consumption in liberalizing economies*. Cambridge: Cambridge University Press.

Baker, Peter. 2019. "Trump declares a national emergency, and provokes a constitutional clash." *New York Times*, February 15.

Baland, Jean-Marie, and James A Robinson. 2008. "Land and power: Theory and evidence from Chile." *American Economic Review* 98 (5): 1737–1765.

Balta, Evren, Cristóbal Rovira Kaltwasser, and Alper H. Yagci. 2022. "Populist attitudes and conspiratorial thinking." *Party Politics* 28 (4): 625–637.

Bandura, Albert. 1977. "Self-efficacy: Toward a unifying theory of behavioral change." *Psychological Review* 84 (2): 191–215.

Bandura, Albert. 1982. "Self-efficacy mechanism in human agency." *American Psychologist* 37 (2): 122–147.

Barber, Benjamin R. 1996. *Jihad vs. McWorld: How globalism and tribalism are reshaping the world.* New York: Ballentine Books.

Bartle, John. 2018. "Why the conservatives lost their majority – but still won." In *None past the post: Britain at the polls, 2017*, edited by Nicholas Allen and John Bartle, 272–319. Manchester: Manchester University Press.

Başok, Emre, and Peter Sayer. 2020. "Language ideologies, language policies and their translation into Fiscal policies in the U.S. perspectives of language education community stakeholders." *Journal of Culture and Values in Education* 3 (2): 54–80.

Becker, Sascha O., Thiemo Fetzer, and Dennis Novy. 2017. "Who voted for Brexit? A comprehensive district-level analysis." *Economic Policy* 32 (92): 601–650.

Berinsky, Adam J. 2018. "Telling the truth about believing the Lies? Evidence for the limited prevalence of expressive survey responding." *The Journal of Politics* 80 (1): 211–224.

Berman, Sherri. 2019. "Populism and the decline of social democracy." *Journal of Democracy* 30 (3): 5–19.

Bermeo, Nancy, and Larry Bartels. 2014. *Mass politics in tough times: Opinions, votes and protest in the Great Recession.* Oxford: Oxford University Press.

Bidegain, Germán, and Víctor Tricot. 2017. "Political opportunity structure, social movements, and malaise in representation in Uruguay, 1985–2014." In *Malaise in representation in Latin American countries*, edited by Alfredo Joignant, Mauricio Morales Quiroga, and Claudio Fuentes, 139–160. New York: Springer.

Birdsall, Nancy, Nora Lustig, and Christian J. Meyer. 2014. "The strugglers: The new poor in Latin America?" *World Development* 60: 132–146.

Booth, John A., and Mitchell Seligson. 2009. *The legitimacy puzzle: Political support and democracy in eight nations.* Cambridge: Cambridge University Press.

Borzutzky, Silvia, and Sarah Perry. 2021. "'It is not about the 30 pesos, it is about the 30 years': Chile's elitist democracy, social movements, and the October 18 protests." *The Latin Americanist* 65 (2): 207–232.

Boucoyannis, Deborah. 2013. "The equalizing hand: Why Adam Smith thought the market should produce wealth without steep inequality." *Perspectives on Politics* 11 (4): 1051–1070.

Brader, Ted, and George E. Marcus. 2013. "Emotion and political psychology." In *The Oxford handbook of political psychology*, edited by Leonie Huddy, David Sears, and Jack Levy, 165–204. Oxford: Oxford University Press.

Breen, Richard, Kristian Bernt Karlson, and Anders Holm. 2013. "Total, direct, and indirect effects in logit and probit models." *Sociological Methods & Research* 42 (2): 164–191.

Brockner, Joel, Mary Konovsky, Rochelle Cooper-Schneider, Robert Folger, Christopher Martin, and Robert J. Bies. 1994. "Interactive effects of procedural justice and outcome negativity on victims and survivors of job loss." *The Academy of Management Journal* 37 (2): 397–409.

Bruder, Martin, Peter Haffke, Nick Neave, Nina Nouripanah, and Roland Imhoff. 2013. "Measuring individual differences in generic beliefs in conspiracy theories across cultures: Conspiracy mentality questionnaire." *Frontiers in Psychology* 4 (225). https://doi.org/10.3389/fpsyg.2013.00225.

Bruton, Henry J. 1998. "A reconsideration of import substitution." *Journal of Economic Literature* 36 (2): 903–936.

Bunce, Valerie. 2001. "Democratization and economic reform." *Annual Review of Political Science* 4 (1): 43–65.

Burkhart, Ross E., and Michael S. Lewis-Beck. 1994. "Comparative democracy: The economic development thesis." *American Political Science Review* 88 (4): 903–910.

Busby, Ethan, Joshua R. Gubler, and Kirk A. Hawkins. 2019. "Framing and blame attribution in populist rhetoric." *Journal of Politics* 81 (2): 616–630.

Campbell, Angus, Gerald Gurin, and Warren E. Miller. 1954. *The voter decides*. Evanston: Row, Peterson.

Campbell, Rosie. 2018. "A coalition of chaos: Where next?" In *None past the post: Britain at the polls, 2017*, edited by Nicholas Allen and John Bartle, 320–353. Manchester: Manchester University Press.

Carr, Marilyn, and Martha Alter Chen. 2002. *Globalization and the informal economy: How global trade and investment impact on the working poor*. Geneva: International Labour Office.

Carreras, Miguel, Yasemin Irepoglu Carreras, and Shaun Bowler. 2019. "Long-term economic distress, cultural backlash, and support for Brexit." *Comparative Political Studies* 52 (9): 1396–1424.

Cassim, Ziyad, Borko Handjiski, Jörg Schubert, and Yassir Zouaoui. 2020. "The $10 trillion rescue: How governments can help deliver impact." McKinsey & Company. www.mckinsey.com/industries/public-and-social-sector/our-insights/the-10-trillion-dollar-rescue-how-governments-can-deliver-impact. Accessed July 22, 2022.

Castanho Silva, Bruno, Ioannis Andreadis, Eva Adnduiza, Nebojsa Blanusa, Yazmin Morlet Corti, Gisela Delfino, Guillem Rico, Saskia P. Ruth-Lovell, Bram Spruyt, Marco Steenbergen, and Levente Littvay. 2018. "Public opinion surveys: A new scale." In *The ideational approach to populism: Concept, theory and analysis*, edited by Kirk A. Hawkins, Ryan E. Carlin and Cristóbal Rovira Kaltwasser, 150–178. New York: Routledge.

Castanho Silva, Bruno, Federico Vegetti, and Levente Littvay. 2017. "The elite is up to something: Exploring the relation between populism and belief in conspiracy theories." *Swiss Political Science Review* 23 (4): 423–443.

Castiglioni, Rossana. 2005. *The politics of social policy change in Chile and Uruguay: Retrenchment versus maintenance 1973–1998*. New York: Routledge.

Castro, Irene. 2013. Diez incumplimientos electorales de Mariano Rajoy. *El Dario*, November 19.

CBC News. 2008. "Barbs fly over economy as leaders return to campaign trail." *CBC News*, October 3. www.cbc.ca/news/canada/barbs-fly-over-economy-as-leaders-return-to-campaign-trail-1.716130. Accessed August 27, 2021.

Chagas-Bastos, Fabrício H. 2019. "Political realignment in Brazil: Jair Bolsonaro and the right turn." *Revista de Estudios Sociales* (69): 92–100.

Chambers, Simone, and Jeffery Kopstein. 2001. "Bad civil society." *Political Theory* 29 (6): 837–865.

Choi, Eunjung, and Jongseok Woo. 2010. "Political corruption, economic performance, and electoral outcomes: A cross-national analysis." *Contemporary Politics* 16 (3): 249–262.

Christin, Thomas, Simon Hug, and Pascal Sciarini. 2002. "Interests and information in referendum voting: An analysis of Swiss voters." *European Journal of Political Research* 41 (6): 759–776.

Clarke, Harold, Matthew Goodwin, and Paul Whiteley. 2017. *Brexit: Why Britain voted to leave the European Union.* Cambridge: Cambridge University Press.

Clarke, Harold, Paul Whiteley, Walter Borges, David Sanders, and Marianne Stewart. 2016. "Modelling the dynamics of support for a right-wing populist party: The case of UKIP." *Journal of Elections, Public Opinion and Parties* 26 (2): 135–154.

Coaston, Jane. 2020. "QAnon, the scarily popular pro-Trump conspiracy theory, explained." *Vox.* www.vox.com/policy-and-politics/2018/8/1/17253444/qanon-trump-conspiracy-theory-4chan-explainer. Accessed September 5, 2021.

Colantone, Italo, and Piero Stanig. 2018a. "Global competition and Brexit." *American Political Science Review* 112 (2): 201–218.

Colantone, Italo, and Piero Stanig. 2018b. "The trade origins of economic nationalism: Import competition and voting behavior in Western Europe." *American Journal of Political Science* 62 (4): 936–953.

Collier, David, and James Mahon. 1993. "Conceptual 'stretching' revisited." *American Political Science Review* 87 (4): 845–855.

Collier, Ruth Berins, and David Collier. 2002. *Shaping the political arena.* South Bend: Notre Dame University Press.

Conover, Pamela Johnston, and Stanley Feldman. 1986. "Emotional reactions to the economy: I'm mad as hell and I'm not going to take it anymore." *American Journal of Political Science* 30 (1): 50–78.

Converse, Philip. 1964. "The nature of belief systems in mass publics." In *Ideology and discontent,* edited by David E. Apter, 206–261. New York: Free Press.

Corrales, Javier. 2010. "The repeating revolution: Chávez's new politics and old economics." In *Leftist governments in Latin America: Successes and shortcomings,* edited by Kurt Weyland, Raúl L Madrid, and Wendy Hunter, 28–56. Cambridge: Cambridge University Press.

Corrales, Javier. 2011. "Why polarize? Advantages and disadvantages of a rational-choice analysis of government–opposition relations under Hugo Chávez." In *The revolution in Venezuela: Social and political change under Chávez,* edited by Thomas Ponniah and Johnathan Eastwood, 67–98. Cambridge, MA: Harvard University Press.

Corrales, Javier, and Michael Penfold. 2015. *Dragon in the tropics: Venezuela and the legacy of Hugo Chávez,* 2nd edition. New York: Brookings Institution Press.

Costello, Thomas E., Shauna M. Bowes, Sean T. Stevens, Irwin D. Waldman, Arber Tasimi, and Scott O. Lilienfeld. 2021. "Clarifying the structure and nature of left-wing authoritarianism." *Journal of Personality and Social Psychology.* https://doi.org/10.1037/pspp0000341.

Cowen, Alan S., and Dacher Keltner. 2017. "Self-report captures 27 distinct categories of emotion bridged by continuous gradients." *Proceedings of the National Academy of Sciences* 114 (38): E7900–E7909.

Cox, Gary W. 1990. "Centripetal and centrifugal incentives in electoral systems." *American Journal of Political Science* 34 (4): 903–935.

Craig, Stephen C., Richard G. Niemi, and Glenn E. Silver. 1990. "Political efficacy and trust: A report on the NES pilot study items." *Political Behavior* 12 (3): 289–314.

Cramer, Katherine J. 2016. *The politics of resentment: Rural consciousness in Wisconsin and the rise of Scott Walker.* Chicago: University of Chicago Press.

Crocker, Jennifer, Riia Luhtanen, Stephanie Broadnax, and Bruce Evan Blaine. 1999. "Belief in US government conspiracies against Blacks among Black and white college students: Powerlessness or system blame?" *Personality and Social Psychology Bulletin* 25 (8): 941–953.

Cropanzano, Russell, and Marueen L. Ambrose. 2002. "Procedural and distributive justice are more similar than you think: A monistic perspective and a research agenda." In *Advances in organizational justice*, edited by Jerald Greenberg and Russell Cropanzano, 119–151. Stanford, CA: Stanford University Press.

Crouch, Colin. 1993. *Industrial relations and European state traditions.* Oxford: Oxford University Press.

Crouch, Colin. 2009. "Privatised Keynesianism: An unacknowledged policy regime." *The British Journal of Politics and International Relations* 11 (3): 382–399.

Crouch, Colin. 2011. *The strange non-death of neo-liberalism.* Cambridge: Polity.

Crouch, Colin. 2018. *The globalization backlash.* Cambridge: Polity.

Crow, David. 2010. "The party's over: Citizen conceptions of democracy and political dissatisfaction in Mexico." *Comparative Politics* 43 (1): 41–61.

Crozier, Michael, Samuel Huntington, and Joji Watanuki. 1975. *The crisis of democracy.* New York: New York University Press.

Dahl, Robert A. 1985. *A preface to economic democracy.* Berkeley: University of California Press.

Dahl, Robert A. 1989. *Democracy and its critics.* New Haven: Yale University Press.

Dahlberg, Stefan, and Jonas Linde. 2016. "Losing happily? The mitigating effect of democracy and quality of government on the winner–loser gap in political support." *International Journal of Public Administration* 39 (9): 652–664.

Dalton, Russell J. 2013. *Citizen politics: Public opinion and political parties in advanced industrial democracies.* Washington, DC: Cq Press.

De la Torre, Carlos. 2019. *Populisms: A quick immersion.* New York: Tibidabo Publishing.

DeCharms, Richard. 1968. *Personal causation: The internal affective determinants of behavior.* New York: Academic Press.

Desposato, Scott W. 2006. "From revolution to Rouba Mas Faz?" *ReVista: Harvard Review of Latin America* 5 (1): 29–32.

Dettrey, Bryan J. 2013. "Relative losses and economic voting: Sociotropic considerations or 'keeping up with the Joneses'?" *Politics & Policy* 41 (5): 788–806.

Díaz Pabón, Fabio Andrés, and María Gabriela Palacio Ludeña. 2021. "Inequality and the socioeconomic dimensions of mobility in protests: The cases of Quito and Santiago." *Global Policy* 12 (S2): 78–90.

Disi Pavlic, Rodolfo. 2018. "Sentenced to debt: Explaining student mobilization in Chile." *Latin American Research Review* 53 (3): 448–465.

Disi Pavlic, Rodolfo. 2021. "The nearness of youth: Spatial and temporal effects of protests on political attitudes in Chile." *Latin American Politics and Society* 63 (1): 72–94.

Donadio, Rachel, and Dale Fuchs. 2010. Spanish Premier insists economic recovery is near. *New York Times*, February 17. www.nytimes.com/2010/02/18/world/europe/18spain.html. Accessed July 20, 2021.

Döring, Holger, and Philip Manow. 2021. Parliaments and governments database (ParlGov): Information on parties, elections and cabinets in modern democracies. https://parlgov.org/data-info/. Accessed July 22, 2022.

Dougherty, Carter. 2008. "Stopping a financial crisis, the Swedish Way." *The New York Times*, September 22. www.nytimes.com/2008/09/23/business/worldbusiness/23krona.html. Accessed July 22, 2022.

Douglas, Karen M., Robbie M. Sutton, and Aleksandra Cichocka. 2017. "The psychology of conspiracy theories." *Current Directions in Psychological Science* 26 (6): 538–542.

Douglas, Karen M., Joseph E. Uscinski, Robbie M. Sutton, Aleksandra Cichocka, Turkay Nefes, Chee Siang Ang, and Farzin Deravi. 2019. "Understanding conspiracy theories." *Political Psychology* 40 (S1): 3–35.

Dowsett, Sonya. 2010. "Spain austerity plan scrapes through parliament." *Reuters*, May 27. www.reuters.com/article/us-spain-idUSTRE64Q54T20100527. Accessed July 20, 2021.

Duckworth, Cheryl. 2008. "Maria Montessori and peace education." In *Encyclopedia of peace education*, edited by Monisha Bajaj, 33–37. Charlotte, NC: Information Age Publishing.

Duque, Debora, and Amy Erica Smith. 2019. "The establishment upside down: A year of change in Brazil." *Revista de Ciencia Política* 39 (2): 165–189:

Eagly, Alice H., and Shelly Chaiken. 1993. *The psychology of attitudes*. San Diego: Harcourt Brace Jovanovich.

Easton, David. 1975. "A reassessment of the concept of political support." *British Journal of Political Science* 5 (4): 435–457.

Edwards, Sam. 2019. "Spain's Watergate: Inside the corruption scandal that changed a nation." *The Guardian*, March 1. www.theguardian.com/news/2019/mar/01/spain-watergate-corruption-scandal-politics-gurtel-case. Accessed July 27, 2021.

Eichengreen, Barry. 2018. *The populist temptation: Economic grievance and political reaction in the modern era*. Oxford: Oxford University Press.

Ekman, Paul, and Wallace V. Friesen. 1971. "Constants across cultures in the face and emotion." *Journal of Personality and Social Psychology* 17 (2): 124–129.

Elchardus, Mark, and Bram Spruyt. 2012. "The contemporary contradictions of egalitarianism: An empirical analysis of the relationship between the old and new left/right alignments." *European Political Science Review* 4 (2): 217–239.

Elchardus, Mark, and Bram Spruyt. 2016. "Populism, persistent republicanism and declinism: An empirical analysis of populism as a thin ideology." *Government and Opposition* 51 (1): 111–133.

Ellis, Faron. 2016. "Conservative campaign: Defeated but not devastated." In *The Canadian federal election of 2015*, edited by Jon H. Pammett and Christopher Dornan, 23–56. Toronto: Dudurn.

Encarnación, Omar G. 2005. "Do political pacts freeze democracy? Spanish and south American lessons." *West European Politics* 28 (1): 182–203.

Enders, Adam M. 2021. "Issues versus affect: How do elite and mass polarization compare?" *The Journal of Politics* 83 (4): 1872–1877.

Engelhardt, Andrew M. 2018. "Racial attitudes through a partisan lens." *British Journal of Political Science* 51 (3): 1062–1079.

Erten, Bilge, and José Antonio Ocampo. 2013. "Super cycles of commodity prices since the mid-nineteenth century." *World Development* 44: 14–30.

Escolar, Ignacio. 2012. "Spain did not swing to the right, the left collapsed." *The Guardian*, February 3. www.theguardian.com/commentisfree/2012/feb/03/spain-left-collapsed. Accessed July 20, 2021.

Etheridge, Eric. 2009. "Rick Santelli: Tea Party time." *The New York Times*, February 20. http://opinionator.blogs.nytimes.com/2009/02/20/rick-santelli-tea-party-time/. Accessed July 22, 2022.

Ferguson, Thomas, Benjamin Page, Jacob Rothschild, Arturo Chang, and Jie Chen. 2018. "The economic and social roots of populist rebellion: Support for Donald Trump in 2016." Institute for New Economic Thinking Working Paper Series 83. https://papers.ssrn.com/sol3/papers.cfm?abstract_id=3306267. Accessed July 22, 2022.

Fernandes, Jorge M., Pedro C. Magalhães, and José Santana-Pereira. 2018. "Portugal's leftist government: From sick man to poster boy?" *South European Society and Politics* 23 (4): 503–524.

Filer, Tanya. 2018. "The hidden and revealed: styles of political conspiracy theory in Kirchnerism." In *Conspiracy theories and the people who believe them*, edited by Joseph Uscinski, 395–409. Oxford: Oxford University Press.

Filindra, Alexandra. 2019. "Is 'threat' in the eye of the researcher? Theory and measurement in the study of state-level immigration policymaking." *Policy Studies Journal* 47 (3): 517–543.

Fishbein, Martin, and Icek Ajzen. 1975. *Belief, attitude, intention and behavior: An introduction to theory and research*. Boston: Addison-Wesley.

Ford, Robert, and Matthew J. Goodwin. 2014. *Revolt on the right: Explaining support for the radical right in Britain*. London: Routledge.

Forgas, Joseph P. 1995. "Mood and judgment: The affect infusion model (AIM)." *Psychological Bulletin* 117 (1): 39–66.

Forgas, Joseph P., and Gordon H. Bower. 1987. "Mood effects on person-perception judgments." *Journal of Personality and Social Psychology* 53 (1): 53–60.

Forgas, Joseph P., William D. Crano, and Klaus Fiedler, eds. 2021. *The psychology of populism: The tribal challenge to liberal democracy.* New York: Routledge.

Forgas, Joseph P., and Stephanie Moylan. 1987. "After the movies: Transient mood and social judgments." *Personality and Social Psychology Bulletin* 13 (4): 467–477.

Fowler, Anthony, and Andrew B. Hall. 2018. "Do shark attacks influence presidential elections? Reassessing a prominent finding on voter competence." *The Journal of Politics* 80 (4): 1423–1437.

Freire, André, Mélany Barragán, Xavier Coller, Marco Lisi, and Emmanouil Tsatsanis. 2020. "Southern Europe and the eurozone crisis: Political representation, party system characteristics and the impact of austerity." In *Political representation in southern Europe and Latin America*, edited by André Freire, Mélany Barragán, Xavier Coller, Marco Lisi, and Emmanouil Tsatsanis, 17–33. New York: Routledge.

Friedman, Milton. 2020. *Capitalism and freedom.* Chicago: University of Chicago Press.

Fuentes, J. Rodrigo. 2011. "Learning how to manage natural resource revenue." In *Plundered nations? Successes and failures in natural resource extraction*, edited by Paul Collier and Anthony J. Venables, 79–113. New York: Palgrave Macmillan.

Fukuyama, Francis. 2006. *The end of history and the last man.* New York: Free Press. Gadarian, Shana Kushner, and Bethany Albertson. 2014. "Anxiety, immigration, and the search for information." *Political Psychology* 35 (2): 133–164.

Gamble, Andrew. 2015. "The economy." *Parliamentary Affairs* 68 (Supplement 1): 154–167.

Garretón, Manuel Antonio. 2003. *Incomplete democracy.* Chapel Hill: University of North Carolina Press.

Garrido, Hugo, Isabel González, and Javier Aguirre. 2019. "El PP perdió 1,6 millones de votos con Vox y 1,4 con Ciudadanos." *El Mundo*, April 30. www.elmundo.es/espana/2019/04/30/5cc76591fdddff52528b469d.html. Accessed August 8, 2021.

Georgiadou, Vasiliki, Lamprini Rori, and Costas Roumanias. 2018. "Mapping the European far right in the 21st century: A meso-level analysis." *Electoral Studies* 54: 103–115.

Gerber, Alan S., and Gregory A. Huber. 2010. "Partisanship, political control, and economic assessments." *American Journal of Political Science* 54 (1): 153–173.

Germani, Gino. 1978. *Authoritarianism, fascism, and national populism.* New Brunswick: Transaction Books.

Gest, Justin. 2016. *The new minority: White working class politics in an age of immigration and inequality.* Oxford: Oxford University Press.

Gidron, Noam, and Peter A. Hall. 2019. "Populism as a problem of social integration." *Comparative Political Studies* 53 (7): 1027–1059.

Gilens, Martin. 2005. "Inequality and democratic responsiveness." *The Public Opinion Quarterly* 69 (5): 778–796.

Gilens, Martin. 2009. *Why Americans hate welfare: Race, media, and the politics of antipoverty policy*. Chicago: University of Chicago Press.

Gilens, Martin, and Benjamin I. Page. 2014. "Testing theories of American politics: Elites, interest groups, and average citizens." *Perspectives on Politics* 12 (3): 564–581.

Gimpel, James G., Nathan Lovin, Bryant Moy, and Andrew Reeves. 2020. "The urban–rural gulf in American political behavior." *Political Behavior* 42 (4): 1343–1368.

Ginsberg, Benjamin, and Martin Shefter. 1999. *Politics by other means: Politicians, prosecutors, and the press from Watergate to Whitewater*. New York: W. W. Norton.

Goetz, Stephan J., Meri Davlasheridze, Yicheol Han, and David A. Fleming-Muñoz. 2019. "Explaining the 2016 vote for President Trump across U.S. counties." *Applied Economic Perspectives and Policy* 41 (4): 703–722.

Goldberg, Julie H., Jennifer S. Lerner, and Philip E. Tetlock. 1999. "Rage and reason: The psychology of the intuitive prosecutor." *European Journal of Social Psychology* 29: 781–795.

Golder, Matt. 2016. "Far right parties in Europe." *Annual Review of Political Science* 19 (1): 477–497.

Gollwitzer, Mario, and Brad J. Bushman. 2012. "Do victims of injustice punish to improve their mood?" *Social Psychological and Personality Science* 3 (5): 572–580.

Gomila, Robin. 2021. "Logistic or linear? Estimating causal effects of experimental treatments on binary outcomes using regression analysis." *Journal of Experimental Psychology* 150 (4): 700–709.

Gonzalez, Ricardo. 2019. *Estudio Nacional de Opinión Pública 84*. Santiago de Chile: Encuesta CEP.

Goodhart, David. 2017. *The road to somewhere: The populist revolt and the future of politics*. Oxford: Oxford University Press.

Goodwin, Matthew J., and Oliver Heath. 2016. "The 2016 referendum, Brexit and the left behind: An aggregate-level analysis of the result." *The Political Quarterly* 87 (3): 323–332.

Goodwin, Matthew, and Caitlin Milazzo. 2015. *UKIP: Inside the campaign to redraw the map of British politics*. Oxford: Oxford University Press.

Green, Donald P., Bradley Palmquist, and Eric Schickler. 2004. *Partisan hearts and minds: Political parties and the social identities of voters*. New Haven, CT: Yale University Press.

Green, Duncan. 2003. *Silent revolution: The rise and crisis of market economics in Latin America*. New York: New York University Press.

Gross, James J. 2013. *Handbook of emotion regulation*, 2nd edition. New York: Guilford Press.

Gross, Justin H., and Kaylee T. Johnson. 2016. "Twitter taunts and tirades: Negative campaigning in the age of Trump." *PS: Political Science & Politics* 49 (4): 748–754.

Guiso, Luigi, Helios Herrera, Massimo Morelli, and Tommaso Sonno. 2017. *Demand and supply of populism*. London: Centre for Economic Policy Research.

Gurr, Ted. 1971. *Why men rebel*. Princeton: Princeton University Press.

Hacker, Jacob S. 2008. *The great risk shift: The new economic insecurity and the decline of the American dream*. Oxford: Oxford University Press.

Hacker, Jacob S., and Paul Pierson. 2020. *Let them eat tweets: How the right rules in an age of extreme inequality*. New York: Liveright.

Handlin, Samuel. 2019. *State crisis in fragile democracies*. Cambridge: Cambridge University Press.

Hawkins, Kirk A. 2009. "Is Chávez populist? Measuring populist discourse in comparative perspective." *Comparative Political Studies* 42 (8): 1040–1067.

Hawkins, Kirk A. 2010. *Venezuela's chavismo and populism in comparative perspective*. Cambridge: Cambridge University Press.

Hawkins, Kirk A. 2018. "The ideational approach." In *Routledge handbook of global populism*, edited by Carlos De la Torre, 57–72 New York: Routledge.

Hawkins, Kirk A., Rosario Aguilar, Bruno Castanho Silva, Erin K. Jenne, Bojana Kocijan, and Cristóbal Rovira Kaltwasser. 2019. "Measuring populist discourse: The global populism database." Presented at the EPSA Annual Conference, Belfast, UK, June 20–22.

Hawkins, Kirk A., and Cristóbal Rovira Kaltwasser. 2017. "The ideational approach to populism." *Latin American Research Review* 52 (4): 513–528.

Hawkins, Kirk A., and Cristóbal Rovira Kaltwasser. 2018. "Measuring populist discourse in the United States and beyond." *Nature Human Behaviour* 2 (4): 241–242.

Hawkins, Kirk A., Cristóbal Rovira Kaltwasser, and Ioannis Andreadis. 2018. "The activation of populist attitudes." *Government and Opposition* 55 (2): 1–25.

Hawley, George. 2011. "Political threat and immigration: Party identification, demographic context, and immigration policy preference." *Social Science Quarterly* 92 (2): 404–422.

Hay, Colin. 2009. "Good inflation, bad inflation: The housing boom, economic growth and the disaggregation of inflationary preferences in the UK and Ireland." *The British Journal of Politics and International Relations* 11 (3): 461–478.

Hay, Colin, Jari Matti Riiheläinen, Nicola J Smith, and Matthew Watson. 2008. "Ireland: The outlier inside." In *The euro at ten: Europeanisation, power and convergence*, edited by Kenneth Dyson, 182–203. Oxford: Oxford University Press.

Hayek, Friederick A. 2007. *The road to serfdom*. Chicago: University of Chicago Press.

Healy, Andrew J., Neil Malhotra, and Cecilia Hyunjung Mo. 2010. "Irrelevant events affect voters: Evaluations of government performance." *Proceedings of the National Academy of Sciences* 107 (29): 12804–12809.

Heneghan, Tom. 2011. "Sarkozy joins allies burying multiculturalism." *Reuters*, February 11.

Herndon, Thomas, Michael Ash, and Robert Pollin. 2014. "Does high public debt consistently stifle economic growth? A critique of Reinhart and Rogoff." *Cambridge Journal of Economics* 38 (2): 257–279.

Hicks, John Donald. 1931a. "The persistence of populism." *Minnesota History* 12 (1): 3–20.

Hicks, John Donald. 1931b. *The populist revolt: A history of the Farmers' Alliance and the People's Party*. Minneapolis: University of Minnesota Press.

Hirschman, Albert O. 1970. *Exit, voice, and loyalty: Response to decline in firms, organizations and states*. Cambridge, MA: Harvard University Press.

Hobolt, Sara B. 2016. "The Brexit vote: A divided nation, a divided continent." *Journal of European Public Policy* 23 (9): 1259–1277.

Hochschild, Arlie Russell. 2016. "The ecstatic edge of politics: Sociology and Donald Trump." *Contemporary Sociology* 45 (6): 683–689.

Hochschild, Arlie Russell. 2018. *Strangers in their own land: Anger and mourning on the American right*. New York: The New Press.

Hofstadter, Richard. 1955. *The Age of Reform: From Bryan to FDR*. New York: Vintage.

Hofstadter, Richard. 2012. *The paranoid style in American politics*. New York: Vintage.

Houle, Christian, and Paul D. Kenny. 2018. "The political and economic consequences of populist rule in Latin America." *Government and Opposition* 53 (2): 256–287.

Hunter, Wendy. 2007. "The normalization of an anomaly: The workers' party in Brazil." *World Politics* 59 (3): 440–475.

Hunter, Wendy, and Timothy J. Power. 2019. "Bolsonaro and Brazil's illiberal backlash." *Journal of Democracy* 30 (1): 68–82.

Huntington, Samuel. 1965. "Political development and decay." *World Politics* 17 (3): 386–430.

Inglehart, Ronald, and Pippa Norris. 2016. "Trump, Brexit, and the rise of populism: Economic have-nots and cultural backlash." Unpublished working paper. https://papers.ssrn.com/sol3/papers.cfm?abstract_id=2818659. Accessed July 22, 2022.

Inglehart, Ronald, and Pippa Norris. 2017. "Trump and the populist authoritarian parties: The silent revolution in reverse." *Perspectives on Politics* 15 (2): 443–454.

Inglehart, Ronald, and Pippa Norris. 2019. *Cultural backlash and the rise of populism: Trump, Brexit, and authoritarian populism*. Cambridge: Cambridge University Press.

Inglehart, Ronald, and Christian Welzel. 2005. *Modernization, cultural change, and democracy*. Cambridge: Cambridge University Press.

International Monetary Fund. 2012. "World economic outlook: October 2012." In *World Economic and Financial Surveys*. Washington, DC: International Monetary Fund.

Isidore, Chris. 2014. "US ends TARP with $15.3 billion profit." *CNN Money*, December 19. https://money.cnn.com/2014/12/19/news/companies/government-bailouts-end/#:~:text=The%20U.S.%20government%20essentially%20closed,and%20the%20U.S.%20auto%20industry. Accessed March 15, 2021.

Iversen, Torben, and David Soskice. 2019. *Democracy and prosperity*. Princeton, NJ: Princeton University Press.

Iyengar, Shanto, and Sean J. Westwood. 2015. "Fear and loathing across party lines: New evidence on group polarization." *American Journal of Political Science* 59 (3): 690–707.

Izquierdo, José María. 2014. "Popular Party awaiting judgment day." *El País*, February 4. https://english.elpais.com/elpais/2014/02/04/inenglish/1391511 180_144115.html. Accessed July 27, 2021.

Jacobson, Gary C. 2013. "Partisan polarization in American politics: A background paper." *Presidential Studies Quarterly* 43 (4): 688–708.

Jardina, Ashley. 2019. *White identity politics*. Cambridge: Cambridge University Press.

Jardina, Ashley, Nathan Kalmoe, and Kimberly Gross. 2021. "Disavowing white identity: How social disgust can change social identities." *Political Psychology* 42 (4): 619–636.

Jeffrey, Brooke. 2016. "Back to the future: The resurgent Liberals." In *The Canadian federal election of 2015*, edited by Jon H. Pammett and Christopher Dornan, 57–84. Toronto: Dundurn.

Jost, John T. 2019. "Anger and authoritarianism mediate the effects of fear on support for the far right – what Vasilopoulos et al. (2019) really found." *Political Psychology* 40 (4): 705–711.

Kahneman, Daniel, and Amos Tversky. 2012. "Prospect theory: An analysis of decision under risk." In *Handbook of the Fundamentals of Financial Decision Making*, edited by Leonard C. Maclean and William T. Ziemba, 99–127. New Jersey: World Scientific.

Kambhampati, Sandhya. 2020. "The coronavirus stimulus package versus the Recovery Act." *Los Angeles Times*, March 26. www.latimes.com/politics/story/2020-2003-26/coronavirus-stimulus-package-versus-recovery-act. Accessed March 12, 2021.

Kamin, Steven B., and Laurie Pounder DeMarco. 2012. "How did a domestic housing slump turn into a global financial crisis?" *Journal of International Money and Finance* 31 (1): 10–41.

Kayam, Orly. 2020. "Straight to the people: Donald Trump's rhetorical style on Twitter in the 2016 U.S. presidential election." *Language and Dialogue* 10 (2): 149–170.

Kazin, Michael. 1998. *The populist persuasion: An American history*, Kindle edition. Ithaca, NY: Cornell University Press.

Kendi, Ibram X. 2019. *How to be an antiracist*. London: One World.

Kinder, Donald R., and Cindy Kam. 2009. *Us and them: Ethnocentric foundations of American opinion*. Chicago: Chicago University Press.

Kinder, Donald R., and D. Roderick Kiewiet. 1981. "Sociotropic politics: The American case." *British Journal of Political Science* 11 (2): 129–161.

Kinder, Donald R., and Lynn M. Sanders. 1996. *Divided by color: Racial politics and democratic ideals*. Chicago: University of Chicago Press.

Klingemann, Hans-Dieter. 1999. "Mapping political support in the 1990s: A global analysis." In *Critical citizens: Global support for democratic governance*, edited by Pipa Norris, 31–56. Oxford: Oxford University Press.

Knight, Laurence. 2012. "Spanish economy: What is to blame for its problems." *BBC News*, May 18. www.bbc.com/news/business-17753891. Accessed July 22, 2022.

Koltai, Jonathan, Francesco Maria Varchetta, Martin McKee, and David Stuckler. 2019. "Deaths of despair and Brexit votes: Cross-local authority statistical analysis in England and Wales." *American Journal of Public Health* 110 (3): 401–406.

Kriesi, Hanspeter, Edgar Grande, Romain Lachat, Martin Dolezal, Simon Born-schier, and Timotheos Frey. 2006. "Globalization and the transformation of the national political space: Six European countries compared." *European Journal of Political Research* 45 (6): 921–956.

Kristjanpoller, Werner, Josephine E. Olson, and Rodolfo I. Salazar. 2016. "Does the commodities boom support the export led growth hypothesis? Evidence from Latin American countries." *Latin American Economic Review* 25 (6). https://doi.org/10.1007/s40503-016-0036-z.

Kurtz, Marcus J. 2004a. "The dilemmas of democracy in the open economy: Lessons from Latin America." *World Politics* 56 (2): 262–302.

Kurtz, Marcus J. 2004b. *Free market democracy and the Chilean and Mexican countryside.* Cambridge: Cambridge University Press.

Kwon, Hyeok Yong. 2004. "Economic reform and democratization: Evidence from Latin America and post-socialist countries." *British Journal of Political Science* 34 (2): 357–368.

Laclau, Ernesto. 1977. *Politics and ideology in Marxist theory.* London: New Left Books.

Laclau, Ernesto. 2005. *On populist reason.* London: Verso.

Laclau, Ernesto, and Chantal Mouffe. 1985. *Hegemony and socialist theory.* London: Verso.

Lamberti, P. 2019. "Millennials just aren't that into starting families; is that such a bad thing?" *Money Under 30,* March 14. www.moneyunder30.com/millennials-waiting-to-start-a-family. Accessed May 4, 2021.

Lapper, Richard. 2021. *Beef, Bible and bullets: Brazil in the age of Bolsonaro.* Manchester: Manchester University Press.

Layton, Matthew L., Amy Erica Smith, Mason W. Moseley, and Mollie J. Cohen. 2021. "Demographic polarization and the rise of the far right: Brazil's 2018 presidential election." *Research & Politics* 8 (1). https://doi.org/10.1177/2053168021990204.

Lazarus, Richard S. 1991. *Emotion and adaptation.* Oxford: Oxford University Press on Demand.

Lee, Frances E. 2016. *Insecure majorities: Congress and the perpetual campaign.* Chicago: University of Chicago Press.

Lelkes, Yphtach. 2016. "Mass polarization: Manifestations and measurements." *Public Opinion Quarterly* 80 (S1): 392–410.

Lerner, Jennifer S., and Dacher Keltner. 2000. "Beyond valence: Toward a model of emotion-specific influences on judgement and choice." *Cognition and Emotion* 14 (4): 473–493.

Levendusky, Matthew. 2009. *The partisan sort: How liberals became Democrats and conservatives became Republicans.* Chicago: University of Chicago Press.

Levitsky, Steven, and Daniel Ziblatt. 2018. *How democracies die.* New York: Broadway Books.

Lichbach, Mark Irving, and Alan S. Zuckerman. 2009. *Comparative politics: Rationality, culture, and structure.* Cambridge: Cambridge University Press.

Lillard, Angeline S., Megan J. Heise, Eve M. Richey, Xin Tong, Alyssa Hart, and Paige M. Bray. 2017. "Montessori preschool elevates and equalizes child outcomes: A longitudinal study." *Frontiers in Psychology* 8 (1783). https://doi .org/10.3389/fpsyg.2017.01783.

Lind, E. Allan. 2001. "Fairness heuristic theory: Justice judgments as pivotal cognitions in organizational relations." In *Advances in Organizational Justice*, edited by Jerald Greenberg and Russell Cropanzano, 56–88. Stanford, CA: Stanford University Press.

Lind, E. Allan, and Tom R. Tyler. 1988. *The social psychology of procedural justice: Critical issues in social justice.* New York: Plenum Press.

Lind, E. Allan, and Kees van den Bos. 2002. "When fairness works: Toward a general theory of uncertainty management." *Research in Organizational Behavior* 24: 181–223.

Lipset, Seymour Martin. 1955. "The radical right: A problem for American democracy." *The British Journal of Sociology* 6 (2): 176–209.

Lipset, Seymour Martin. 1963. *Political man: The social bases of politics.* Garden City: Anchor Books.

Lisi, Marco. 2016. "U-turn: The Portuguese radical left from marginality to government support." *South European Society and Politics* 21 (4): 541–560.

Locke, John. 2003. *Two treatises of government: Rethinking the Western tradition.* New Haven, CT: Yale University Press.

López-Calva, Luis Felipe, and Nora Claudia Lustig. 2010. *Declining inequality in Latin America: A decade of progress?* Washington, DC: Brookings Institution Press.

Lupu, Noam. 2011. "Party brands in crisis: Partisanship, brand dilution, and the breakdown of political parties in Latin America." PhD thesis, Department of Politics, Princeton University.

Luther, Kurt Richard, and Ferdinand Müller-Rommel. 2002. *Political parties in the new Europe: Political and analytical challenges.* Oxford: Oxford University Press.

Macdougall, Alex I., Allard R. Feddes, and Bertjan Doosje. 2020. "'They've put nothing in the pot!': Brexit and the key psychological motivations behind voting 'remain' and 'leave'." *Political Psychology* 41 (5): 979–995.

Madariaga, Aldo, and Cristóbal Rovira Kaltwasser. 2020. "Right-wing moderation, left-wing inertia and political partelisation in post-transition Chile." *Journal of Latin American Studies* 52 (2): 343–371.

Madsen, Douglass, and Peter G. Snow. 1991. *The charismatic bond: Political behavior in a time of crisis.* Cambridge, MA: Harvard University Press.

Magalhães, Pedro C. 2016. "Economic evaluations, procedural fairness, and satisfaction with democracy." *Political Research Quarterly* 69 (3): 552–534.

Magalhães, Pedro C., and Luís Aguiar-Conraria. 2018. "Procedural fairness, the economy, and support for political authorities." *Political Psychology* 40 (1): 165–181.

Maioni, Antonia. 1997. "Parting at the crossroads: The development of health insurance in Canada and the United States, 1940–1965." *Comparative Politics* 29 (4): 411–431.

Malbin, Michael J., Anne H. Bedlington, Robert G. Boatright, James E. Campbell, Alexandra Cooper, Anthony Corrado, Diana Dwyre, John C. Green, Paul S.

Herrnson, Robin Kolodny, Raymond J. La Raja, Lynda Powell, Jason Reifler, Mark J. Rozell, Richard Skinner, Jennifer A. Steen, Benjamin A. Webster, and Clyde Wilcox. 2003. *Life after Reform: When the Bipartisan Campaign Reform Act Meets Politics*. Lanham, MD: Rowman & Littlefield.

Malik, Kenan. 2015. "The failure of multiculturalism: Community versus society in Europe." *Foreign Affairs* 94: 21.

Manzetti, Luigi, and Carole J. Wilson. 2007. "Why do corrupt governments maintain public support?" *Comparative Political Studies* 40 (8): 949–970.

Marcos-Marne, Hugo, Carolina Plaza-Colodro, and Tina Freyburg. 2020. "Who votes for new parties? Economic voting, political ideology and populist attitudes." *West European Politics* 43 (1): 1–21.

Marcus, George E. 2010. *Sentimental citizen: Emotion in democratic politics*. University Park: Penn State Press.

Marcus, George E. 2021. "The rise of populism: The politics of justice, anger, and grievance." In *The psychology of populism*, edited by Klaus Fiedler, William D. Crano and Joseph P. Forgas, 81–104. New York: Routledge.

Marcus, George E., and Ted Brader. 2014. "Emotion and political psychology." In *The Oxford handbook of political psychology*, edited by Leonie Huddy, David Sears, and Jack Levy, 165–204. Oxford: Oxford University Press.

Marcus, George E., and Michael B. MacKuen. 1993. "Anxiety, enthusiasm, and the vote: The emotional underpinnings of learning and involvement during presidential campaigns." *American Political Science Review* 87 (3): 672–685.

Marcus, George E., Michael MacKuen, and W. Russell Neuman. 2011. "Parsimony and complexity: Developing and testing theories of affective intelligence." *Political Psychology* 32 (2): 323–336.

Marcus, George E., W. Russell Neuman, and Michael MacKuen. 2000. *Affective intelligence and political judgment*. Chicago: University of Chicago Press.

Marcus, George E., Nicholas Valentino, and Pavlos Vasilopoulos. 2019. "Applying the theory of affective intelligence to support for authoritarian policies and parties." *Political Psychology* 40 (S1): 109–139. https://doi.org/10.1111/pops.12571.

Mariner, Wendy K., George J. Annas, and Leonard H. Glantz. 2005. "Jacobson v Massachusetts: It's not your great-great-grandfather's public health law." *American Journal of Public Health* 95 (4): 581–590.

Martínez, Guillem. 2015. "15-M, four years on: Caught between rupture and regeneration." *El País*, May 15. https://english.elpais.com/elpais/2015/05/15/inenglish/1431703911_191382.html?rel=mas. Accessed July 20, 2021.

Mason, Liliana. 2018. *Uncivil agreement: How politics became our identity*. Chicago: University of Chicago Press.

Matsusaka, John G. 2010. "Popular control of public policy: A quantitative approach." *Quarterly Journal of Political Science* 5: 133–167.

McCarty, Nolan, Keith T. Poole, and Howard Rosenthal. 2006. *Polarized America: The dance of ideology and unequal riches*. Cambridge, MA: MIT Press.

McDonnell, Duncan, and Stefano Ondelli. 2020. "The language of right-wing populist leaders: Not so simple." *Perspectives on Politics*, 1–14. https://doi.org/10.1017/S1537592720002418.

McFarlin, Dean B., and Paul D. Sweeney. 1992. "Distributive and procedural justice as predictors of satisfaction with personal and organizational outcomes." *Academy of Management Journal* 35 (3): 626–637.

McGrane, David. 2016. "From third to first and back to third: The 2015 NDP campaign." In *The Canadian federal election of 2015*, edited by Jon H. Pammett and Christopher Dornan, 85–116. Toronto: Dundurn.

Meléndez, Carlos, and Cristóbal Rovira Kaltwasser. 2017. "Political identities: The missing link in the study of populism." *Party Politics* 25 (4): 520–533.

Melgar, Pablo. 2019. "El Jair Bolsonaro uruguayo y sus amigos tupamaros." *Perfil*, March 13. www.perfil.com/noticias/internacional/el-jair-bolsonaro-uruguayo-y-sus-amigos-tupamaros.phtml. Accessed August 25, 2021.

Mendes, Mariana S., and James Dennison. 2021. "Explaining the emergence of the radical right in Spain and Portugal: Salience, stigma and supply." *West European Politics* 44 (4): 752–775.

Merolla, Jennifer L., Jennifer M. Ramos, and Elizabeth J. Zechmeister. 2007. "Crisis, charisma, and consequences: Evidence from the 2004 US presidential election." *The Journal of Politics* 69 (1): 30–42.

Merolla, Jennifer L., and Elizabeth J. Zechmeister. 2009. *Democracy at risk: How terrorist threats affect the public.* Chicago: University of Chicago Press.

Merolla, Jennifer L., and Elizabeth J. Zechmeister. 2011. "The nature, determinants, and consequences of Chávez's Charisma: Evidence from a study of Venezuelan public opinion." *Comparative Political Studies* 44 (1): 28–54.

Michels, Robert. 2001. *Political parties: A sociological study of the oligarchical tendencies of modern democracy.* Translated by Eden Paul and Cedar Paul. Kitchener, ON: Batoche Books.

Miller, Joanne M., Kyle L. Saunders, and Christina E. Farhart. 2016. "Conspiracy endorsement as motivated reasoning: The moderating roles of political knowledge and trust." *American Journal of Political Science* 60 (4): 824–844.

Miller, Steven V. 2020. "Economic anxiety or ethnocentrism? An evaluation of attitudes toward immigration in the U.S. from 1992 to 2016." *The Social Science Journal.* https://doi.org/10.1080/03623319.2020.1782638.

Minder, Raphael. 2010. "Spain hit by strikes over austerity measures." *New York Times*, June 8. www.nytimes.com/2010/06/09/world/europe/09iht-spain.html. Accessed July 20, 2021.

Minder, Raphael. 2017. *The struggle for Catalonia: Rebel politics in Spain.* London: Hurst & Company.

Monestier, Felipe. 2011. *Movimientos sociales, partidos polîtcos y democracia directa desde abajo en Uruguay: 1985–2004.* Buenos Aires: CLASCO.

Montesquieu, Charles. 2001. *The spirit of the laws.* Kitchener, ON: Batoche Books.

Montestier, Felipe, Lihuen Nocetto, and Fernando Rosenblatt. 2021. "Cabildo Abierto: oportunidades y desafíos para la construcción partidaria en un sistema de partidos institucionalizado." In *De la estabilidad al equilibrio inestable: elecciones y comportamiento electoral*, edited by Juan Andrés Moraes and Verónica Pérez Bentancur. Montevideo: Instituto de Ciencia Política.

Morgan, Stephen L., and Jiwon Lee. 2018. "Trump voters and the white working class." *Sociological Science* 5: 234–245.

Mouffe, Chantal. 2000. *The democratic paradox.* London: Verso.

Mounk, Yascha. 2018. *The people vs. democracy: Why our freedom is in danger and how to save it.* Cambridge, MA: Harvard University Press.

Mudde, Cas. 2007. *Populist radical right parties in Europe.* Cambridge: Cambridge University Press.

Mudde, Cas. 2010. "The populist radical right: A pathological normalcy." *West European Politics* 33 (6): 1167–1186.

Mudde, Cas, and Cristóbal Rovira Kaltwasser. 2013a. "Exclusionary vs. inclusionary populism: Comparing contemporary Europe and Latin America." *Government and Opposition* 48 (2): 147–174.

Mudde, Cas, and Cristóbal Rovira Kaltwasser. 2013b. "Populism." In *The Oxford handbook of political ideologies*, edited by Michael Freeden, Lyman Tower Sargent, and Marc Stears, 493–512. Oxford: Oxford University Press.

Mudde, Cas, and Cristóbal Rovira Kaltwasser. 2013c. "Populism and (liberal) democracy: A framework for analysis." In *Populism in Europe and the Americas: Threat or corrective for democracy?*, edited by Cas Mudde and Cristóbal Rovira Kaltwasser, 1–26. Cambridge: Cambridge University Press.

Mudde, Cas, and Cristóbal Rovira Kaltwasser. 2018. "Studying populism in comparative perspective: Reflections on the contemporary and future research agenda." *Comparative Political Studies* 51 (13): 1667–1693.

Muller, Edward N., and Karl-Dieter Opp. 1986. "Rational choice and rebellious collective action." *American Political Science Review* 80 (2): 471–488.

Müller, Jan-Werner. 2016. *What is populism?* Philadelphia: University of Pennsylvania Press.

Müller, Jan-Werner. 2021. *Democracy rules.* New York: Farrar, Straus and Giroux.

Muro, Diego, and Guillem Vidal. 2017. "Political mistrust in southern Europe since the Great Recession." *Mediterranean Politics* 22 (2): 197–217.

Nadeau, Richard, Michael S. Lewis-Beck, and Éric Bélanger. 2012. "Economics and elections revisited." *Comparative Political Studies* 46 (5): 551–573.

Navarre, Rachel. 2020. "Immigration policy under the Trump administration." In *The future of US empire in the Americas*, edited by Timothy Gill, 307–327. New York: Routledge.

Navarre, Rachel, Matthew Rhodes-Purdy, and Stephen M. Utych. 2020. "Measuring cultural discontent." Presented at the Annual Meeting of the Midwest Political Science Association, Chicago.

Navarre, Rachel, Matthew Rhodes-Purdy, and Stephen M. Utych. 2021. "Conspiracies, emotions and populism: What they don't want you to know." Presented at the Annual Meeting of the Midwest Political Science Association, Chicago.

Navia, Patricio. 2019. "Chile's riots: Frustration at the gate of the promised land." *Americas Quarterly*, October 21. www.americasquarterly.org/article/chiles-riots-frustration-at-the-gate-of-the-promised-land/. Accessed July 13, 2021.

Navia, Patricio, and Lucas Perelló. 2019. "One-night stands and long-term commitments: Presidential approval for Sebastián Piñera in Chile, 2009–2014." *Revista de Ciencia Política* 39 (1): 49–73.

Neubeck, Kenneth J., and Noel A. Cazenave. 2001. *Welfare racism: Playing the race card against America's poor.* New York: Psychology Press.

Niemi, Richard G., Stephen C. Craig, and Franco Mattei. 1991. "Measuring internal political efficacy in the 1988 national election study." *American Political Science Review* 85 (4): 1407–1413.

Norris, Pippa, ed. 1999. *Critical citizens.* Oxford: Oxford University Press.

Ocampo, José Antonio. 2017. "Commodity-led development in Latin America." In *Alternative pathways to sustainable development: Lessons from Latin America,* edited by Gilles Carbonnier, Humberto Campodónico, and Sergio Tezanos Vázquez, 51–76. Leiden: Brill.

OECD. 2022. "Unemployment rate." Indicator. https://doi.org/10.1787/52570002-en. Accessed July 22, 2022.

OIG. 2018. *Special review: Initial observations regarding family separation issues under the Zero Tolerance Policy.* Washington, DC: DHS Office of the Inspector General.

Olson, Mancur. 1971. *The logic of collective action: Public goods and the theory of groups.* Cambridge, MA: Harvard University Press.

Opp, Karl-Dieter, Kate Burow-Auffarth, and Uwe Heinrichs. 1981. "Conditions for conventional and unconventional political participation: An empirical test of economic and sociological hypotheses." *European Journal of Political Research* 9 (2): 147–168.

Orpen, Christopher. 1994. "The effects of self-esteem and personal control on the relationship between job insecurity and psychological well-being." *Social Behavior and Personality* 22 (1): 53–56.

Orr, Martin, and Ginna Husting. 2018. "Media marginalization of racial minorities: Conspiracy theorists in US ghettos and on the Arab street." Working paper. https://scholarworks.boisestate.edu/cgi/viewcontent.cgi?article=1061&context=sociology_facpubs. Accessed July 22, 2022.

Orriols, Lluis, and Guillermo Cordero. 2018. "The breakdown of the Spanish two party system: The upsurge of Podemos and Cuidadanos in the 2015 general election." In *Crisis elections, new contenders and government formation: Breaking the mould in southern Europe,* edited by Anna Bosco and Susannah Verney, 87–110. New York: Routledge.

Page, Benjamin I., Larry M. Bartels, and Jason Seawright. 2013. "Democracy and the policy preferences of wealthy Americans." *Perspectives on Politics* 11 (1): 51–73.

Panizza, Francisco. 2005. "Introduction: Populism and the mirror of democracy." In *Populism and the mirror of democracy,* edited by Francisco Panizza, 1–31. New York: Verso.

Parkin, Andrew. 2021. *Support for democracy in Canada.* Toronto: Environics Institute.

Pastine, Ivan, Tuvana Pastine, and Paul Redmond. 2014. "Incumbent-quality advantage and counterfactual electoral stagnation in the US Senate." *Politics* 35 (1): 32–45.

Patenaude III, Willis. 2019. "Modern American populism: Analyzing the economics behind the 'silent majority,' the Tea Party, and Trumpism." *American Journal of Economics and Sociology* 78 (3): 787–834.

Pérez Bentancur, Verónica, Rafael Piñeiro Rodríguez, and Fernando Rosenblatt. 2018. "Efficacy and the reproduction of political engagement: Evidence from the Broad Front in Uruguay." *Comparative Political Studies* 52 (6): 838–867.

Pérez Bentancur, Verónica, Rafael Piñeiro Rodríguez, and Fernando Rosenblatt. 2019. *How party activism survives: Uruguay's Frente Amplio*. Cambridge: Cambridge University Press.

Pérez Bentancur, Verónica, Rafael Piñeiro Rodríguez, and Fernando Rosenblatt. 2020. "Efficacy and the reproduction of political activism: Evidence from the broad front in Uruguay." *Comparative Political Studies* 52 (6): 838–867.

Peterson-Withorn, Chase. 2019. "Michael Cohen says Trump ran for president as a 'marketing opportunity.' If so, it isn't working." *Forbes*, February 27. www .forbes.com/sites/chasewithorn/2019/02/27/michael-cohen-says-trump-ran-for-president-as-a-marketing-opportunity-if-so-it-isnt-working/?sh=65776c52adeo. Accessed September 3, 2021.

Pettigrew, Thomas F., Oliver Christ, Ulrich Wagner, and Jost Stellmacher. 2007. "Direct and indirect intergroup contact effects on prejudice: A normative interpretation." *International Journal of Intercultural Relations* 31 (4): 411–425.

Pharr, Susan, and Robert D. Putnam, eds. 2000. *Disaffected democracies*. Princeton, NJ: Princeton University Press.

Piketty, Thomas. 2018. *Capital in the twenty-first century*. Cambridge, MA: Harvard University Press.

Piñeiro, Rafael, Matthew Rhodes-Purdy, and Fernando Rosenblatt. 2016. "The engagement curve: Populism and political engagement in Latin America." *Latin American Research Review* 51 (4): 3–23.

Plotke, David. 1997. "Representation is democracy." *Constellations* 4 (1): 19–34.

Politico. 2018. "Full text: Trump's executive order ending family separations." *Politico*, June 20. www.politico.com/story/2018/06/20/full-text-trump-executive-order-family-separations-transcript-658639. Accessed September 16, 2021.

Prebisch, Raul. 1962. "The economic development of Latin America and its principal problems." *Economic Bulletin for Latin America* 7 (1): 1–22.

Przeworski, Adam, and Fernando Limongi. 1997. "Modernization: Theories and facts." *World Politics* 49 (2): 155–183.

Putnam, Robert D. 2000. *Bowling alone: The collapse and revival of American community*. New York: Simon and Schuster.

Pytlik, Nico, Daniel Soll, and Stephanie Mehl. 2020. "Thinking preferences and conspiracy belief: Intuitive thinking and the jumping to conclusions-bias as a basis for the belief in conspiracy theories." *Frontiers in Psychiatry* 11 (987). https://doi.org/10.3389/fpsyt.2020.568942.

Qin, Xin, Run Ren, Zhi-Xue Zhang, and Russel E. Johnson. 2015. "Fairness heuristics and substitutability effects: Inferring the fairness of outcomes, procedures and interpersonal treatment when employees lack clear information." *Journal of Applied Psychology* 100 (3): 749–766.

Quadagno, Jill S. 1994. *The color of welfare: How racism undermined the war on poverty*. Oxford: Oxford University Press.

Quattrone, George A., and Amos Tversky. 1988. "Contrasting rational and psychological analyses of political choice." *American Political Science Review* 82 (3): 719–736.

Quintas da Silva, Rodrigo. 2018. "A Portuguese exception to right-wing populism." *Palgrave Communications* 4 (7).

Rama, José, Lisa Zanotti, Stuart J. Turnbull-Dugarte, and Andrés Santana. 2021. *VOX: The rise of the Spanish populist radical right.* New York: Routledge.

Reise, Steven P., Tyler M. Moore, and Mark G. Haviland. 2010. "Bifactor models and rotations: Exploring the extent to which multidimensional data yield univocal scale scores." *Journal of Personality Assessment* 92 (6): 544–559.

Rennó, Lucio. 2020. "The Bolsonaro voter: Issue positions and vote choice in the 2018 Brazilian presidential elections." *Latin American Politics and Society* 62 (4): 1–23.

Reuters. 2012. "Timeline: Spain's economic crisis." *Reuters*, March 29. www.reuters.com/article/us-spain-strike-economy/timeline-spains-economic-crisis-idUSBRE82S0L420120329. Accessed July 20, 2021.

Rhodes-Purdy, Matthew. 2012. "Participation paradoxes: Voting, contention and support for democracy." Presented at the American Political Science Association Annual Meeting, New Orleans.

Rhodes-Purdy, Matthew. 2015. "Participatory populism: Theory and evidence from Bolivarian Venezuela." *Political Research Quarterly* 68 (3): 415–427.

Rhodes-Purdy, Matthew. 2017a. "Beyond the balance sheet: Performance, participation and regime support in Latin America." *Comparative Politics* 49 (2): 252–286.

Rhodes-Purdy, Matthew. 2017b. "Participatory governance in Latin America: Promises and limitations." *Latin American Politics and Society* 59 (3): 122–131.

Rhodes-Purdy, Matthew. 2017c. *Regime support beyond the balance sheet: Participation and policy performance in Latin America.* Cambridge: Cambridge University Press.

Rhodes-Purdy, Matthew. 2021a. "I am your voice! Populism and external efficacy." Presented at the Annual Meeting of the Midwest Political Science Association, Chicago.

Rhodes-Purdy, Matthew. 2021b. "Lock them up! Punitive aggression and populism as political vigilantism." *Electoral Studies* 74. https://doi.org/10.1016/j.electstud.2021.102415.

Rhodes-Purdy, Matthew. 2021c. "Procedures matter: Strong voice, evaluations of policy performance, and regime support." *Political Studies* 69 (2): 412–433.

Rhodes-Purdy, Matthew, and Raúl L Madrid. 2020. "The perils of personalism." *Democratization* 27 (2): 321–339.

Rhodes–Purdy, Matthew, Rachel Navarre, and Stephen M. Utych. 2020. *The Political Systems Attitudes Study (PSAS) – Pilot Wave.* v03062020. https://doi.org/10.7910/DVN/XMNLTA.

Rhodes-Purdy, Matthew, Rachel Navarre, and Stephen M. Utych. 2021a. "Measuring simultaneous emotions: Existing problems and a new way forward." *Journal of Experimental Political Science* 8 (1): 1–14.

Rhodes-Purdy, Matthew, Rachel Navarre, and Stephen M. Utych. 2021b. "Populist psychology: Economics, culture, and emotions." *Journal of Politics* 83 (4): 1559–1572.

Rhodes-Purdy, Matthew, and Fernando Rosenblatt. 2021. "Raising the red flag: Democratic elitism and the protests in Chile." *Perspectives on Politics*: 1–13. https://doi.org/10.1017/S1537592721000050.

Rico, Guillem, and Robert Liñeira. 2014. "Bringing secessionism into the mainstream: The 2012 regional election in Catalonia." *South European Society and Politics* 19 (2): 257–280.

Rihoux, Benoit, and Charles Ragin, eds. 2009. *Configurational comparative methods: Qualitative comparative analysis (QCA) and related techniques.* Thousand Oaks, CA: Sage Publications.

Riker, William H. 1988. *Liberalism against populism: A confrontation between the theory of democracy and the theory of social choice.* San Francisco: W. H. Freeman and Company.

Robb, Amanda. 2017. "Anatomy of a fake news scandal." *Rolling Stone*, November 16. www.rollingstone.com/feature/anatomy-of-a-fake-news-scandal-125877/. Accessed September 5, 2021.

Roberts, Kenneth M. 1998. *Deepening democracy? The modern left and social movements in Chile and Peru.* Stanford, CA: Stanford University Press.

Roberts, Kenneth M. 2006. "Populism, political conflict, and grass-roots organization in Latin America." *Comparative Politics* 38 (2): 127–148.

Roberts, Kenneth M. 2015. "Populism, political mobilizations, and crises of political representation." In *The promise and perils of populism: Global perspectives*, edited by Carlos de la Torre, 140–158. Lexington: University Press of Kentucky.

Roberts, Kenneth M. 2017. "State of the field." *European Journal of Political Research* 56 (2): 218–233.

Roberts, Kenneth M. 2019. "Bipolar disorders: Varieties of capitalism and populist out-flanking on the left and right." *Polity* 51 (4): 641–653.

Rodrik, Dani. 2018. "Populism and the economics of globalization." *Journal of International Business Party* 1 (2): 12–33.

Rooduijn, Matthijs, Stijn van Kessel, Caterina Froio, Andrea Pirro, Sarah de Lange, Daphne Halikiopoulou, Paul Lewis, Cas Mudde, and Paul Taggart. 2019. *The PopuList: An overview of populist, far right, far left and Eurosceptic parties in Europe.* www.popu-list.org/. Accessed July 22, 2022.

Roseman, Ira J. 1996. "Appraisal determinants of emotions: Constructing a more accurate and comprehensive theory." *Cognition and Emotion* 10 (3): 241–278.

Rosenblatt, Fernando. 2018. *Party vibrancy and democracy in Latin America.* Oxford: Oxford University Press.

Rosenblatt, Fernando. 2021. Interviewed by Matthew Rhodes-Purdy.

Rosenblum, Nancy L. and Russell Muirhead. 2019. *A lot of people are saying: The new conspiracism and the assault on democracy.* Princeton: Princeton University Press.

Rosenbluth, Frances, and Ian Shapiro. 2018. *Responsible parties: Saving democracy from itself.* New Haven, CT: Yale University Press.

Rothwell, Jonathan T., and Pablo Diego-Rosell. 2016. "Explaining nationalist political views: The case of Donald Trump." *SSRN*. https://papers.ssrn.com/sol3/papers.cfm?abstract_id=2822059. Accessed July 22, 2022.

Rovira Kaltwasser, Cristóbal. 2015. "Explaining the emergence of populism in Europe and the Americas." In *The Promise and Perils of Populism*, edited by Carlos de la Torre, 189–227. Lexington: University of Kentucky Press.

RTVE.es. 2019. "Un millón de votantes de Cs se fueron a la abstención y 233.000 del PSOE se pasaron a Vox, según una encuesta." *RTVE*, November 18.

www.rtve.es/noticias/20191118/encuesta-gad3-millon-votantes-ciudada-nos-se-fueron-abstencion-10n/1991407.shtml. Accessed August 25, 2021.

Rueschemeyer, Dietrich, Evelyne Stephens, and John Stephens. 1992. *Capitalist development and democracy*. Chicago: University of Chicago Press.

Rydgren, Jens. 2005. *Movements of exclusion: Radical right-wing populism in the Western world*. New York: Nova Publishers.

Saad-Filho, Alfredo. 2013. "Mass protests under 'left neoliberalism': Brazil, June–July 2013." *Critical Sociology* 39 (5): 657–669.

Samuels, David, and Cesar Zucco. 2018. *Partisans, antipartisans, and nonpartisans: Voting behavior in Brazil*. Cambridge: Cambridge University Press.

Sartori, Giovanni. 1970. "Concept misformation in comparative politics." *American Political Science Review* 64 (4): 1033–1053.

Scala, Dante J., and Kenneth M. Johnson. 2017. "Political polarization along the rural–urban continuum? The geography of the presidential vote, 2000–2016." *The ANNALS of the American Academy of Political and Social Science* 672 (1): 162–184.

Schäfer, Armin. 2021. "Cultural backlash? How (not) to explain the rise of authoritarian populism." *British Journal of Political Science*: 1–17. https://doi.org/10.1017/S0007123421000363.

Schonfeld, Irvin Sam, and Joseph J. Mazzola. 2015. "A qualitative study of stress in individuals self-employed in solo businesses." *Journal of Occupational Health Psychology* 20 (4): 501–513.

Schumpeter, Joseph A. 2008. *Capitalism, socialism, and democracy*, 3rd edition. New York: Harper Perennial Modern Classics.

Schwarz, Norbert, and Gerald L. Clore. 1983. "Mood, misattribution, and judgments of well-being: Informative and directive functions of affective states." *Journal of Personality and Social Psychology* 45 (3): 513.

Schwarz, Norbert, Fritz Strack, Detlev Kommer, and Dirk Wagner. 1987. "Soccer, rooms, and the quality of your life: Mood effects on judgments of satisfaction with life in general and with specific domains." *European Journal of Social Psychology* 17 (1): 69–79.

Scott, James C. 2008. *Weapons of the weak*. New Haven, CT: Yale University Press.

Sears, David O., and Carolyn L. Funk. 1999. "Evidence of the long-term persistence of adults' political predispositions." *The Journal of Politics* 61 (1): 1–28.

Seawright, Jason. 2012. *Party-system collapse: The roots of crisis in Peru and Venezuela*. Stanford, CA: Stanford University Press.

Shelbourne, Mallory. 2018. "Trump's infrastructure plan hits a dead end." *The Hill*, May 17. https://thehill.com/policy/transportation/388071-trumps-infrastructure-plan-hits-a-dead-end. Accessed September 4, 2021.

Shiller, Robert J. 2020. *Narrative economics: How stories go viral and drive major economic events*. Princeton, NJ: Princeton University Press.

Shilts, Randy. 1982. *The mayor of Castro Street*. New York: St. Martin's Press.

Siavelis, Peter M. 2016. "Crisis of representation in Chile? The institutional connection." *Journal of Politics in Latin America* 8 (3): 61–93.

Sibbel, Lejo. 2007. "Linking trade with labour rights: The ILO Garment Sector Working Conditions Improvement Project in Cambodia." *Arizona Journal of International And Comparative Law* 24 (1): 235–249.

Sides, John, Michael Tesler, and Lynn Vavreck. 2017. "The 2016 US election: How Trump lost and won." *Journal of Democracy* 28 (2): 34–44.

Sides, John, Michael Tesler, and Lynn Vavreck. 2018. "Hunting where the ducks are: Activating support for Donald Trump in the 2016 Republican primary." *Journal of Elections, Public Opinion and Parties* 28 (2): 135–156.

Sides, John, Michael Tesler, and Lynn Vavreck. 2019. *Identity crisis: The 2016 presidential campaign and the battle for the meaning of America.* Princeton, NJ: Princeton University Press.

Silva, Patricio. 1991. "Technocrats and politics in Chile: From the Chicago boys to the CIEPLAN monks." *Journal of Latin American Studies* 23 (2): 385–410.

Simón, Pablo. 2016. "The challenges of the new Spanish multipartism: Government formation failure and the 2016 general election." *South European Society and Politics* 21 (4): 493–517.

Skocpol, Theda, and Vanessa Williamson. 2012. *The Tea Party and the remaking of Republican conservatism.* Oxford: Oxford University Press.

Slothuus, Rune. 2016. "Assessing the influence of political parties on public opinion: The challenge from pretreatment effects." *Political Communication* 33 (2): 302–327.

Smith, Craig A., and Phoebe C. Ellsworth. 1985. "Patterns of cognitive appraisal in emotion." *Journal of Personality and Social Psychology* 48 (4): 813.

Sobolewska, Maria, and Robert Ford. 2020. *Brexitland.* Cambridge: Cambridge University Press.

Somma, Nicolás M., Matías Bargsted, Rodolfo Disi Pavlic, and Rodrigo M. Medel. 2021. "No water in the oasis: The Chilean spring of 2019–2020." *Social Movement Studies* 20 (4): 495–502.

Spalding, Hobart A. Jr. 1977. *Organized labor in Latin America.* New York: New York University Press.

Spring, Marianna, and Mike Wendling. 2020. "How Covid-19 myths are merging with QAnon conspiracy theory." *BBC News*, September 3. www.bbc.com/news/blogs-trending-53997203. Accessed September 19, 2021.

Spruyt, Bram, Gil Keppens, and Filip van Droogenbroeck. 2016. "Who supports populism and what attracts people to it?" *Political Research Quarterly* 69 (2): 335–346.

Stefani, Silvia. 2021. "Building mistrust: 'Minha Casa Minha Vida' and its political effects in Rio de Janeiro." *Bulletin of Latin American Research.* https://doi.org/10.1111/blar.13261.

Sugiyama, Natasha Borges, and Wendy Hunter. 2013. "Whither clientelism? Good governance and Brazil's Bolsa Família program." *Comparative Politics* 46 (1): 43–62.

Sunstein, Cass R., and Adrian Vermeule. 2009. "Conspiracy theories: Causes and cures." *Journal of Political Philosophy* 17 (2): 202–227.

Taggart, Paul. 2000. *Populism.* Maidenhead: Open University Press.

Tajfel, Henri, John C. Turner, William G. Austin, and Stephen Worchel. 1979. "An integrative theory of intergroup conflict." *Organizational Identity: A Reader*, edited by Mary Jo Hatch and Majken Schultz, 56–65. Oxford: Oxford University Press.

Tarrow, Sidney. 1998. *Power in movement: Social movements and contentious politics.* Cambridge: Cambridge University Press.

Tarrow, Sidney. 2000. "Mad cows and social activists: Contentious politics in the trilateral democracies." In *Disaffected democracies: What's troubling the trilateral countries?* edited by Susan Pharr and Robert D. Putnam, 270–290. Princeton, NJ: Princeton University Press.

Taylor, Charles. 1994. *Multiculturalism: Examining the politics of recognition.* Washington, DC: ERIC.

Teles, Miguel Galvão. 1998. "A segunda plataforma de acordo constitucional entre o Movimento das Forças Armadas e os partidos políticos." *Perspectivas Constitucionais* 20: 54–69.

Teney, Céline, Onawa Promise Lacewell, and Pieter De Wilde. 2014. "Winners and losers of globalization in Europe: Attitudes and ideologies." *European Political Science Review* 6 (4): 575–595.

Tesler, Michael. 2016. *Post-racial or most-racial? Race and politics in the Obama era.* Chicago: University of Chicago Press.

Thibaut, John, and Laurens Walker. 1975. *Procedural justice: A psychological analysis.* Hillsdale, NJ: Lawrence Erlbaum Associates.

Thompson, Derek. 2016. "Who are Donald Trump's supporters, really?" *The Atlantic*, 1 March.

Torcal, Mariano. 2014. "The decline of political trust in Spain and Portugal: Economic performance or political responsiveness?" *American Behavioral Scientist* 58 (12): 1542–1567.

Torcal, Mariano. 2019. "¿Ideología, nacionalismo español o inmigración? Las claves del voto a la ultraderecha." *Contexto y Acción*, November 11. https://ctxt.es/es/20191120/Politica/29662/Mariano-Torcal-ultraderecha-ideologia-nacionalismo-inmigracion-Vox.htm. Accessed July 22, 2022.

Tsebelis, George. 1990. *Nested games.* Berkeley: University of California Press.

Tsebelis, George. 1995. "Decision making in political systems: Veto players in presidentialism, parliamentarism, multicameralism and multipartyism." *British Journal of Political Science* 25 (3): 289–325.

Turnbull-Dugarte, Stuart J. 2019. "Explaining the end of Spanish exceptionalism and electoral support for Vox." *Research & Politics* 6 (2). https://doi.org/10.1177/2053168019851680.

Turnbull-Dugarte, Stuart J., José Rama, and Andrés Santana. 2020. "The Baskerville's dog suddenly started barking: Voting for VOX in the 2019 Spanish general elections." *Political Research Exchange* 2 (1). https://doi.org/10.1080/2474736X.2020.1781543.

Uscinski, Joseph E., Casey Klofstad, and Matthew D. Atkinson. 2016. "What drives conspiratorial beliefs? The role of informational cues and predispositions." *Political Research Quarterly* 69 (1): 57–71.

Uscinski, Joseph E., and Joseph M Parent. 2014. *American conspiracy theories.* Oxford: Oxford University Press.

Utych, Stephen M., Rachel Navarre, and Matthew Rhodes-Purdy. 2021. "Fear or loathing? The affective political economy of prejudice." *Journal of Race, Ethnicity, and Politics.* https://doi.org/10.1017/rep.2021.32.

Utych, Stephen M., Rachel Navarre, and Matthew Rhodes-Purdy. 2022. "White identity, anti-elitism, and opposition to COVID-19 restrictions in the United States." *Representation* 58 (2): 301–310.

Vampa, Davide. 2020. "Competing forms of populism and territorial politics: The cases of Vox and Podemos in Spain." *Journal of Contemporary European Studies* 28 (3): 304–321.

Van den Bos, Kees, E. Allen Lind, and Henk A. M. Wilke. 2001. "The psychology of procedural and distributive justice viewed from the perspective of fairness heuristic theory." In *Justice in the workplace: From theory to practice*, edited by Russell Cropanzano, 49–66. Mahwah, NJ: Lawrence Erlbaum Associates.

Van Prooijen, Jan-Willem. 2017. *The moral punishment instinct.* Oxford: Oxford University Press.

Van Prooijen, Jan-Willem. 2018. *The psychology of conspiracy theories.* New York: Routledge.

Vasilopoulos, Pavlos, George E. Marcus, Nicholas A. Valentino, and Martial Foucault. 2018. "Fear, anger, and voting for the far right: Evidence from the November 13, 2015 Paris terror attacks." *Political Psychology* 40 (4): 679–704.

Vasilopoulos, Pavlos, George E. Marcus, Nicholas Valentino, and Martial Foucault. 2019. "Anger mediates the effects of fear on support for the far right: A rejoinder." *Political Psychology* 40 (4): 713–717.

Volkens, Andrea, Tobias Burst, Theres Matthieß, and Lisa Zehnter. 2020. Manifesto Project dataset. https://doi.org/10.25522/MANIFESTO.MPDS.2020B. Accessed 7/22/2022

Walker, Jan. 2001. *Control and the psychology of health: Theory, measurement and applications.* Maidenhead: Open University Press.

Wampler, Brian. 2007. *Participatory budgeting in Brazil.* University Park: Pennsylvania State University Press.

Wampler, Brian. 2015. *Activating democracy in Brazil: Popular participation, social justice, and interlocking institutions.* South Bend, IL: University of Notre Dame Press.

Wang, Amy B. 2017. "Did the 2011 White House correspondents' dinner spur Trump to run for president?" *Chicago Tribune*, February 26. www.chicagotribune.com/nation-world/ct-white-house-correspondents-dinner-trump-20170226-story.html. Accessed July 22, 2022.

Watson, David, Lee Anna Clark, and Auke Tellegen. 1988. "Development and validation of brief measures of positive and negative affect: the PANAS scales." *Journal of Personality and Social Psychology* 54 (6): 1063–1070.

Watson, Katy. 2020. "Chile's choice: Out with the old, in with the new?" *BBC News*, October 24. www.bbc.com/news/world-latin-america-54643589. Accessed July 13, 2021.

Weaver, Matthew. 2010. "Angela Merkel: German multiculturalism has 'utterly failed'." *The Guardian*, October 17. www.theguardian.com/world/2010/oct/17/angela-merkel-german-multiculturalism-failed. Accessed July 22, 2022.

Webber, Jude. 2018. "Mexico's López Obrador vows to end neo-liberalism in inauguration." *Financial Times*, December 2. www.ft.com/content/fdb0c912-f3a6-11e8-ae55-df4bf4of9dod. Accessed September 12, 2021.

Werner, Anika, Onawa Promise Lacewell, and Andrea Volkens. 2015. *Manifesto Project coding instructions*, 5th edition. Berlin: Manifesto Project.

Weyland, Kurt. 1996. "Risk taking in Latin American economic restructuring: Lessons from prospect theory." *International Studies Quarterly* 40 (2): 185–207.

Weyland, Kurt. 1999. "Neoliberal populism in Latin America and eastern Europe." *Comparative Politics* 31 (4): 379–401.

Weyland, Kurt. 2001. "Clarifying a contested concept: Populism in the study of Latin American politics." *Comparative Politics* 34 (1): 1–22.

Weyland, Kurt. 2017. "A political-strategic approach." In *The Oxford handbook of populism*, edited by Cristóbal Rovira Kaltwasser, Paul Taggart, Paulina Ochoa Espejo, and Pierre Ostiguy, 48–72. Oxford: Oxford University Press.

Weyland, Kurt, and Raúl L. Madrid. 2019. *When democracy trumps populism: European and Latin American lessons for the United States.* Cambridge: Cambridge University Press.

White, Robert W. 1959. "Motivation reconsidered: The concept of competence." *Psychological Review* 66 (5): 297–333.

Whiteley, Paul F. and David Sanders. 2014. "British Election Study, 2010: Face-to-face survey." UK Data Archive, Colchester.

Williams, Joan C. 2019. *White working class: Overcoming class cluelessness in America.* Cambridge, MA: Harvard Business Press.

Williamson, Vanessa. 2013. "The Tea Party and the shift to 'austerity by gridlock' in the United States." Presented at the Annual Meeting of the American Political Science Association, Chicago.

Williamson, Vanessa, Theda Skocpol, and John Coggin. 2011. "The Tea Party and the remaking of republican conservatism." *Perspectives on Politics* 9 (1): 25–43.

Wilson, Trevor. 2011. *The downfall of the Liberal Party, 1914–1935.* London: Faber & Faber.

Winter, Brian. 2017. "Revisiting Brazil's 2013 protests: What did they really mean." *Americas Quarterly.* www.americasquarterly.org/article/revisiting-brazils-2013-protests-what-did-they-really-mean/. Accessed July 22, 2022.

Winthrop, Rebecca. 2020. *The need for civic education in 21st-century schools.* Washington, DC: Brookings Institute.

Woodward, Bob. 2021. *Rage.* New York: Simon and Schuster.

Wright, Stephen C., Arthur Aron, Tracy McLaughlin-Volpe, and Stacy A. Ropp. 1997. "The extended contact effect: Knowledge of cross-group friendships and prejudice." *Journal of Personality and Social Psychology* 73 (1): 73–90.

Wuttke, Alexander, Christian Schimpf, and Harald Schoen. 2020. "When the whole is greater than the sum of its parts: On the conceptualization and measurement of populist attitudes and other multidimensional constructs." *American Political Science Review* 114 (2): 356–374.

Ybarra, Vickie D., Lisa M. Sanchez, and Gabriel R. Sanchez. 2016. "Anti-immigrant anxieties in state policy: The great recession and punitive immigration policy in the American states, 2005–2012." *State Politics & Policy Quarterly* 16 (3): 313–339.

Zaller, John R. 1992. *The nature and origins of mass opinion.* Cambridge: Cambridge University Press.

Zarzalejos, Javier. 2016. "Populism in Spain: An analysis of Podemos." *European View* 15 (2): 183–191.

Index